The Other in Palestine
Matei Glass

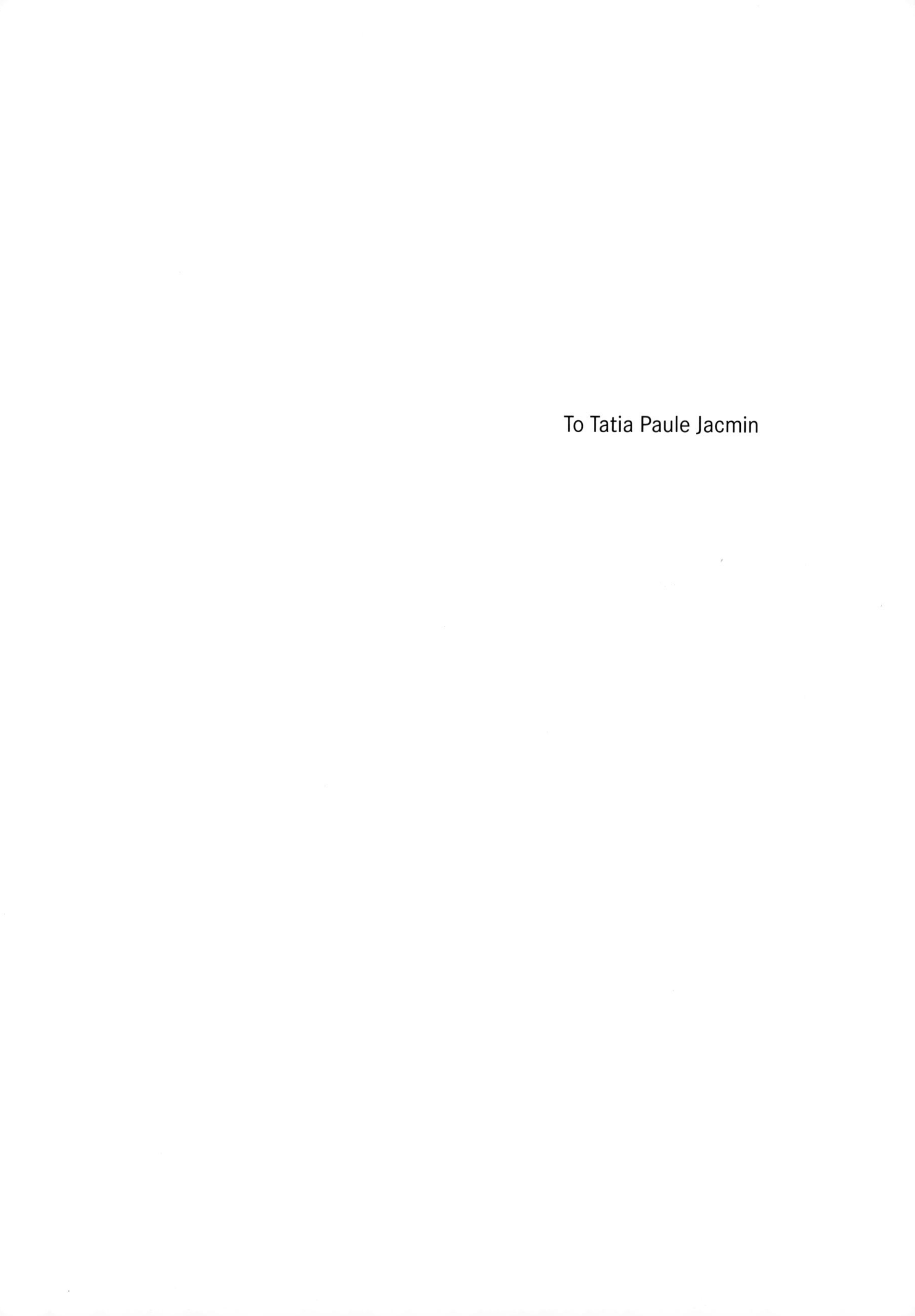

To Tatia Paule Jacmin

We are the mirror as well as the face of it.
We are tasting the taste this minute of eternity.
We are the pain and what cures the pain, both.
We are the sweet cold water and the jar that pours.

Jelaledin Rumi (1207 – 1273)

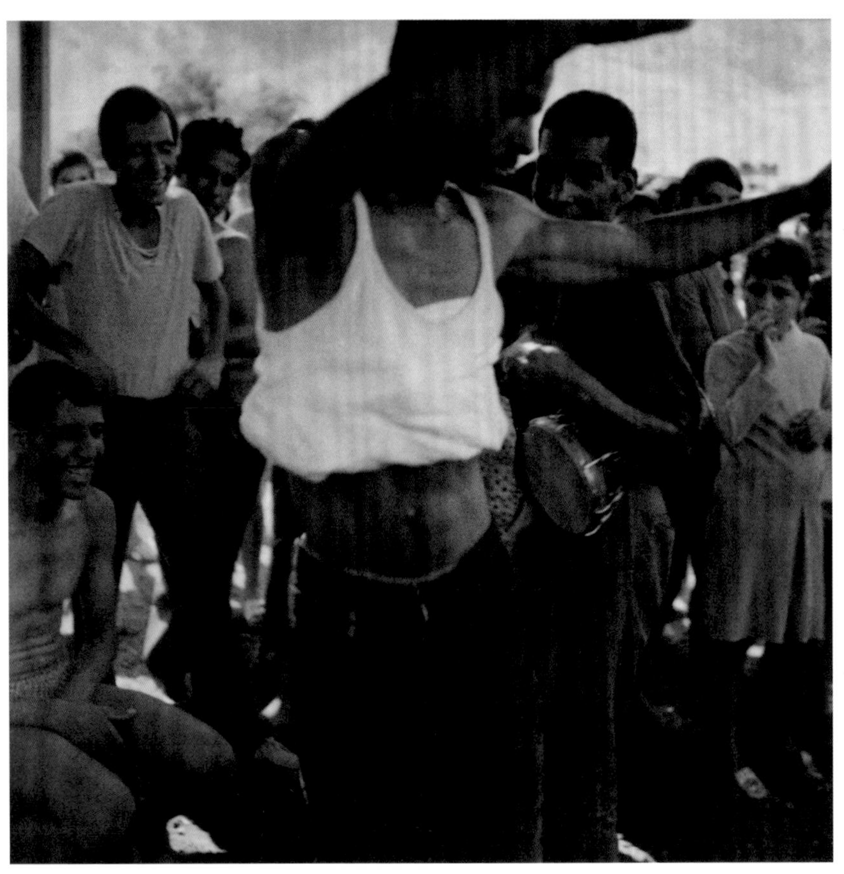

... 33 years ago at the age of 13.

Can a gap in one's identity be filled?
Can an identity ever be in focus and above all separate and exclusive?
The other defines us while we define ourselves.
Also we may try to define ourselves by trying to define the other.
These images from my photographic travel journal are mainly
of Palestine and Palestinians.
They are also somehow of myself and are about my need to identify
and redefine a people about whom I learned little as I grew up.
I was a child of Holocaust survivors whose support for Israel
could not be other than unquestioning.
Somehow, it is my need to fill in the blanks in my personal
and collective memory that brought me to Palestine with my camera.
With the passing of the years I began to know there was much more
to the story… much more to be seen. Israel was never simply that heroic
far away place, the brave homeland whose imagery stirred me as a child.
She was other things to other people who I can no longer simply think
of as the enemy… dangerous… terrorists.
It is a force of absence in the image of the utopia
in which I once believed, that has moved me to continue
the photographic journal I began when I first visited Israel,
33 years ago at the age of 13.
I needed to travel through the mirror, to see utopia's otherside,
its forgotten twin.

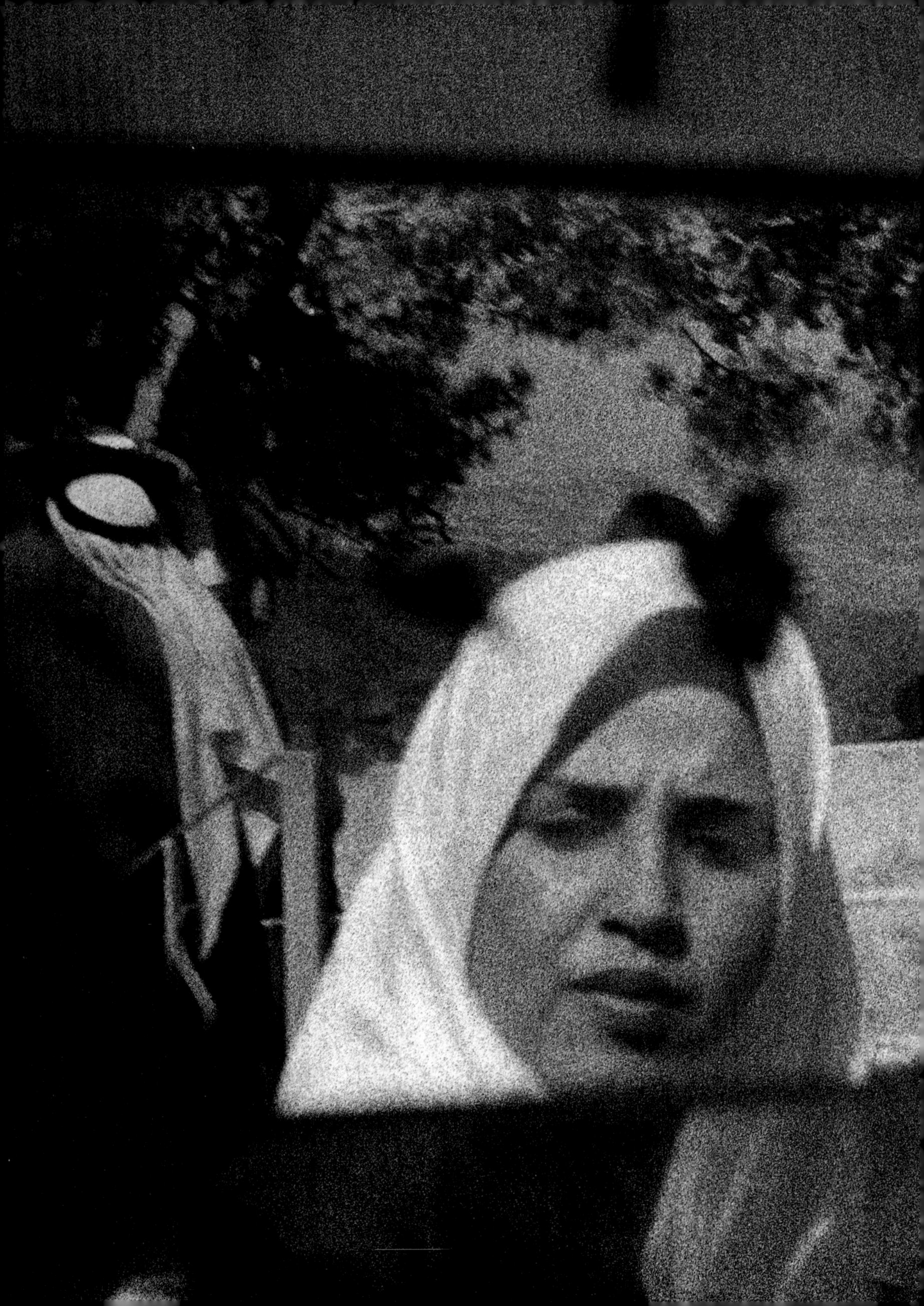

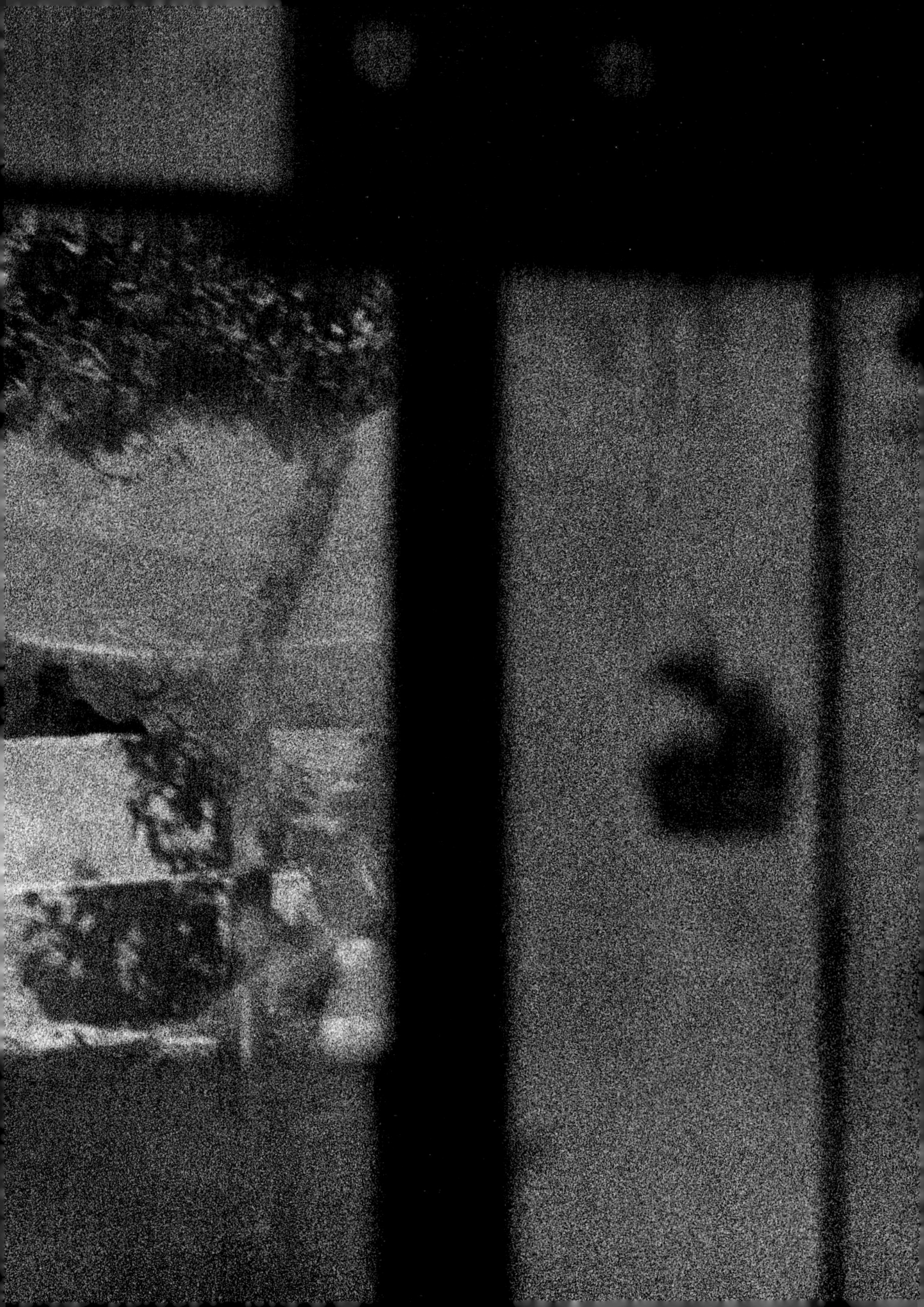

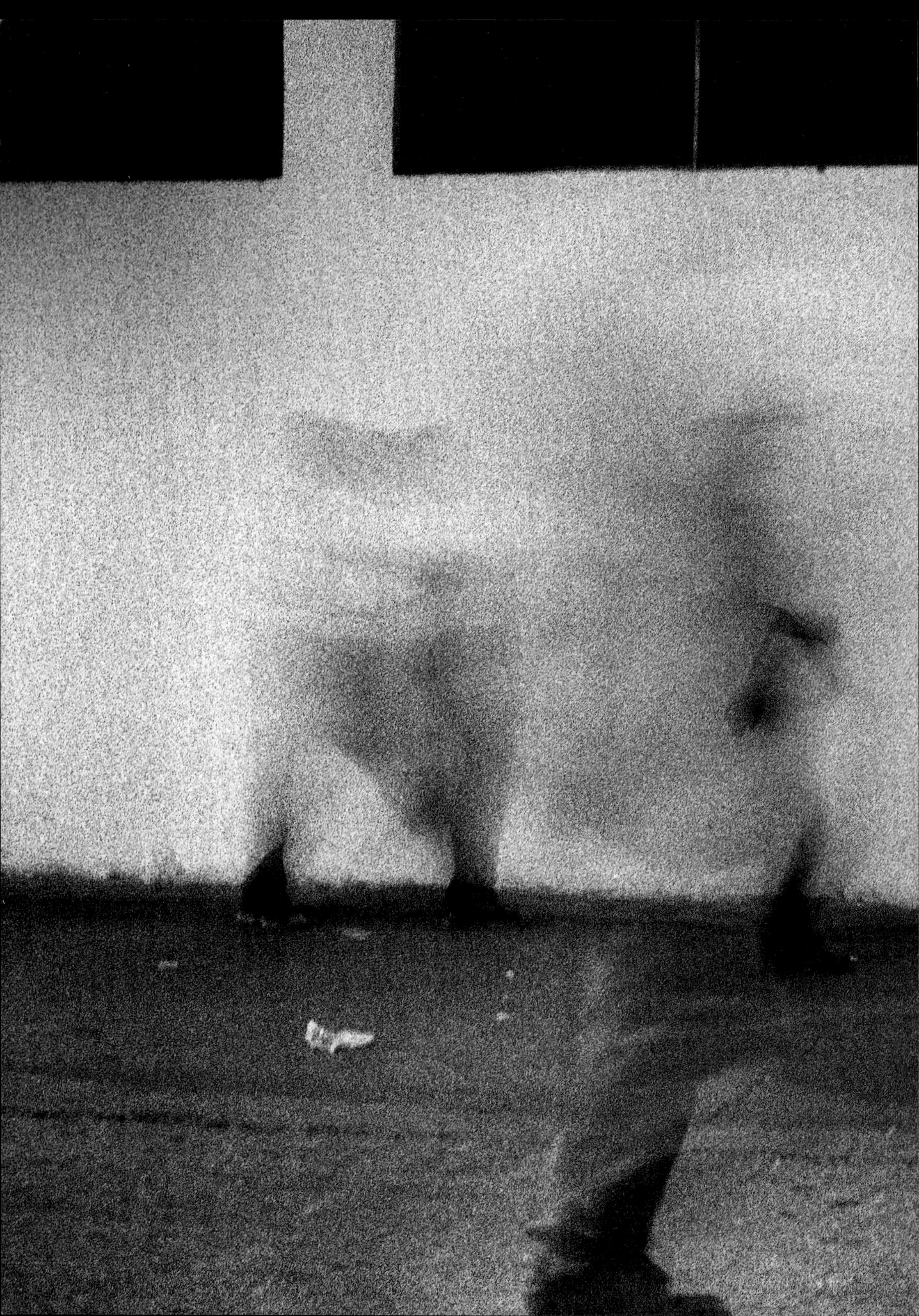

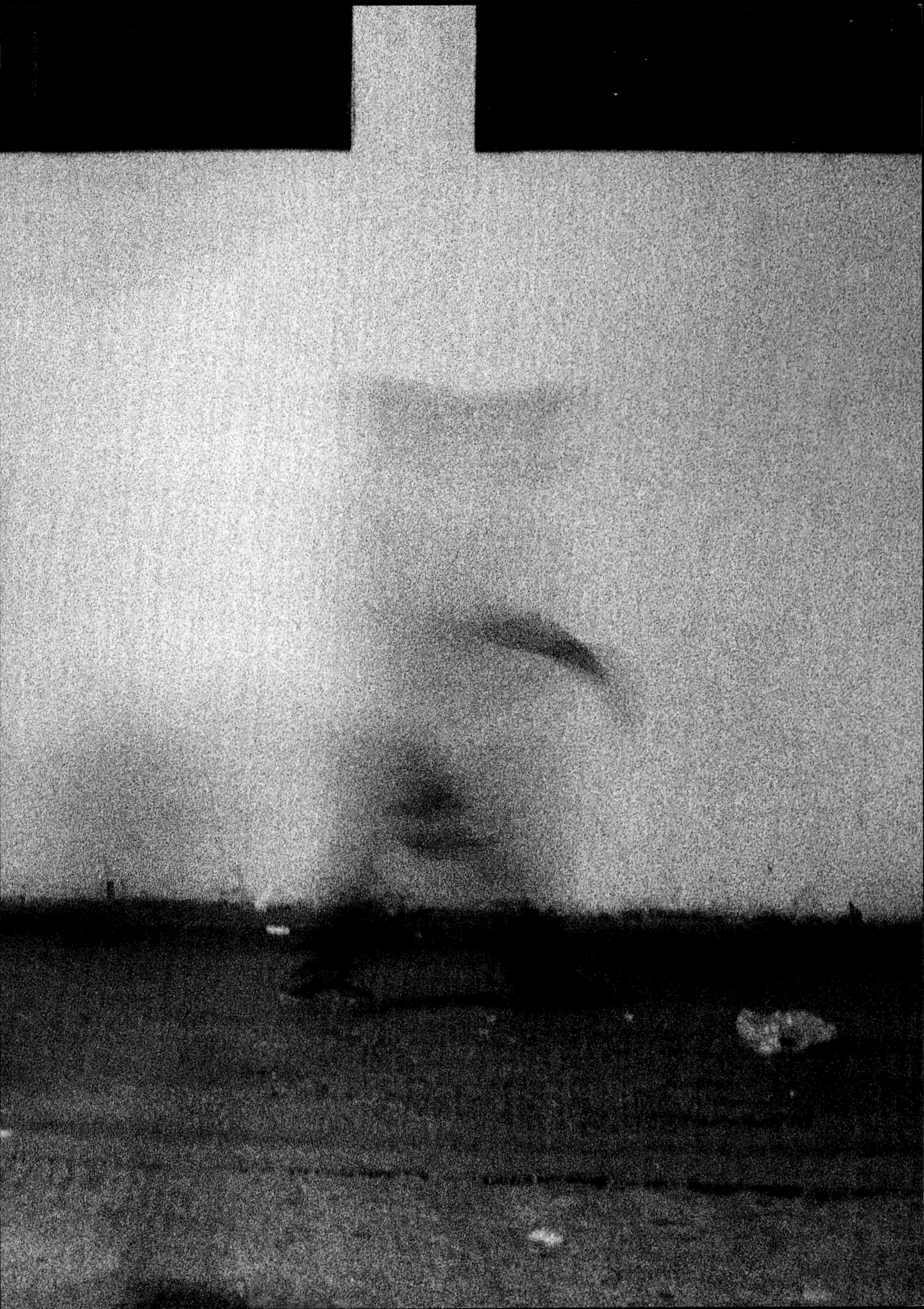

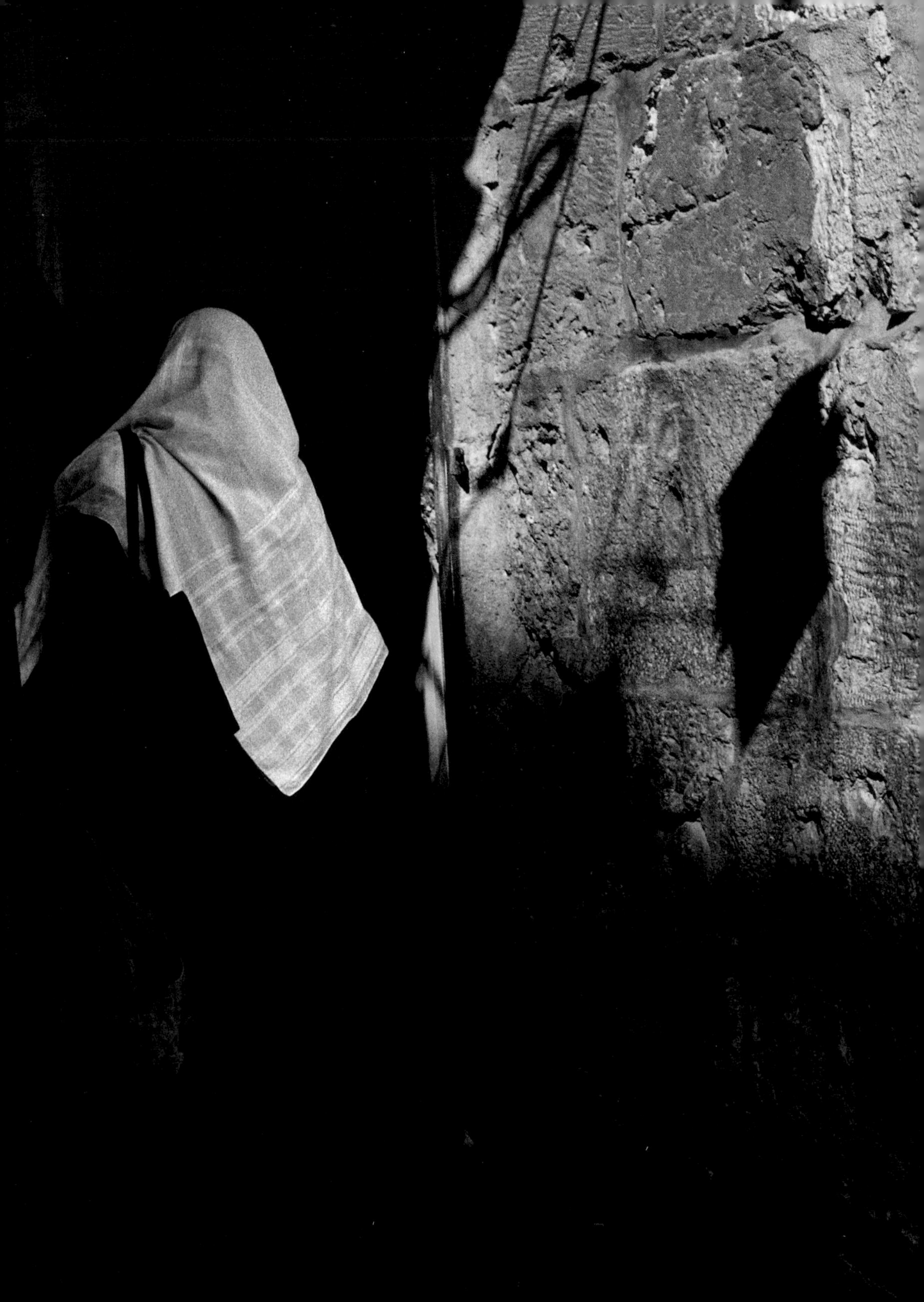

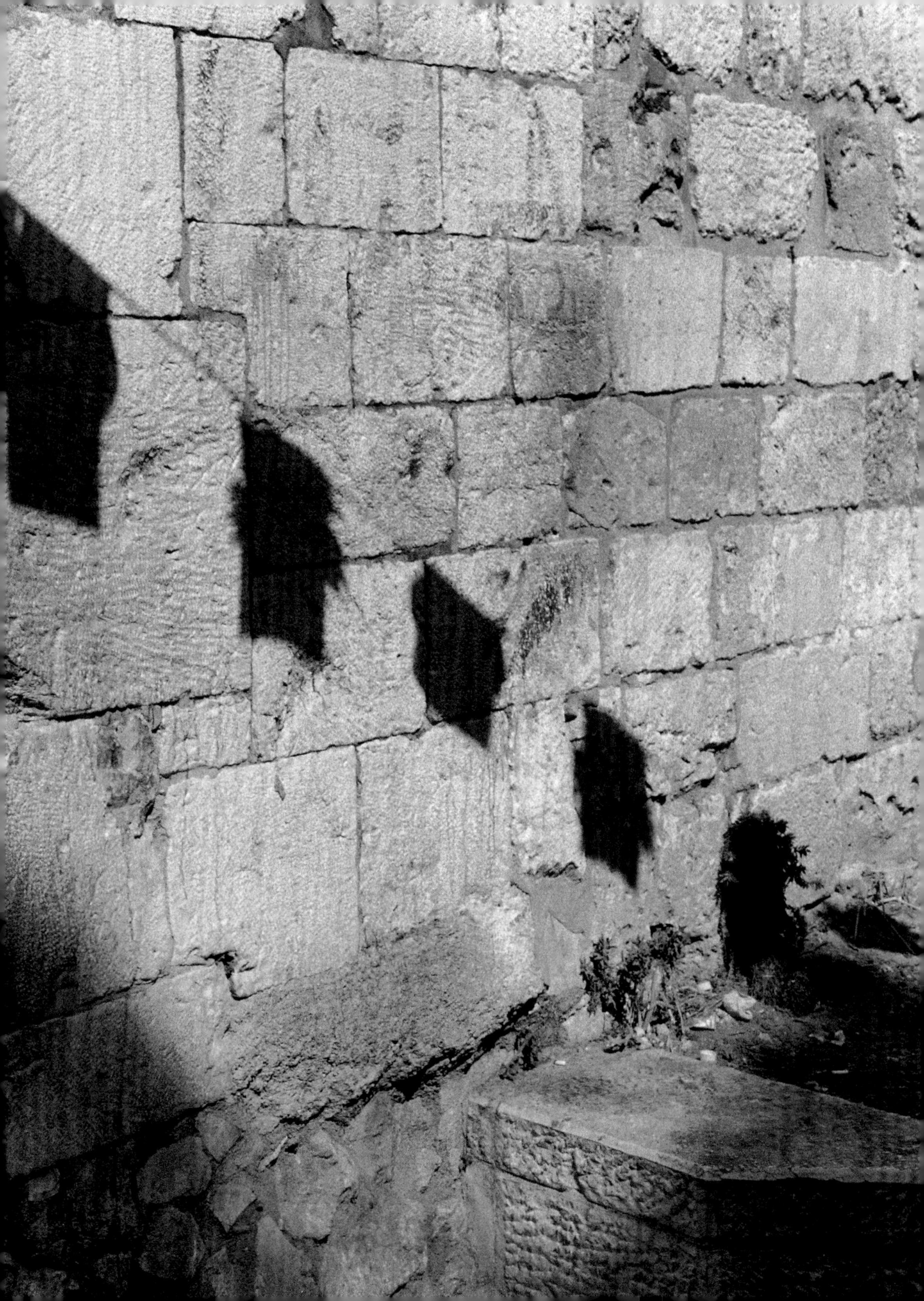

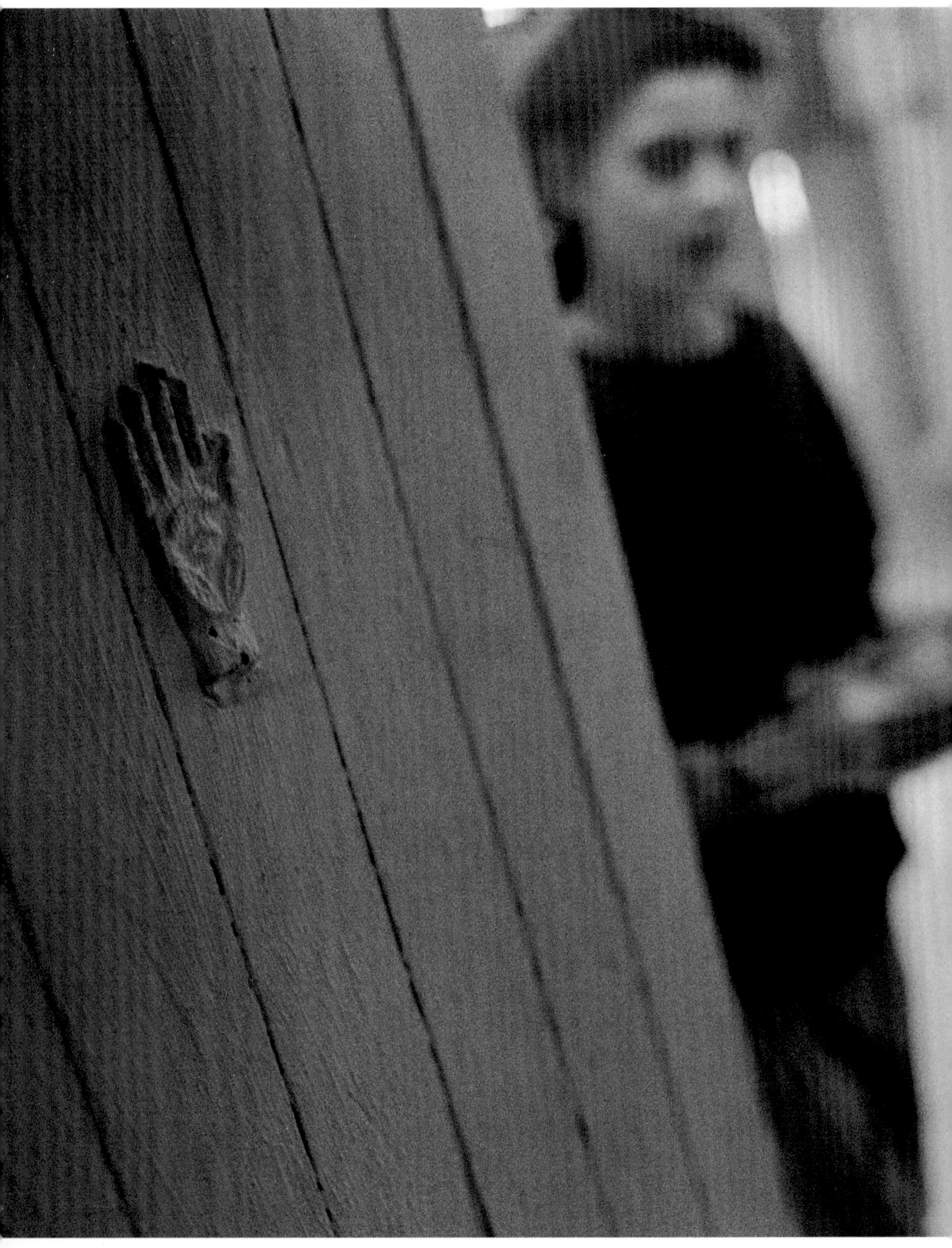

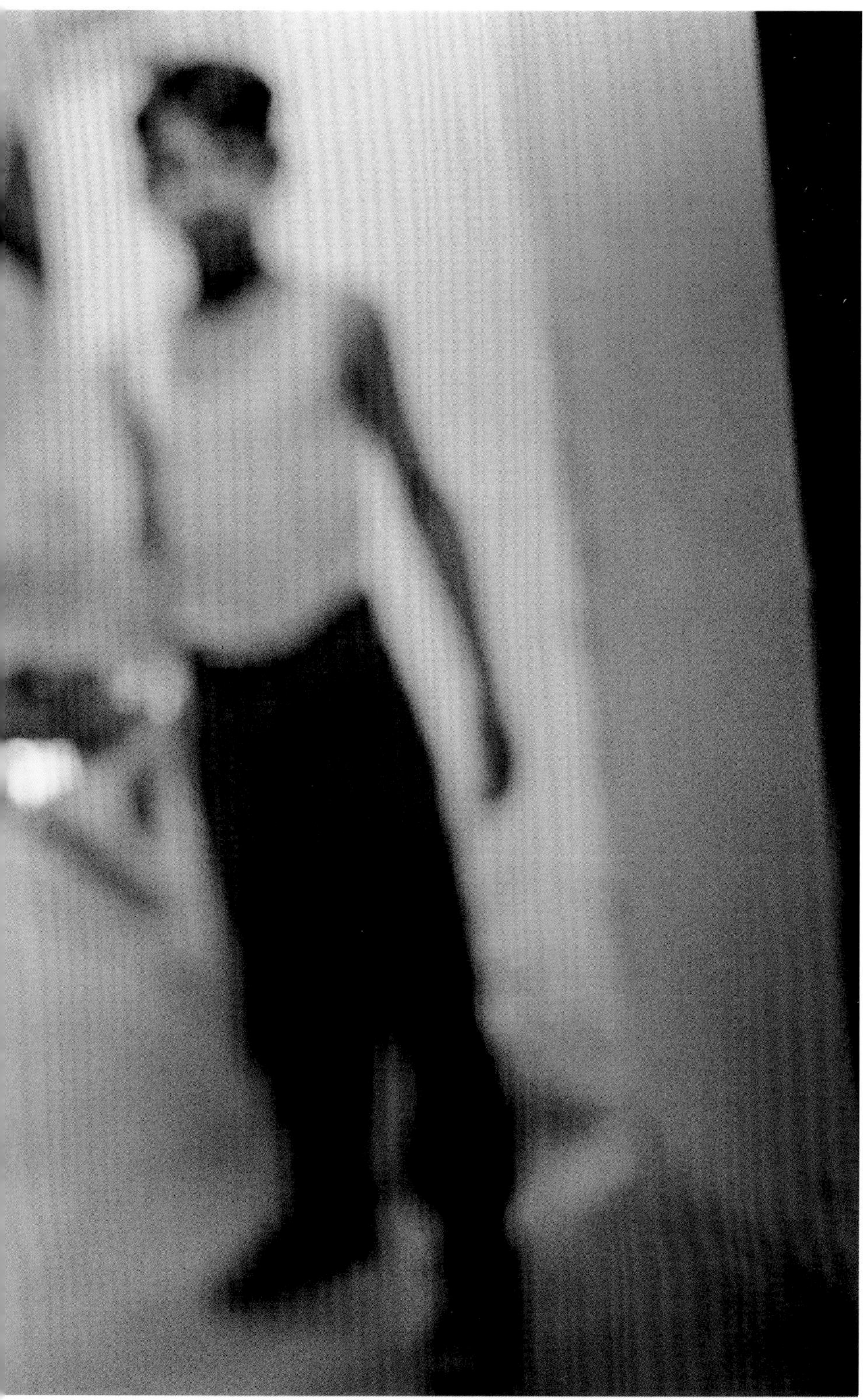

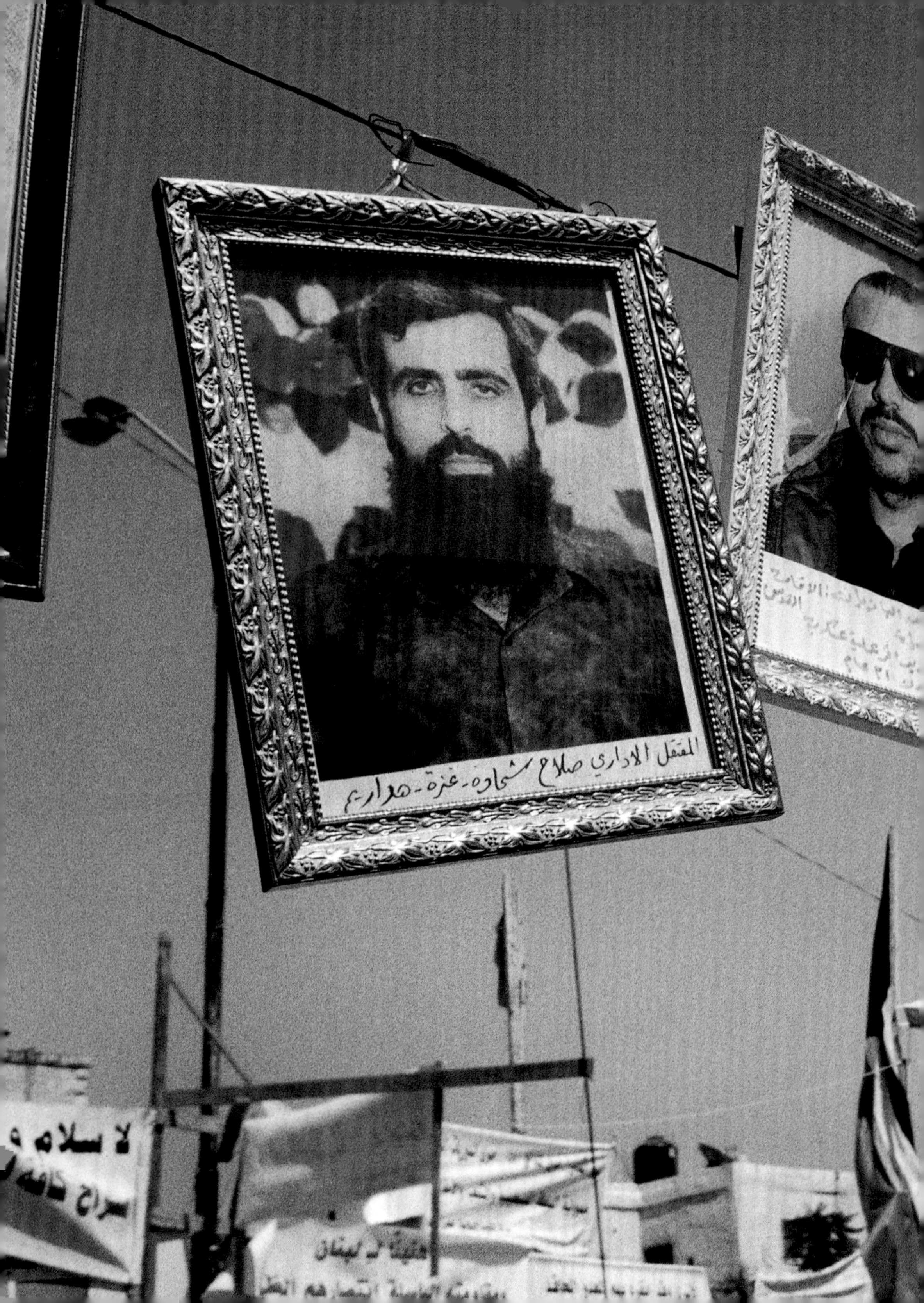

المعتقل الإداري صلاح شحادة - غزة - هدارم

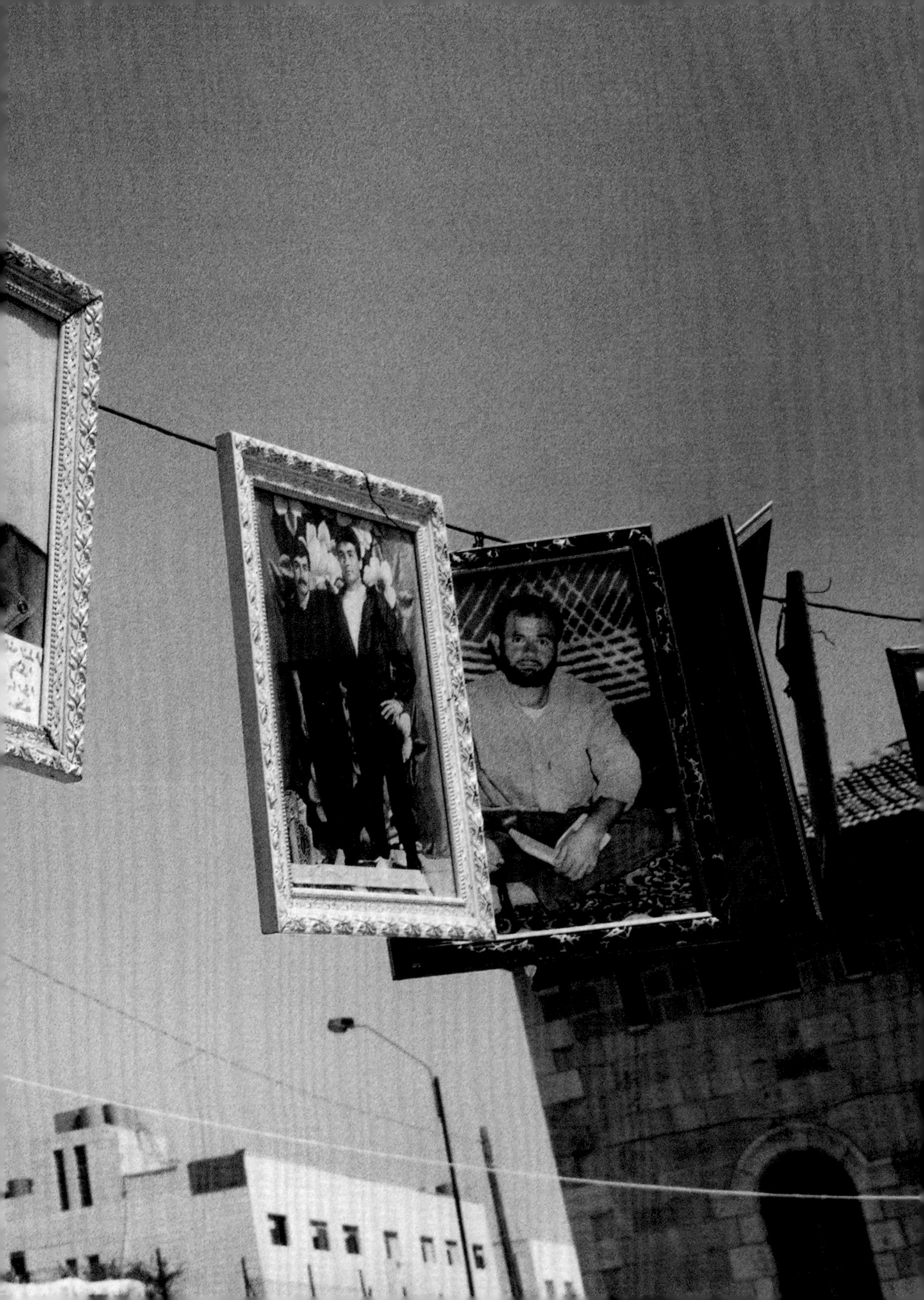

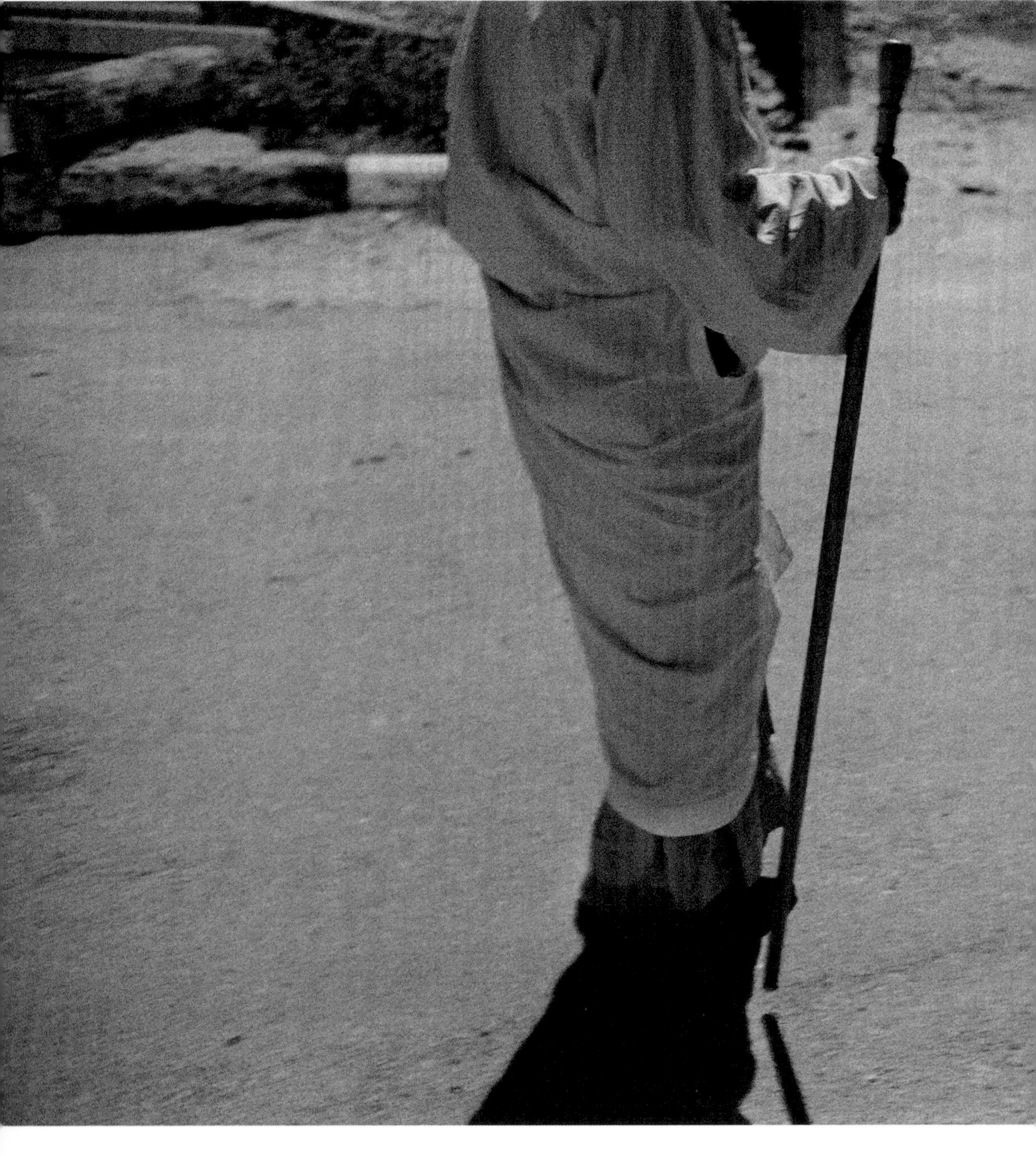

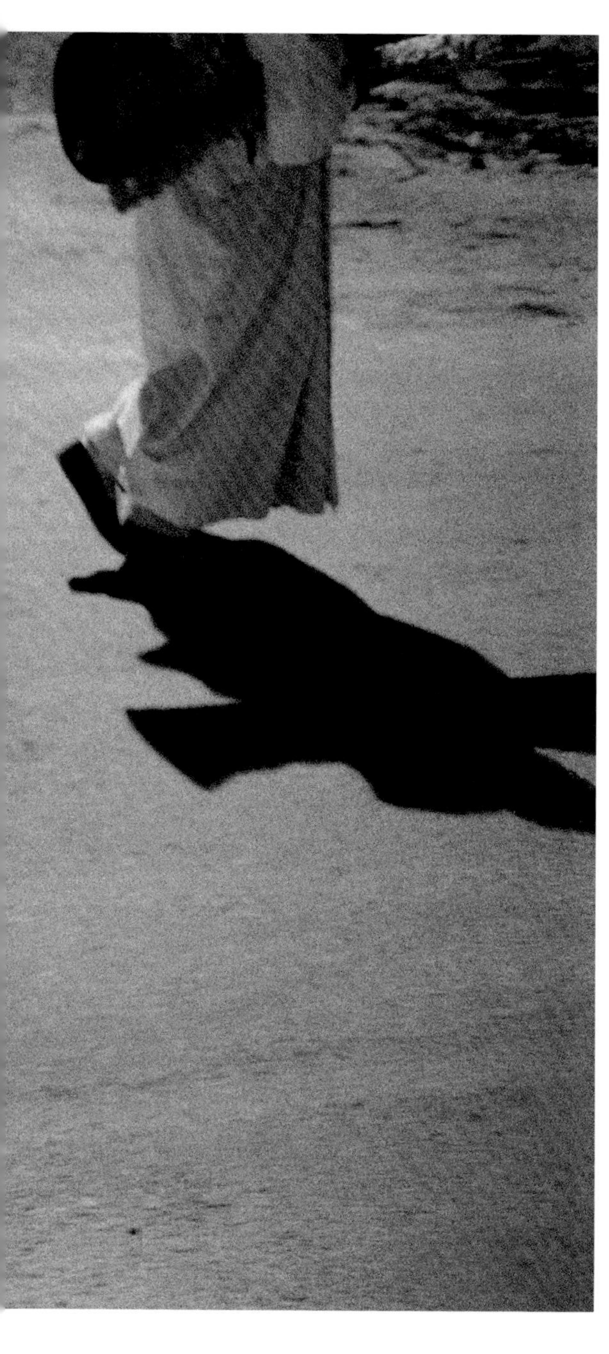

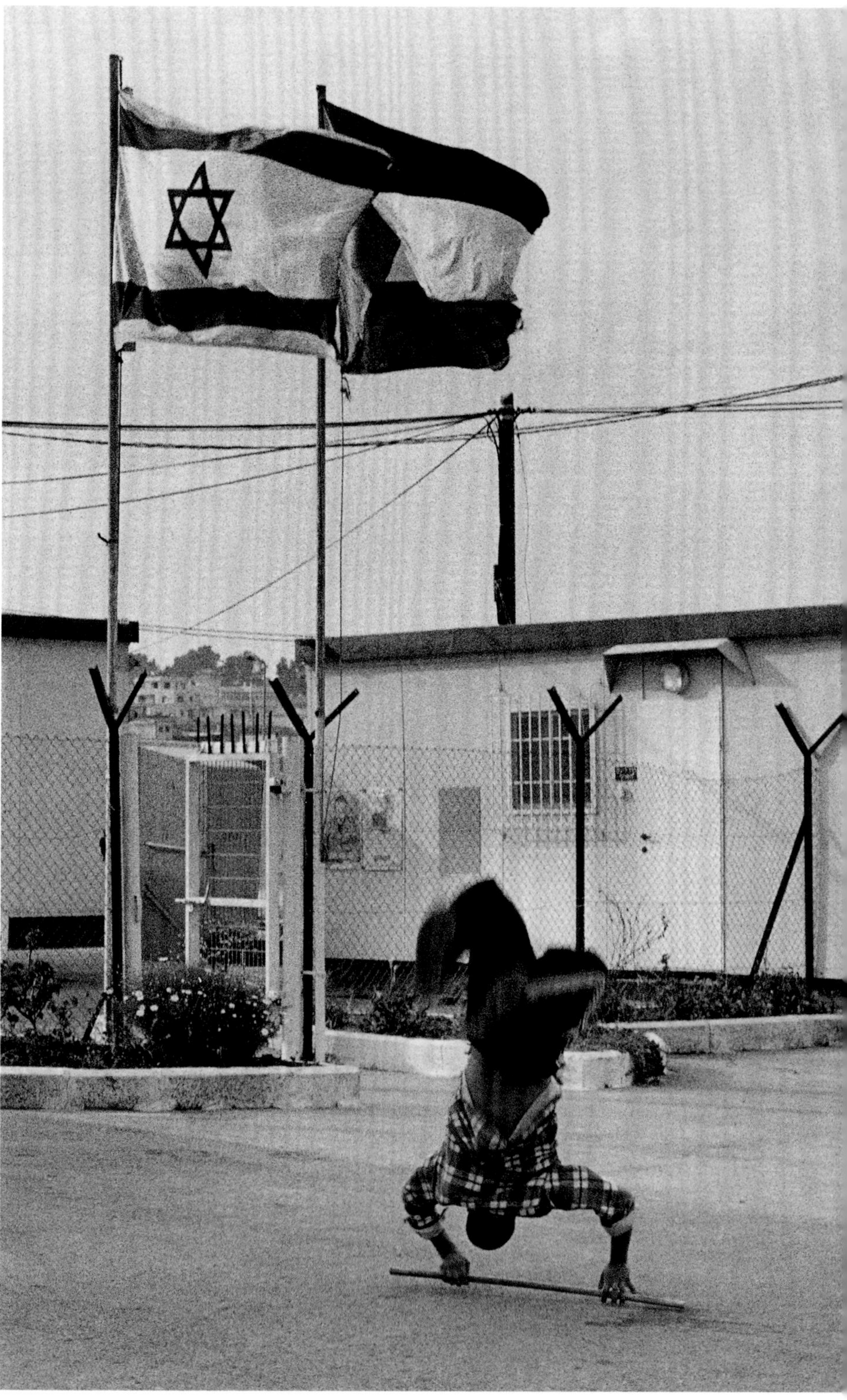

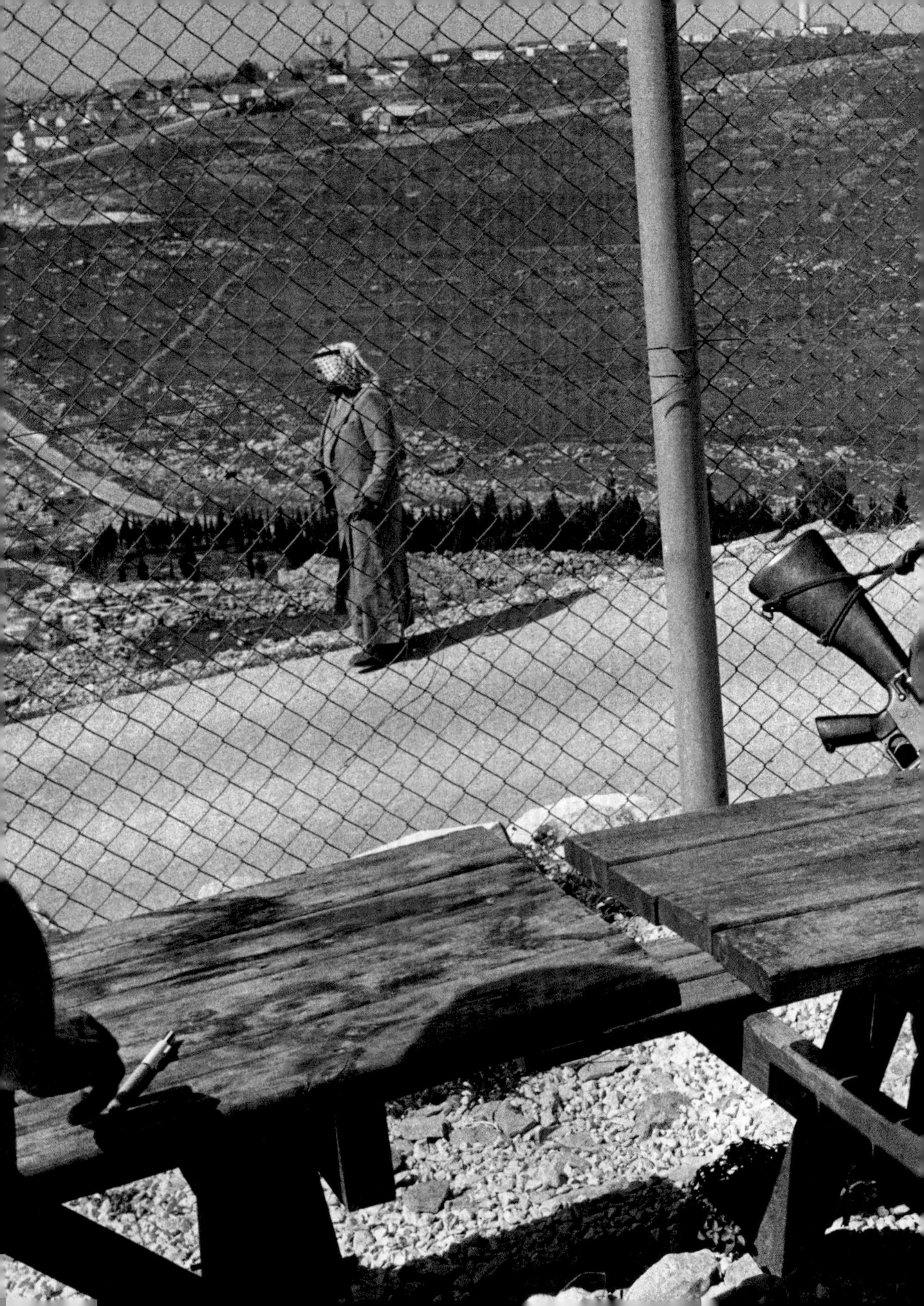

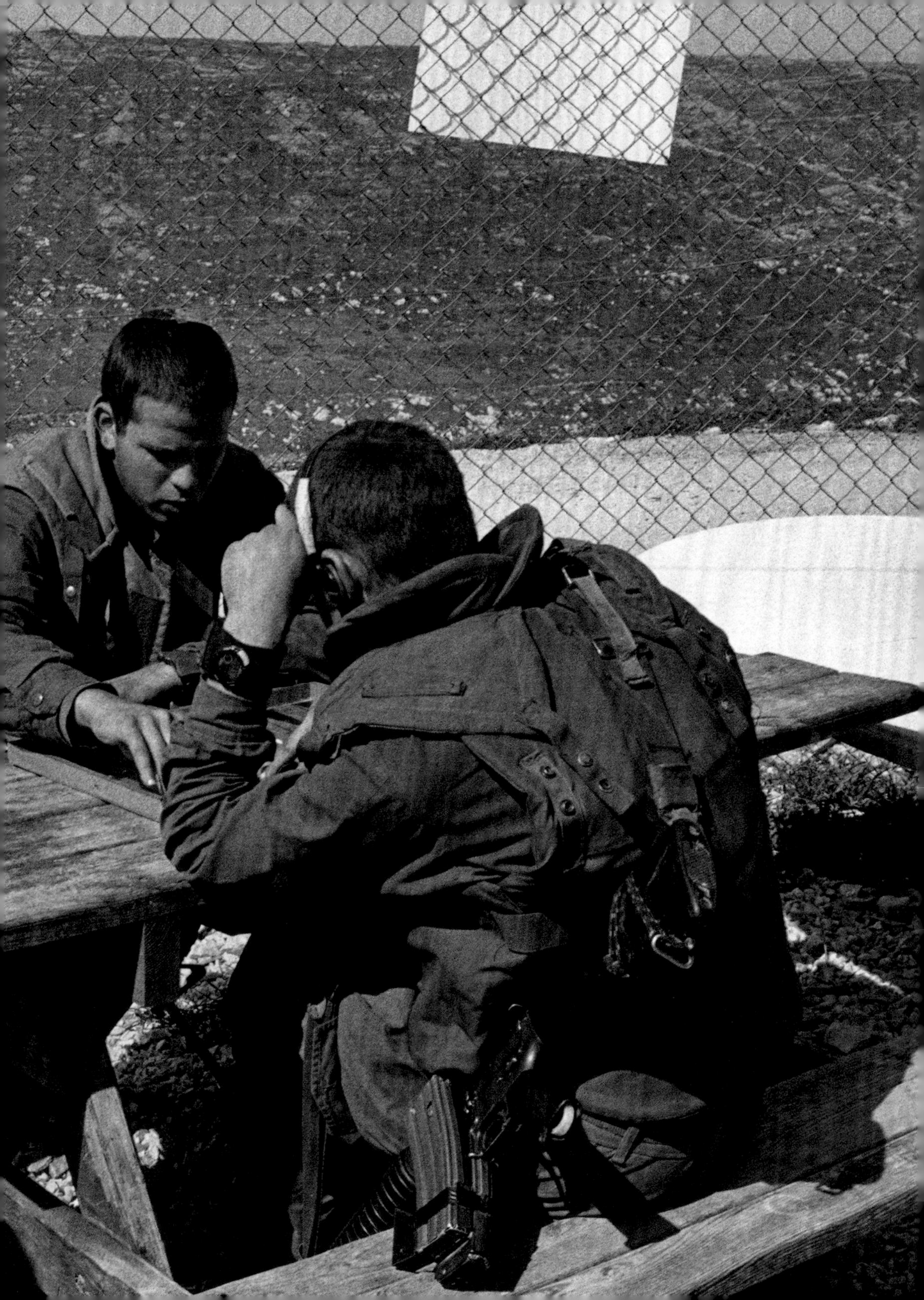

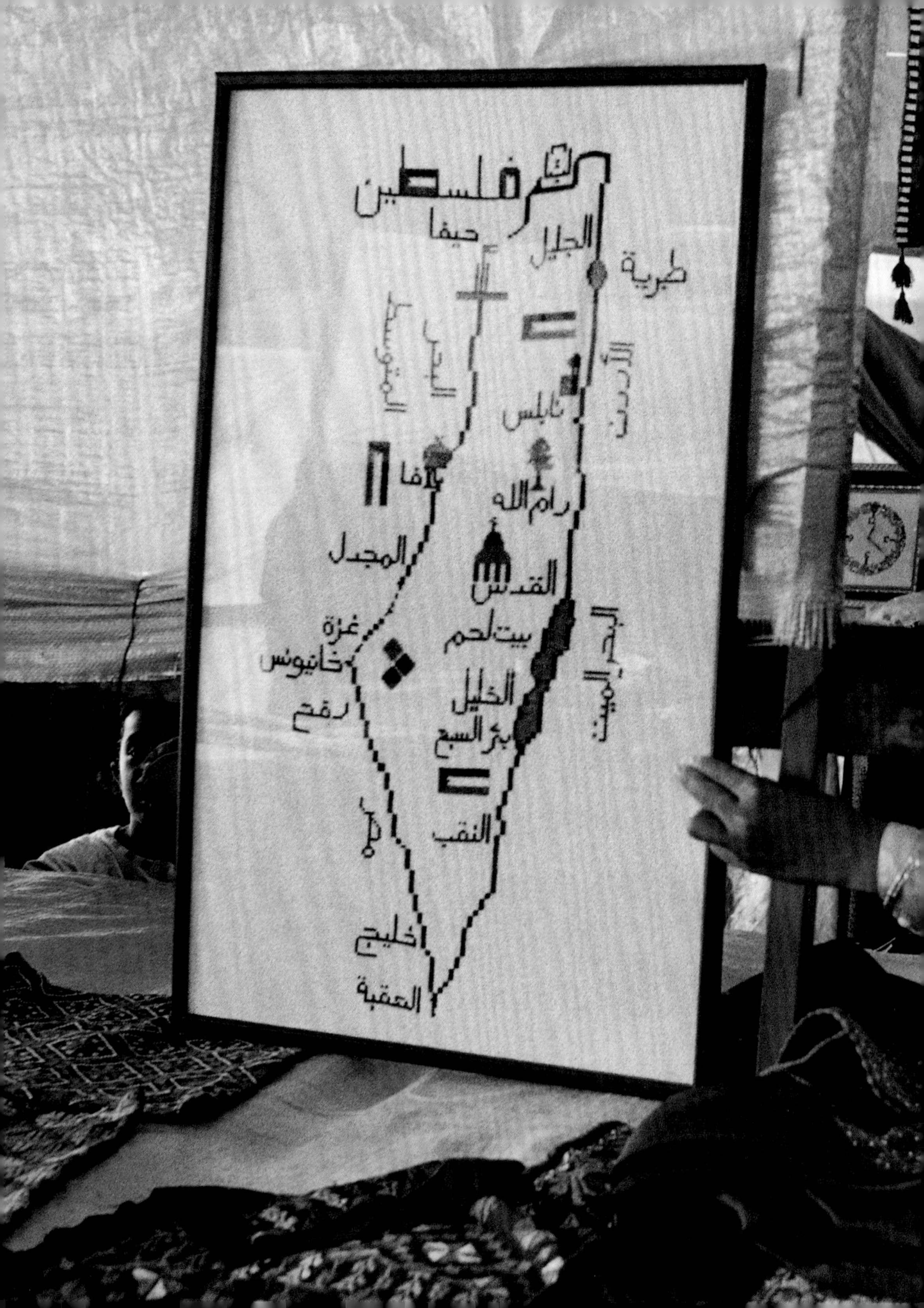

فلسطين
الجليل
حيفا
طبرية
الأردن
نابلس
رام الله
يافا
القدس
المجدل
بيت لحم
غزة
الخليل
خانيونس
بئر السبع
رفح
النقب
خليج
العقبة

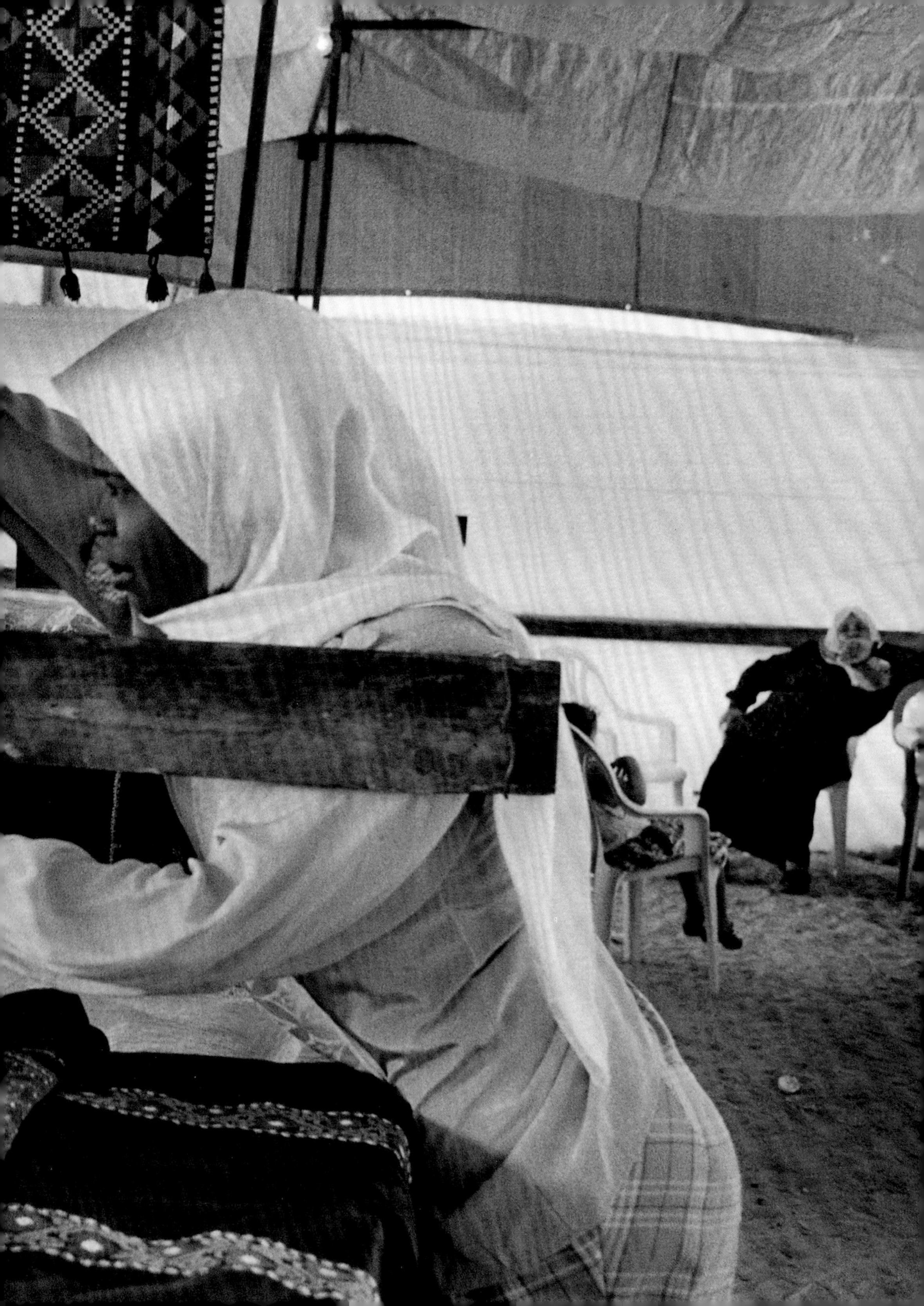

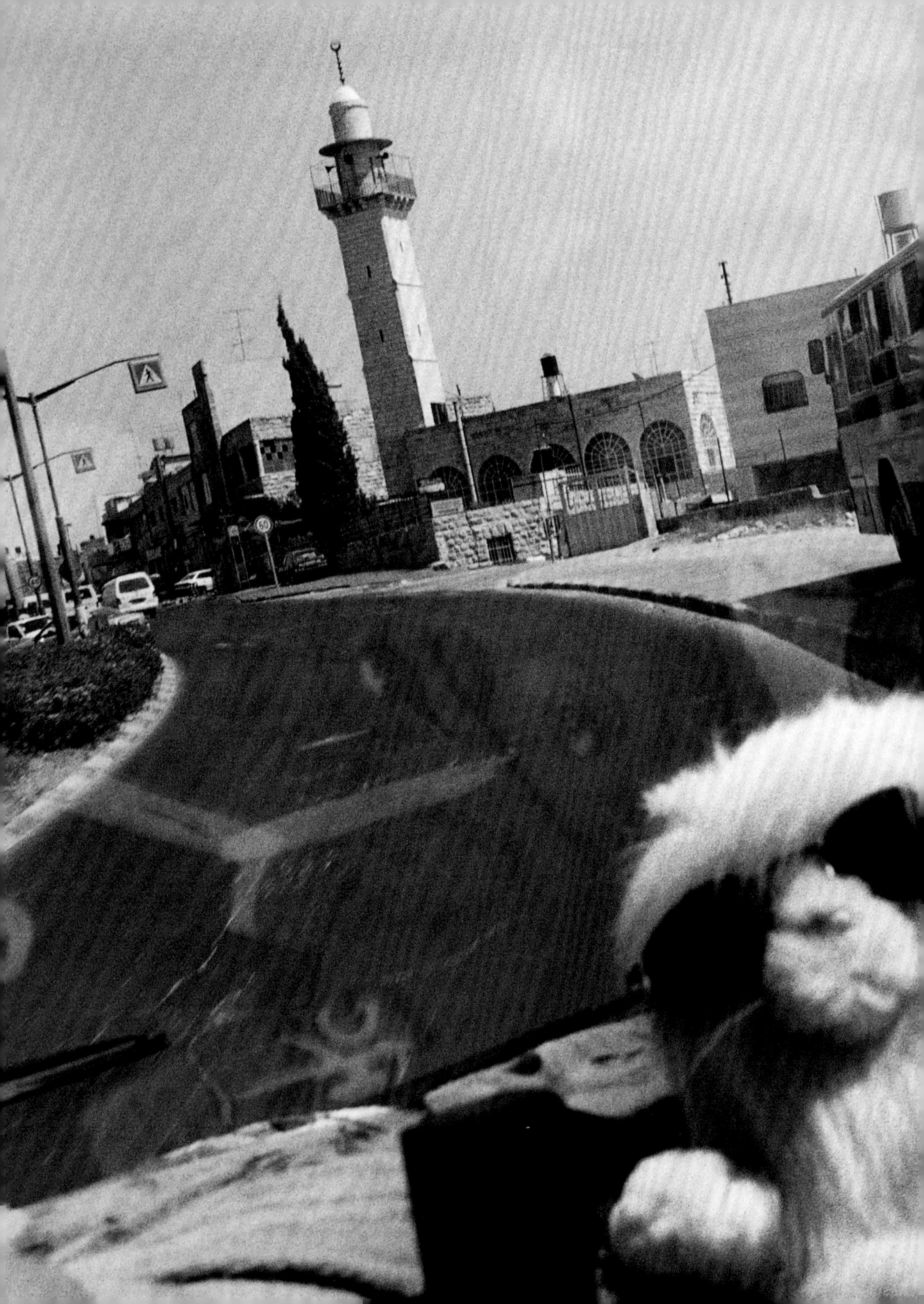

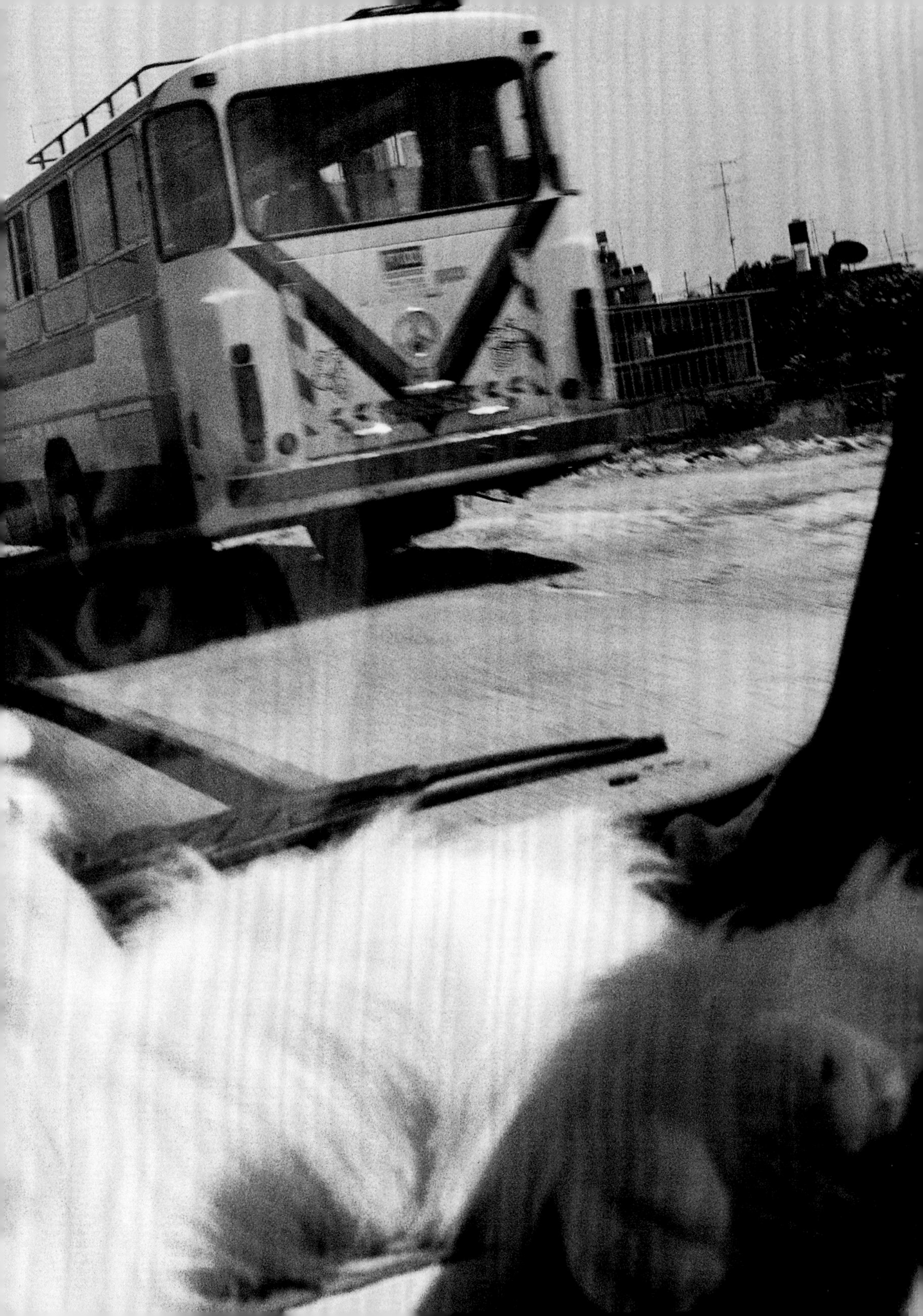

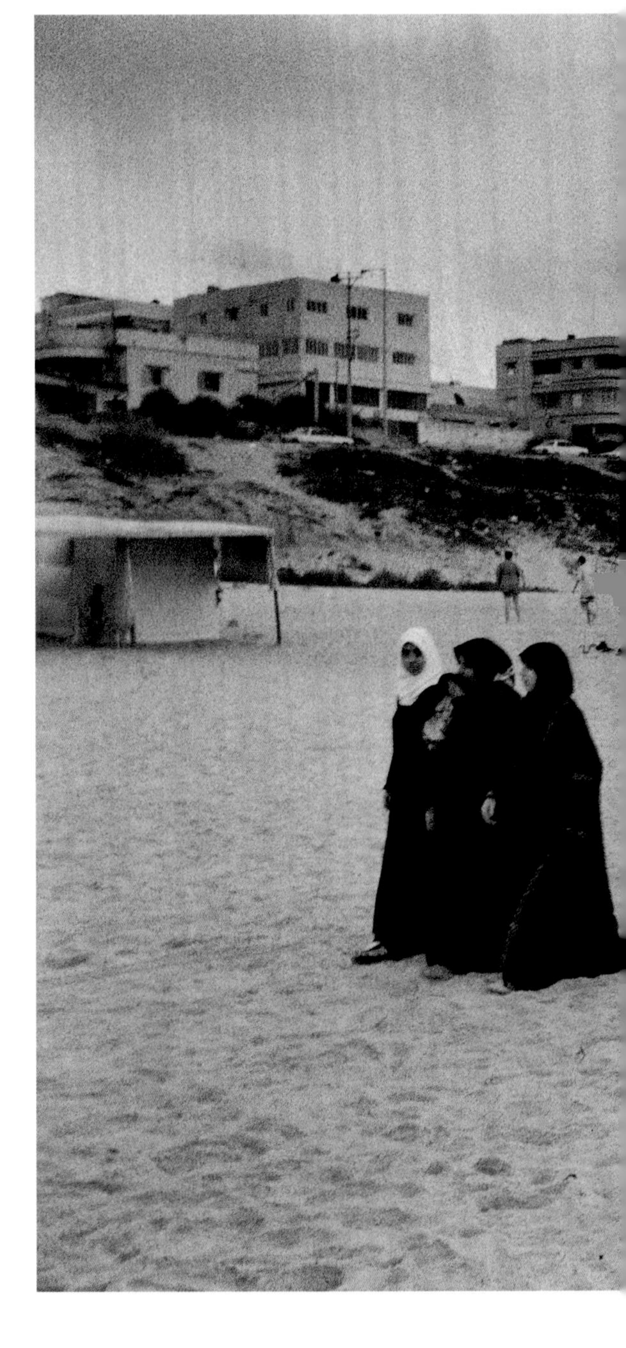

SBITANY

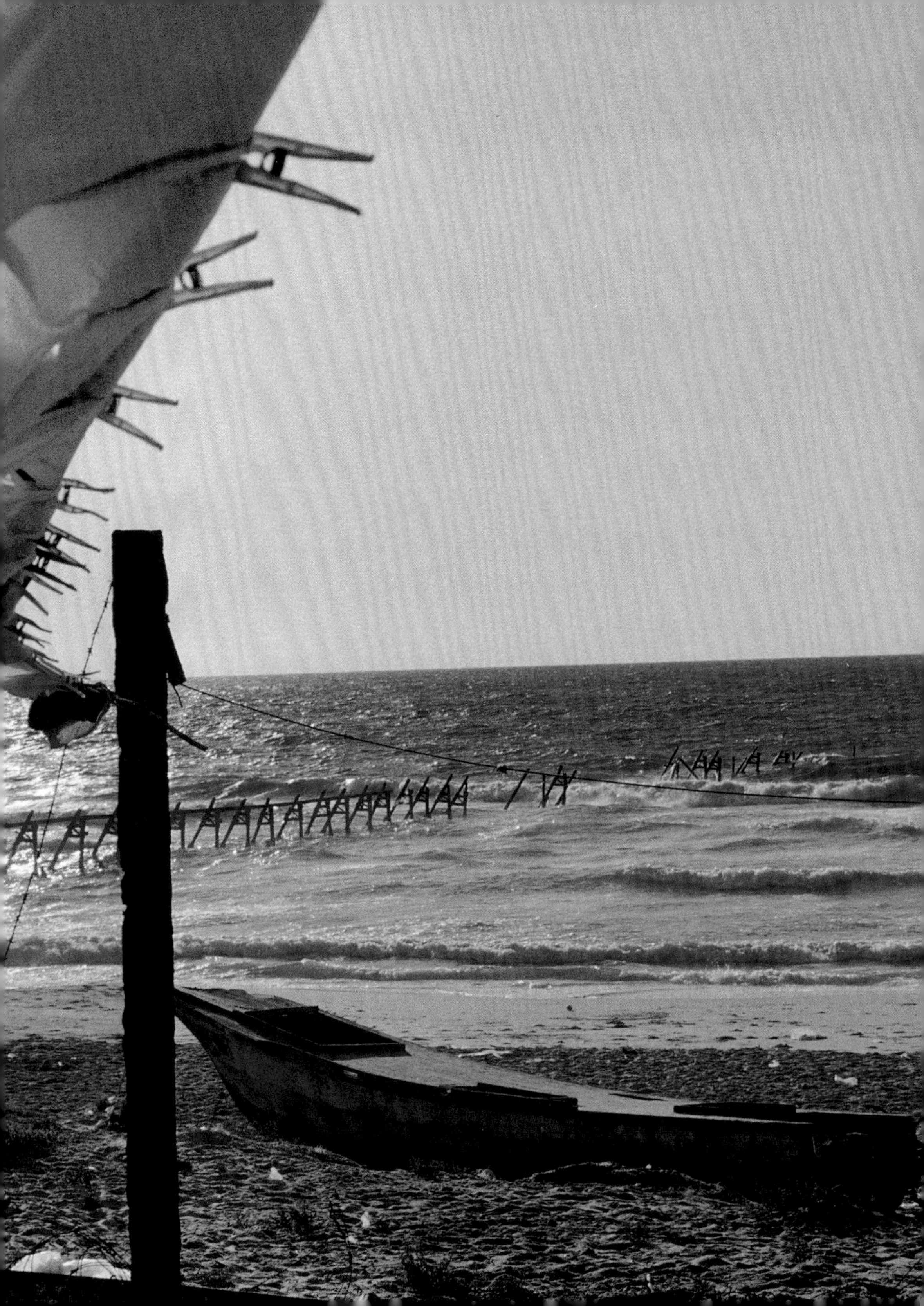

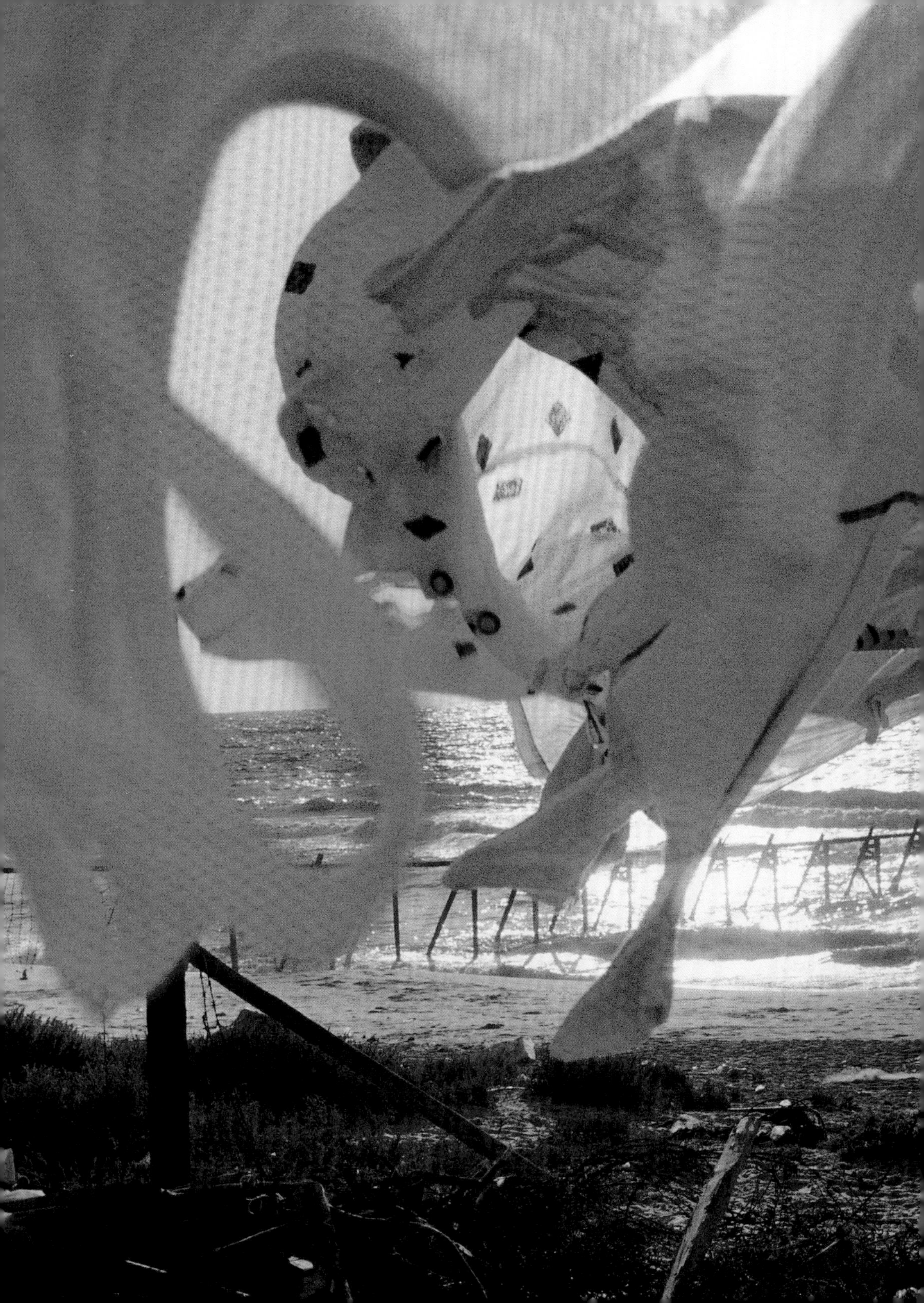

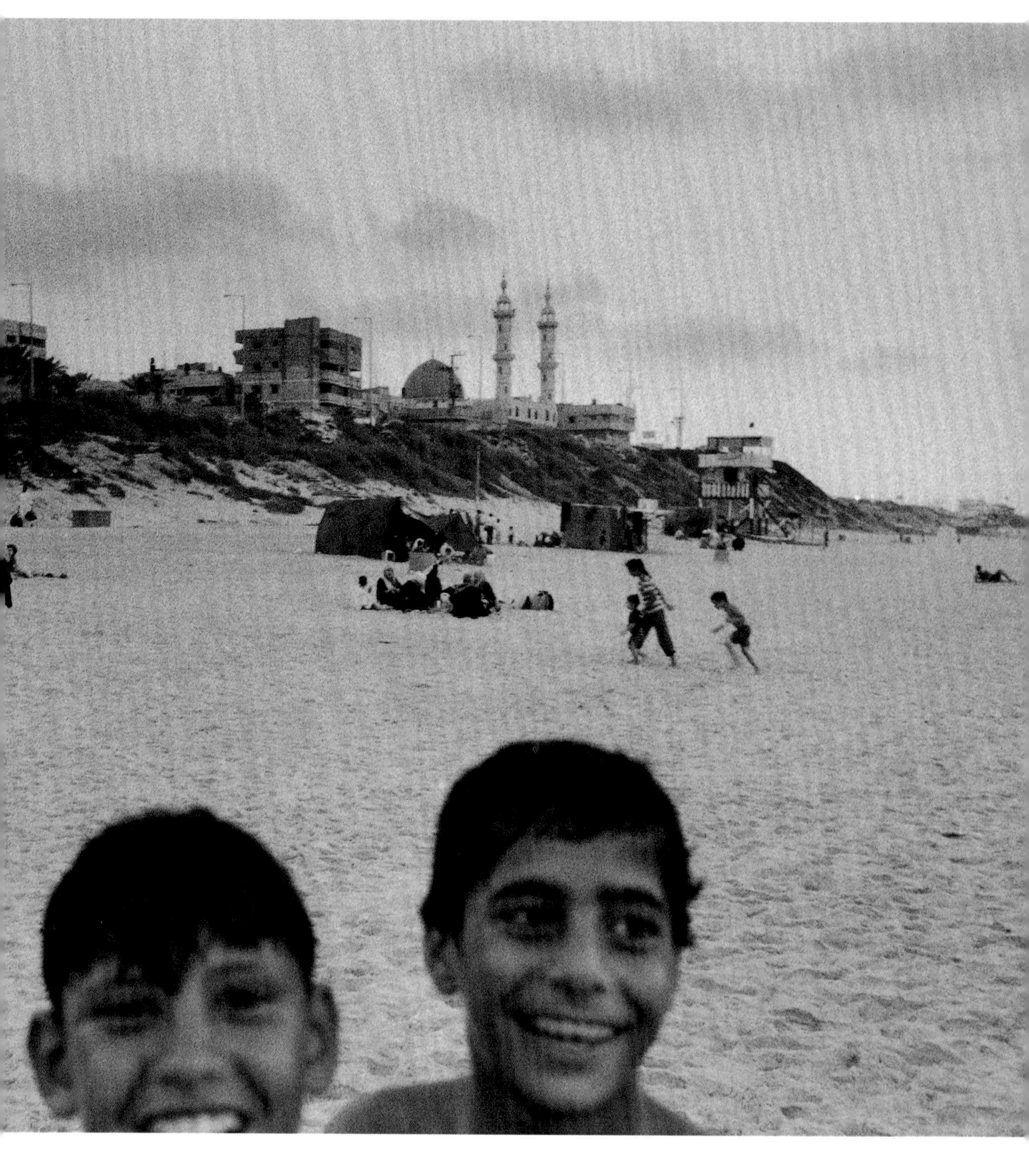

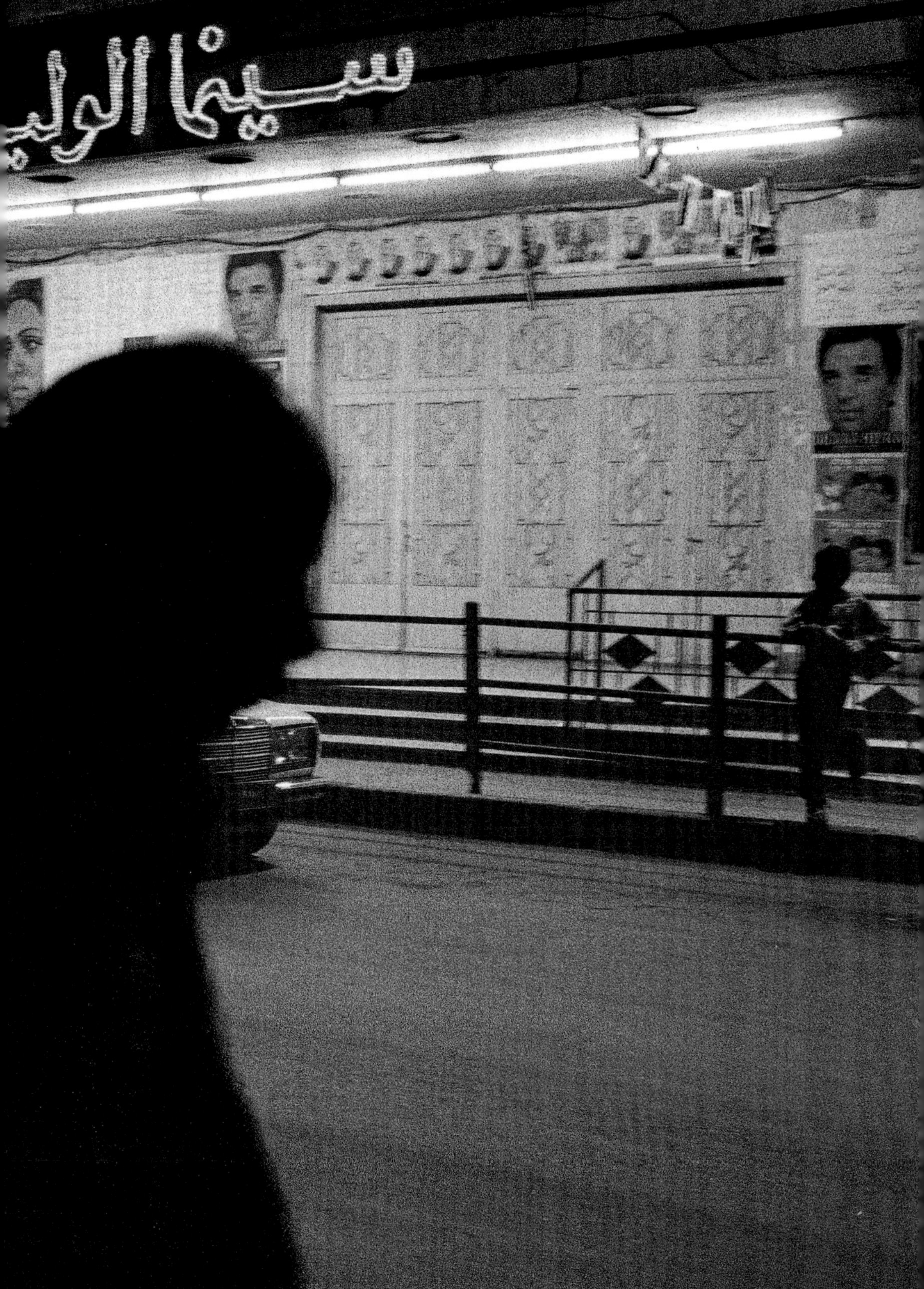

سينما الوليد

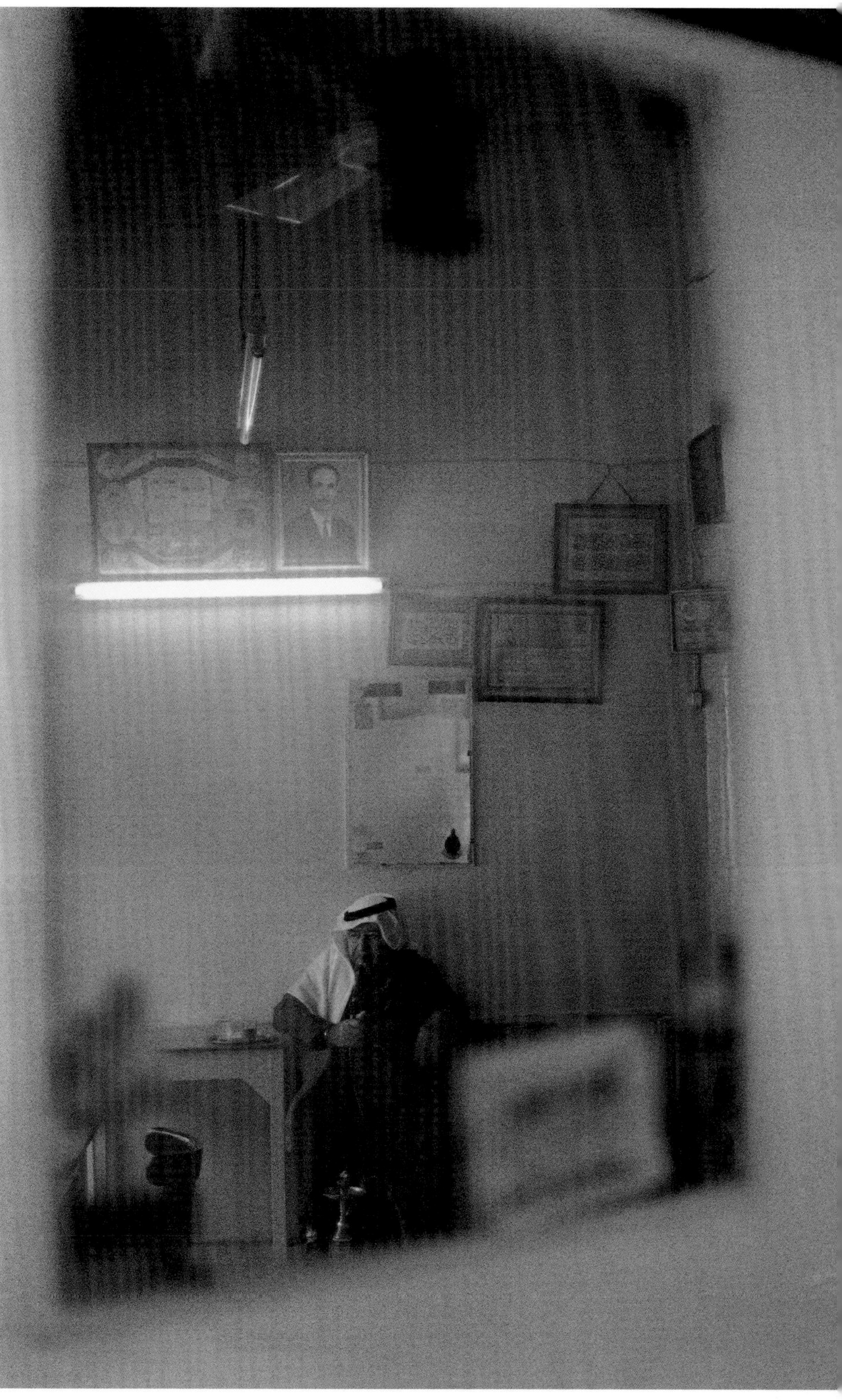

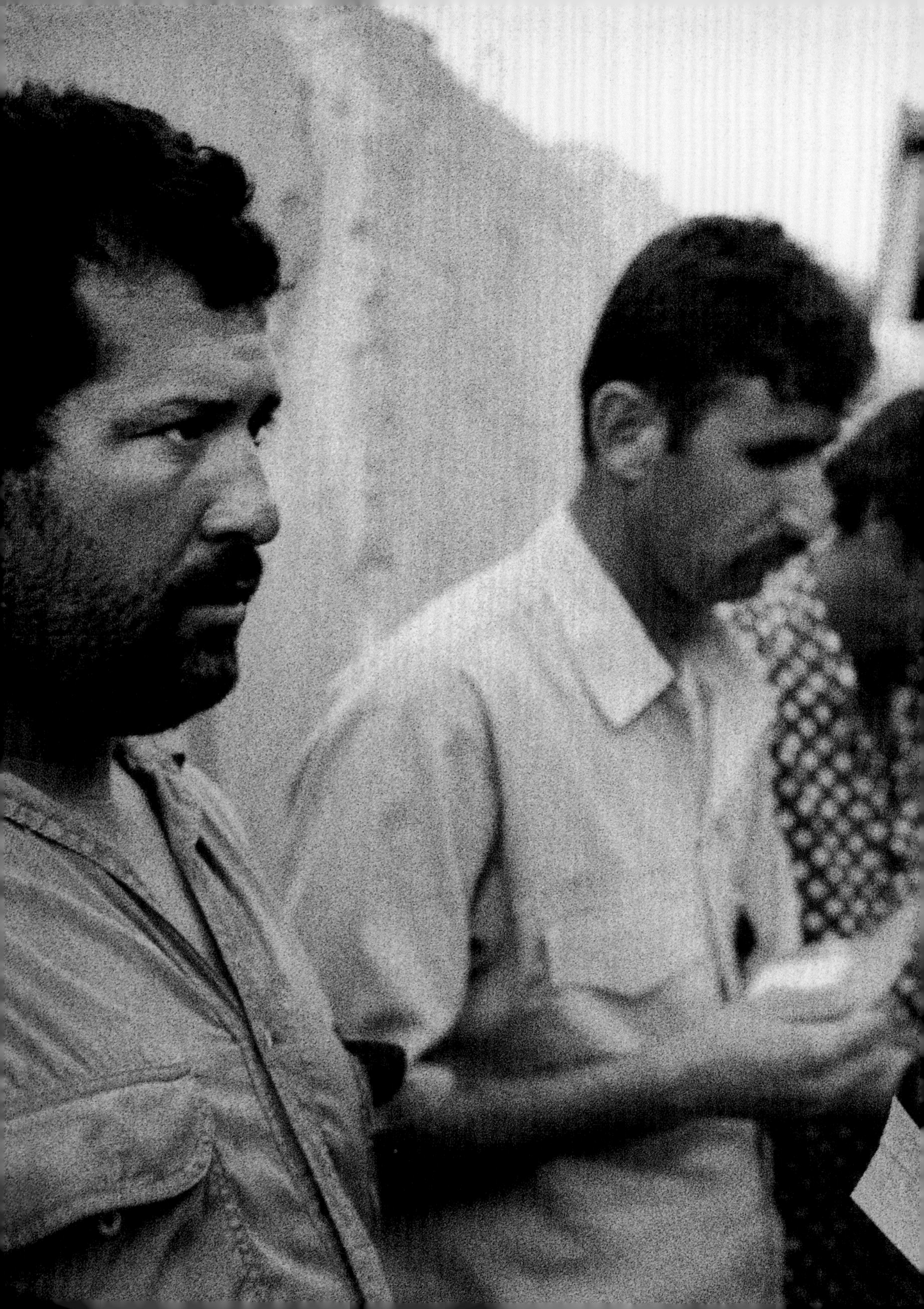

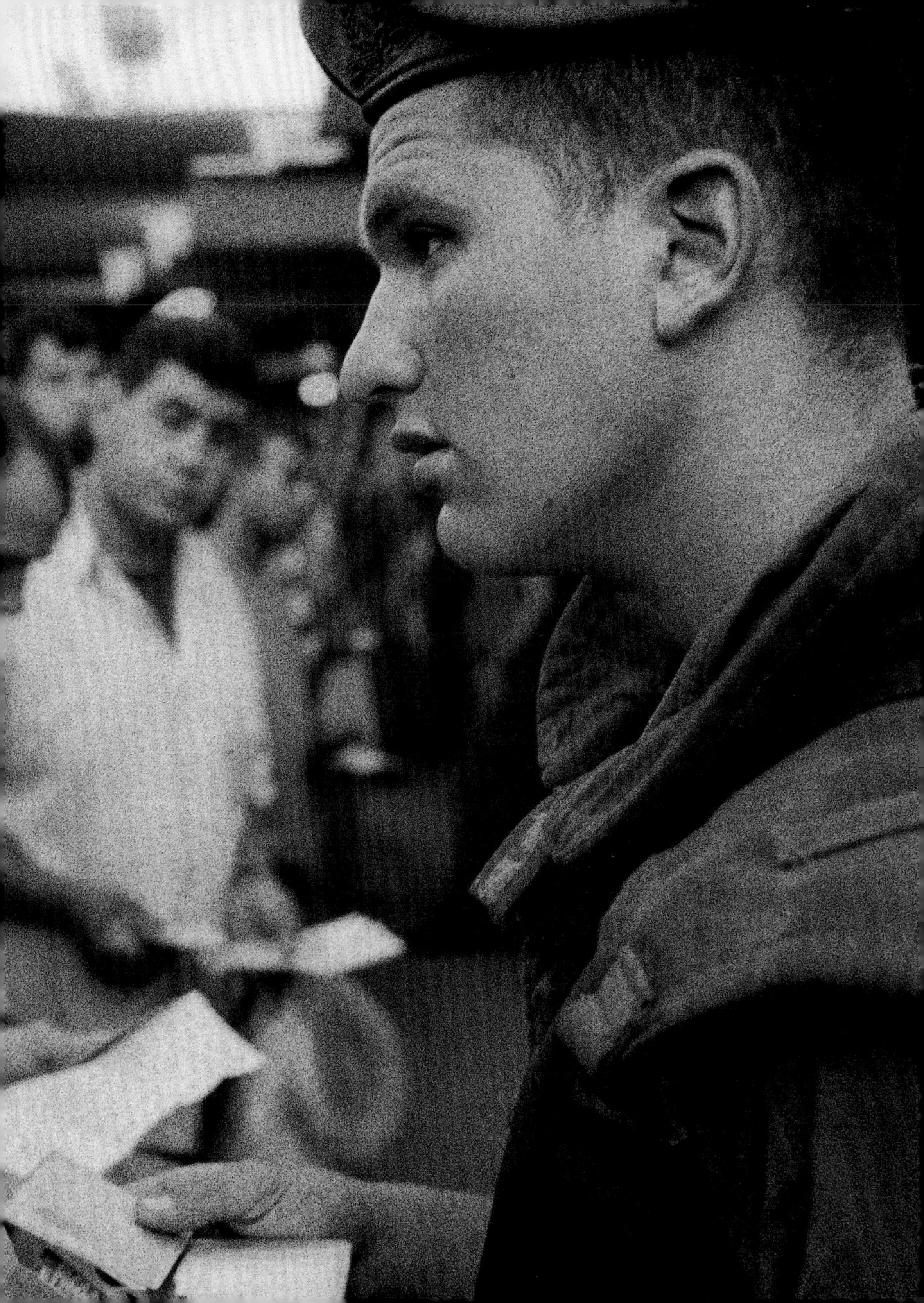

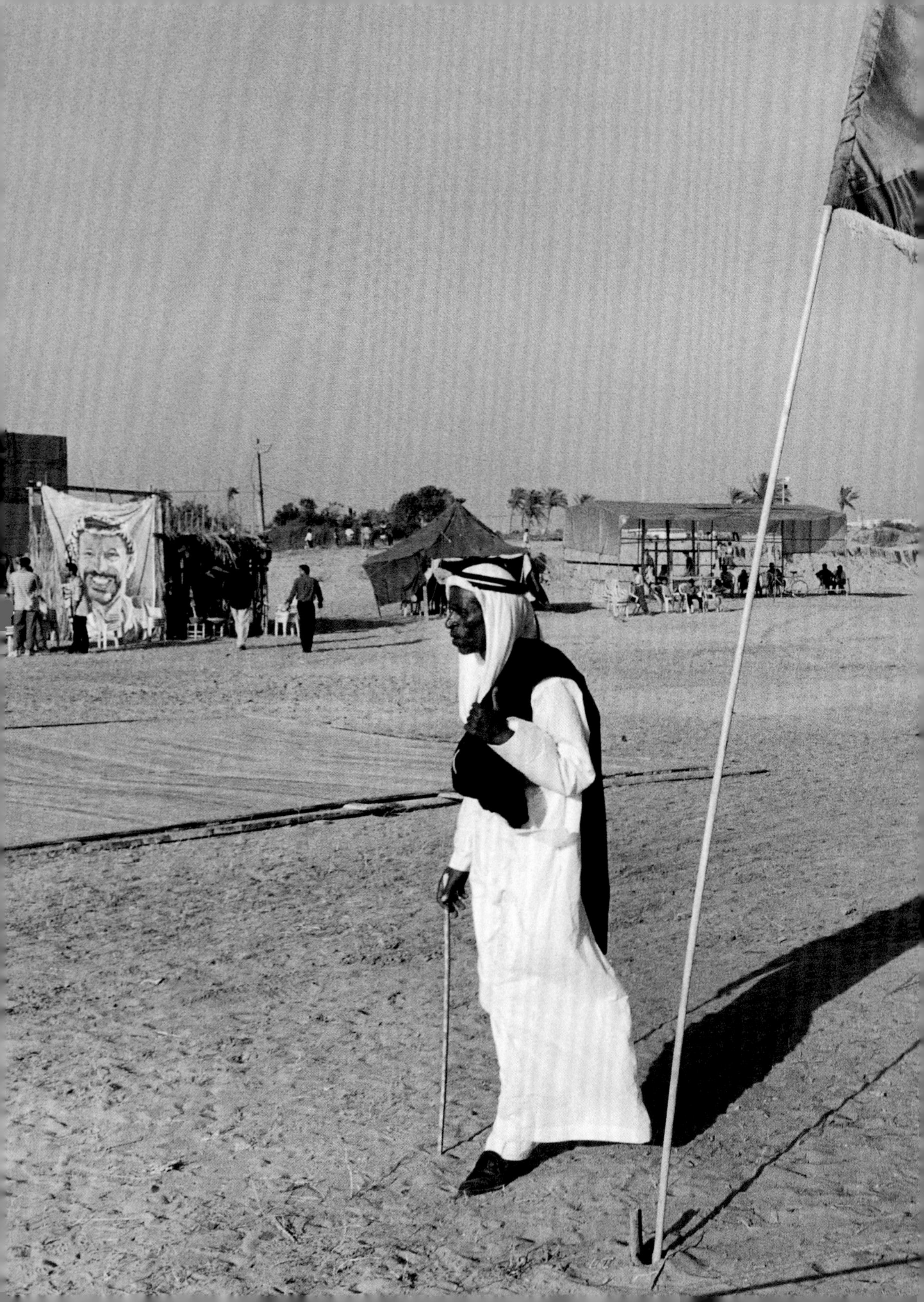

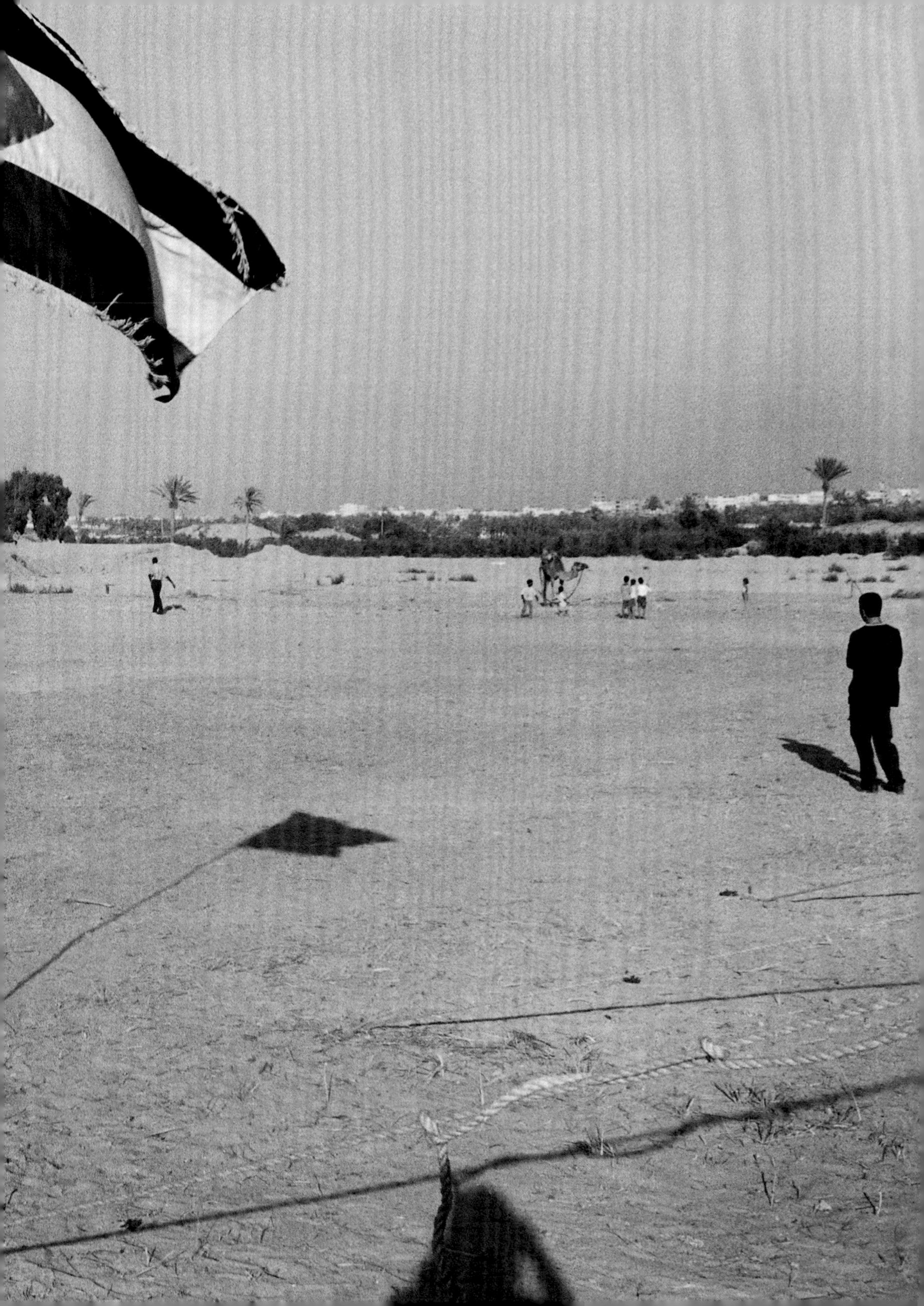

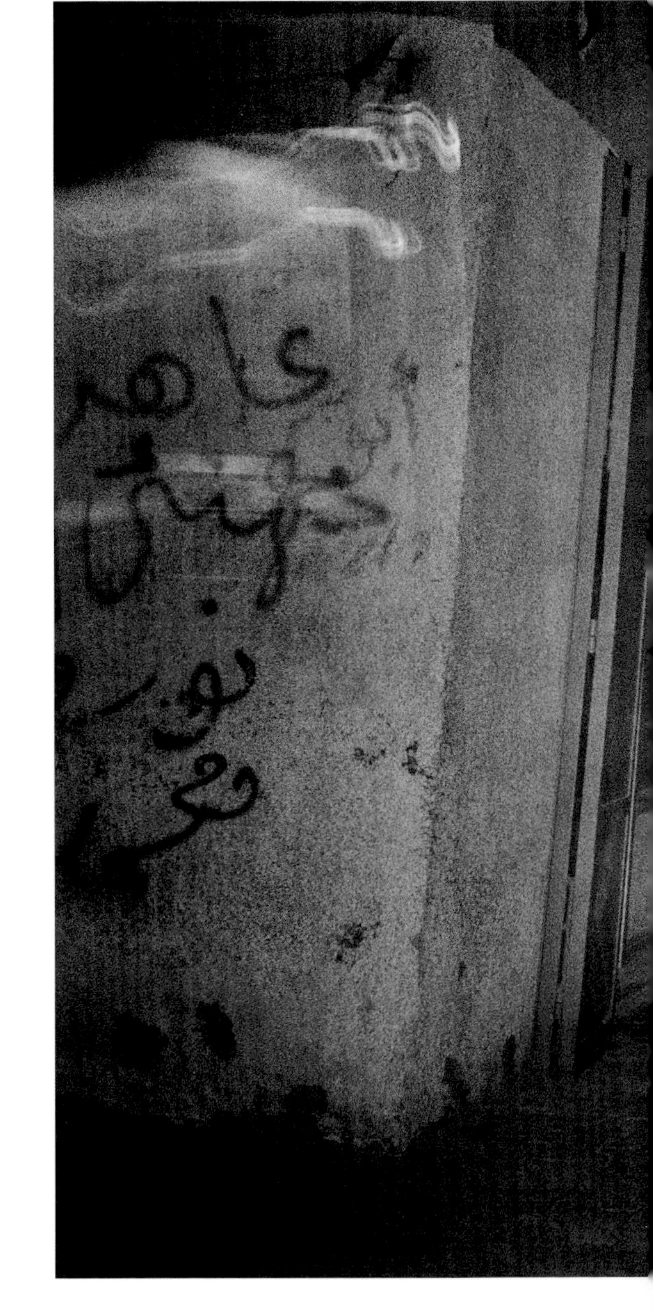

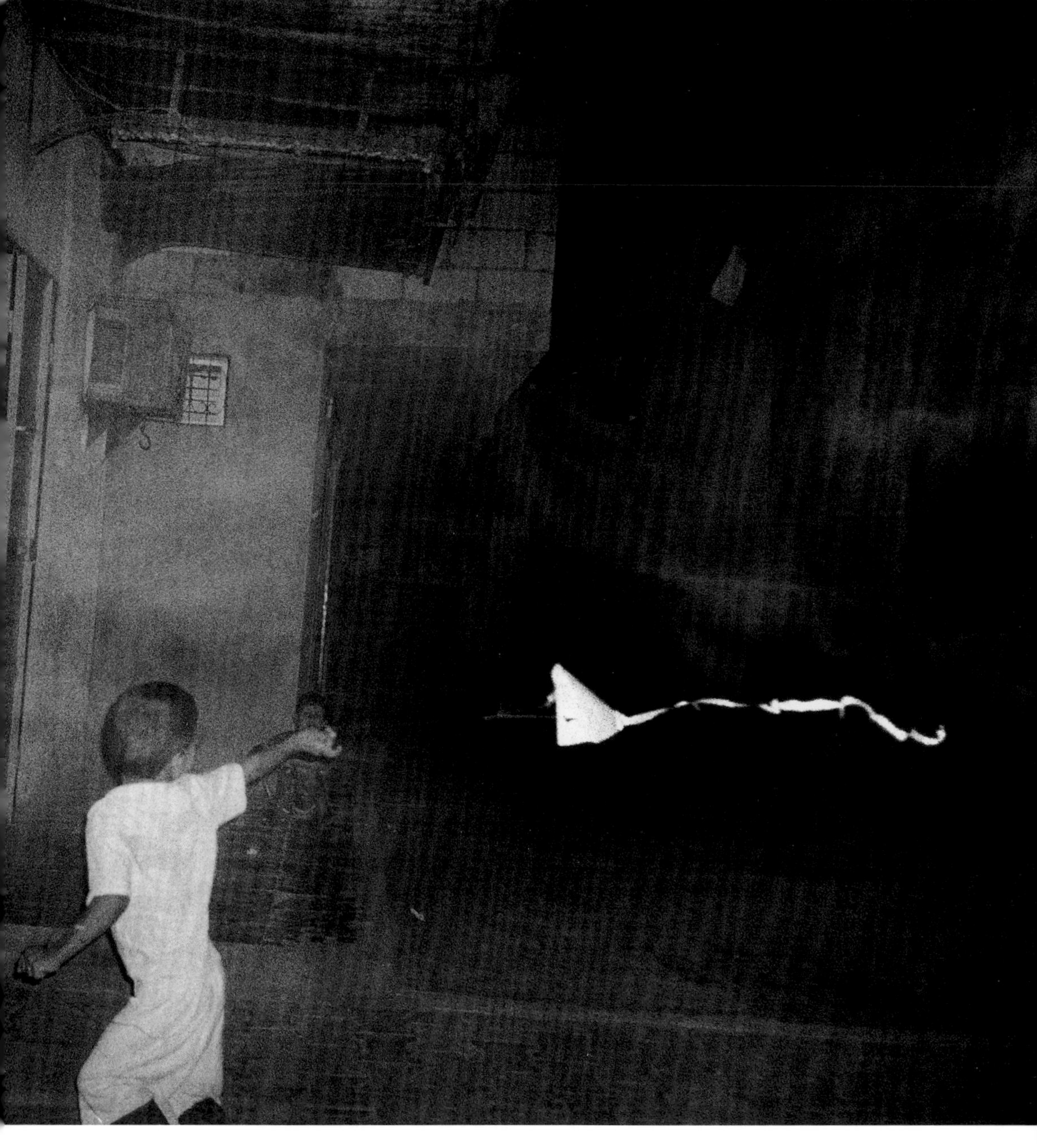

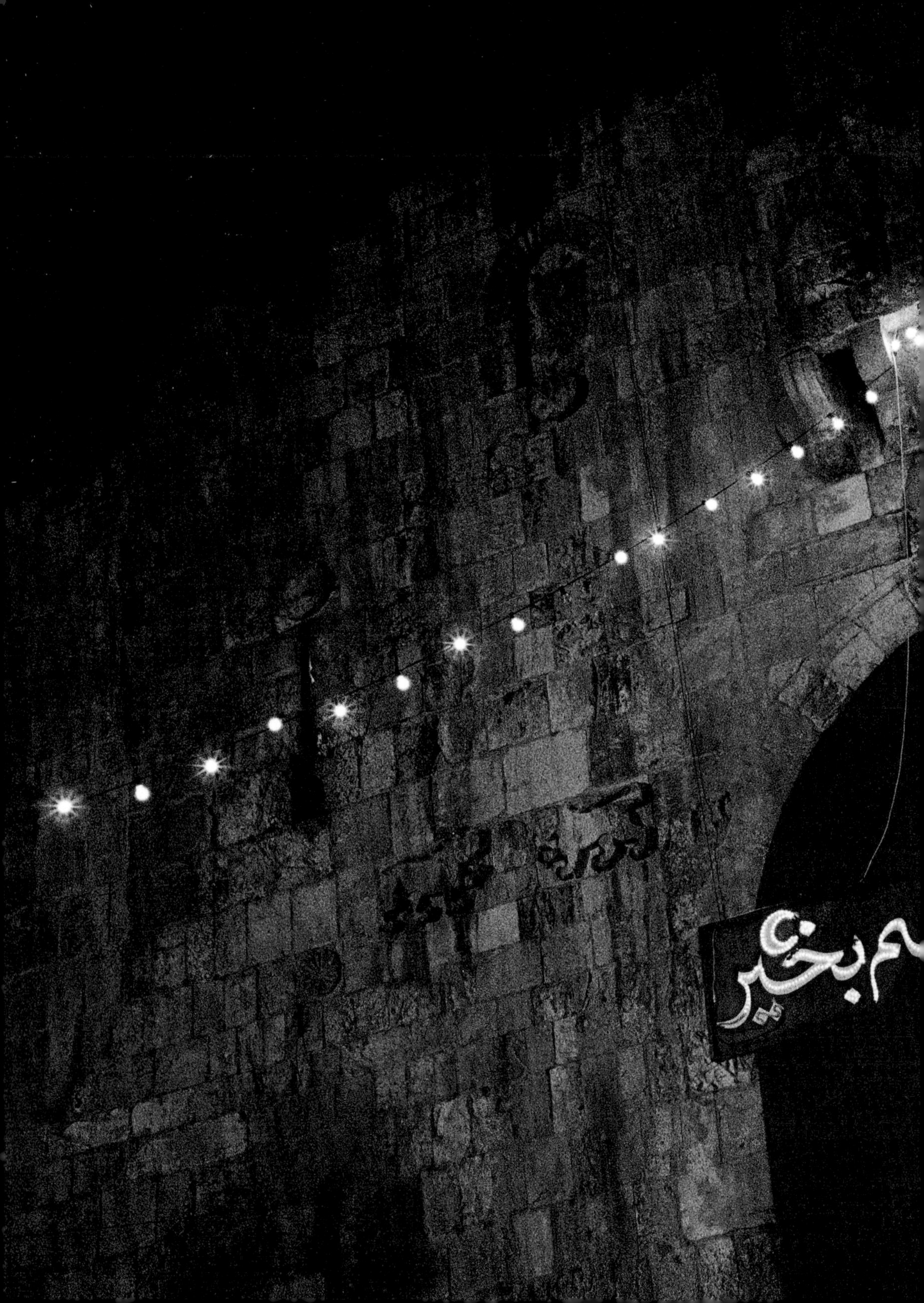
م بخير

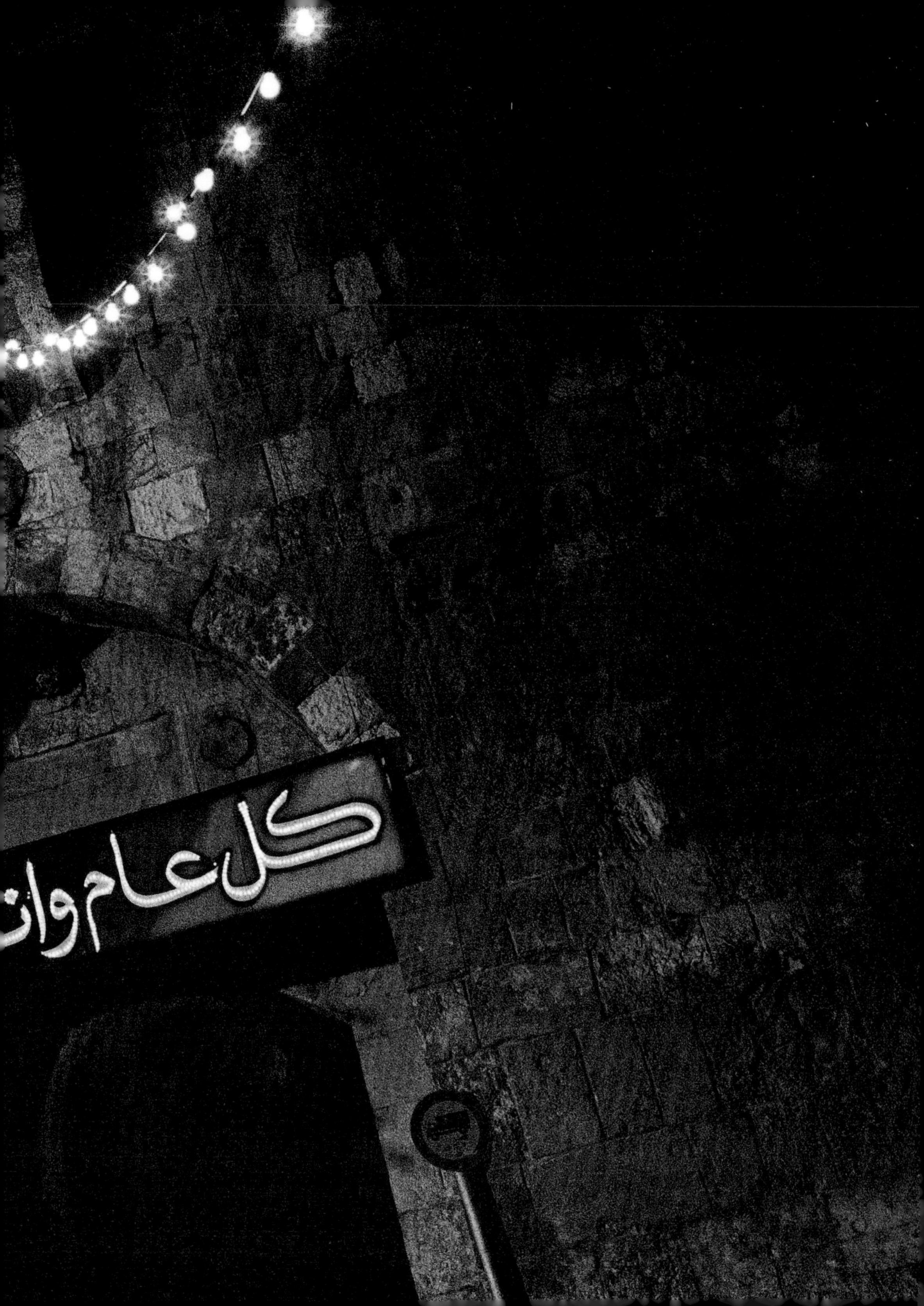

كل عام
وانت

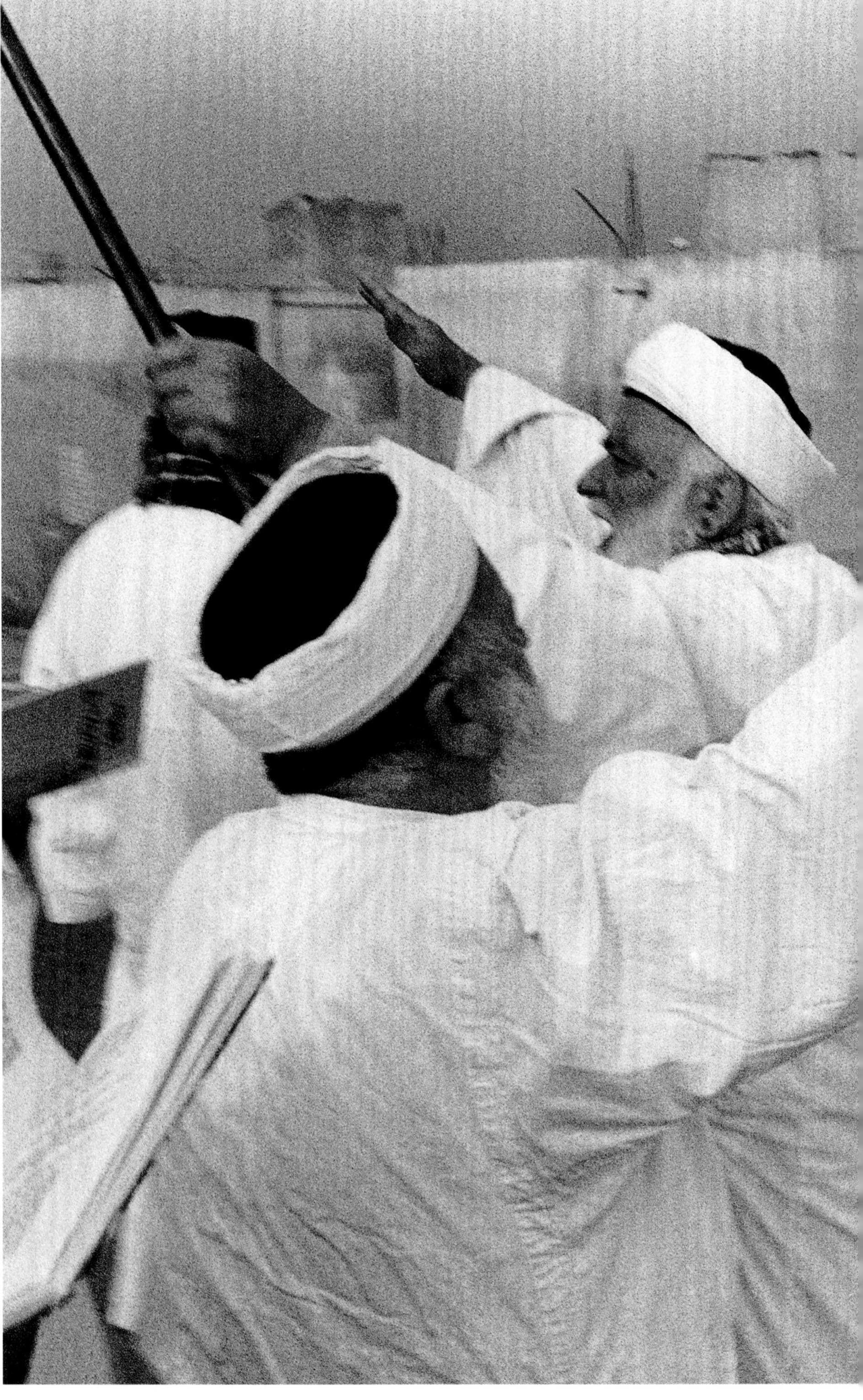

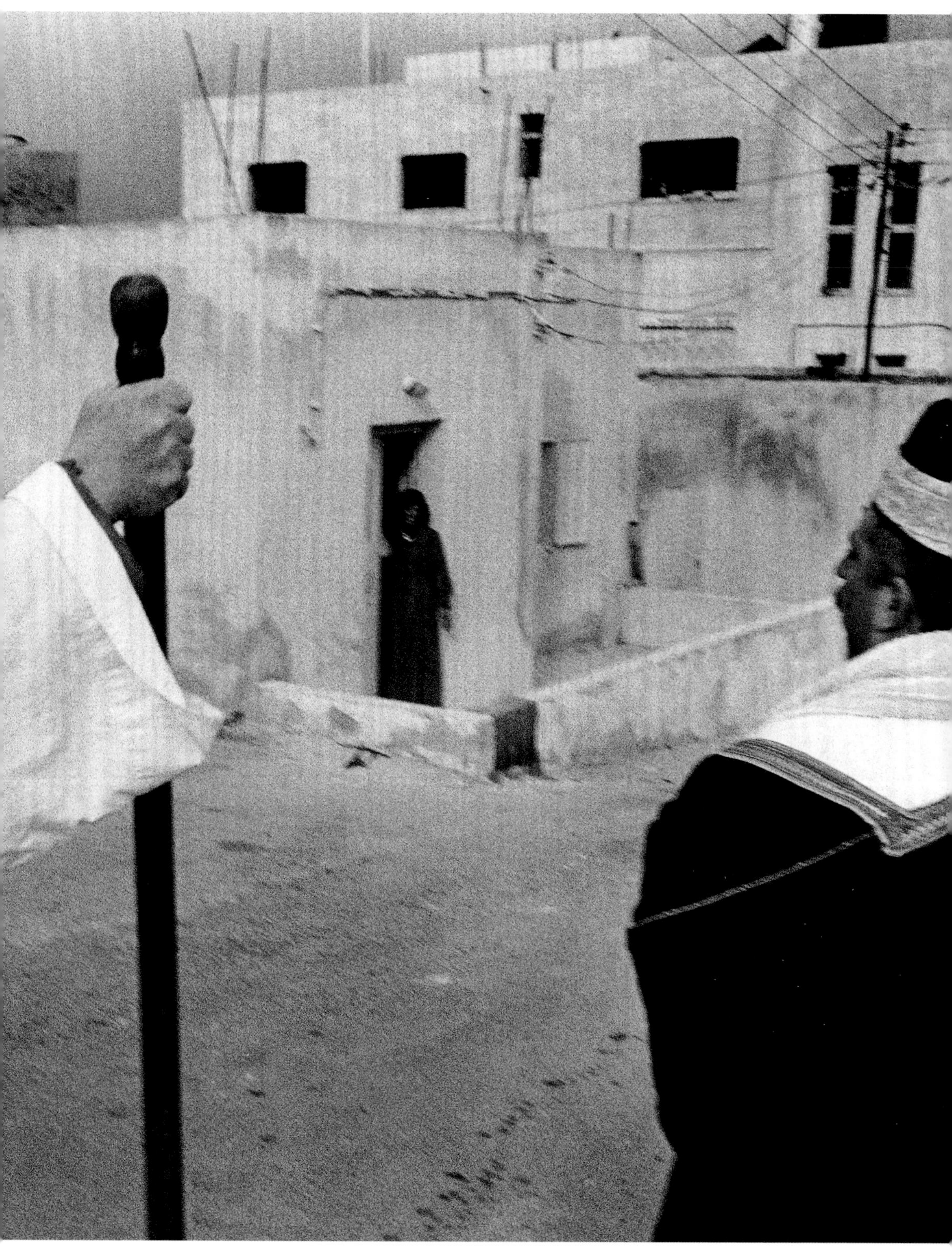

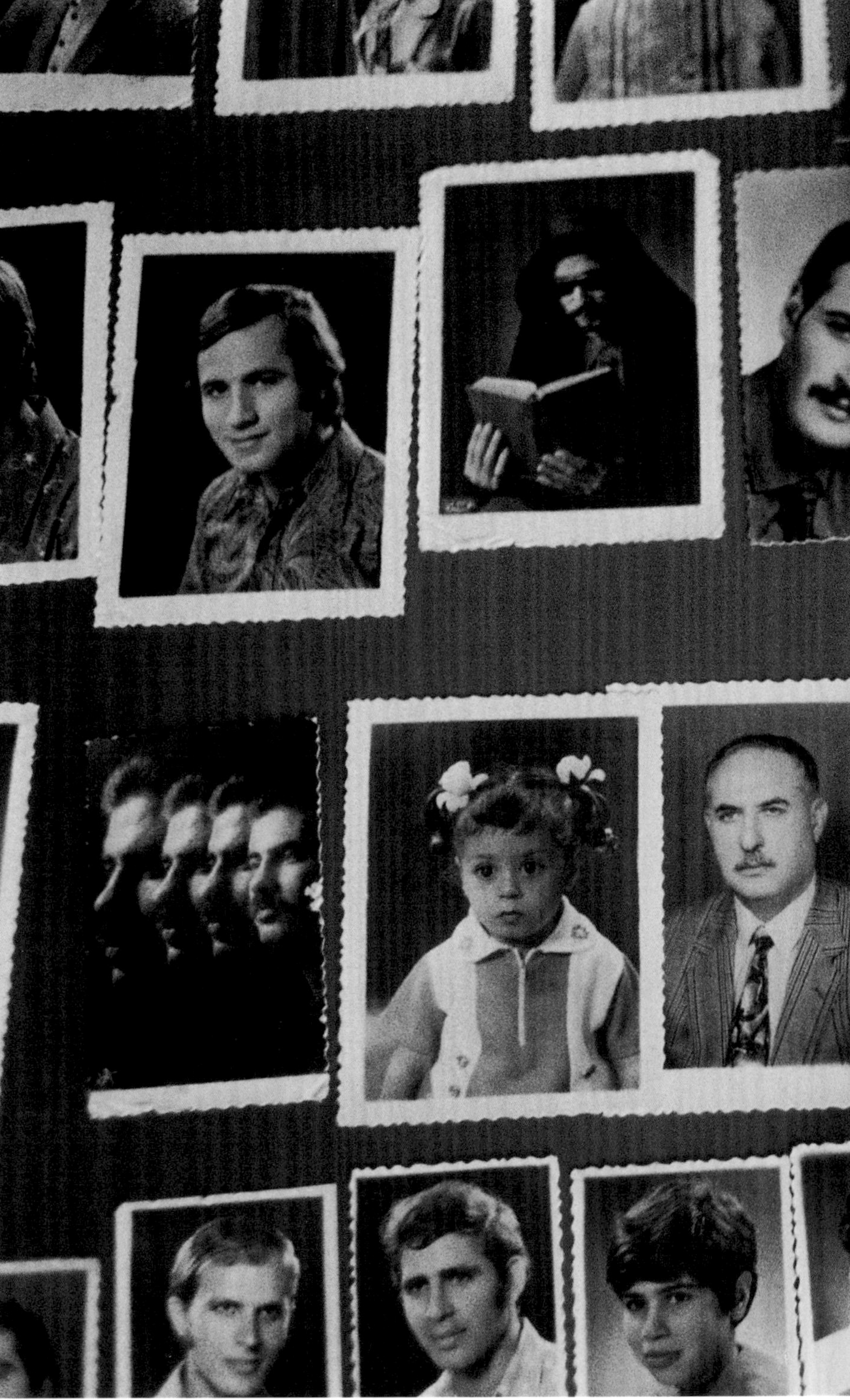

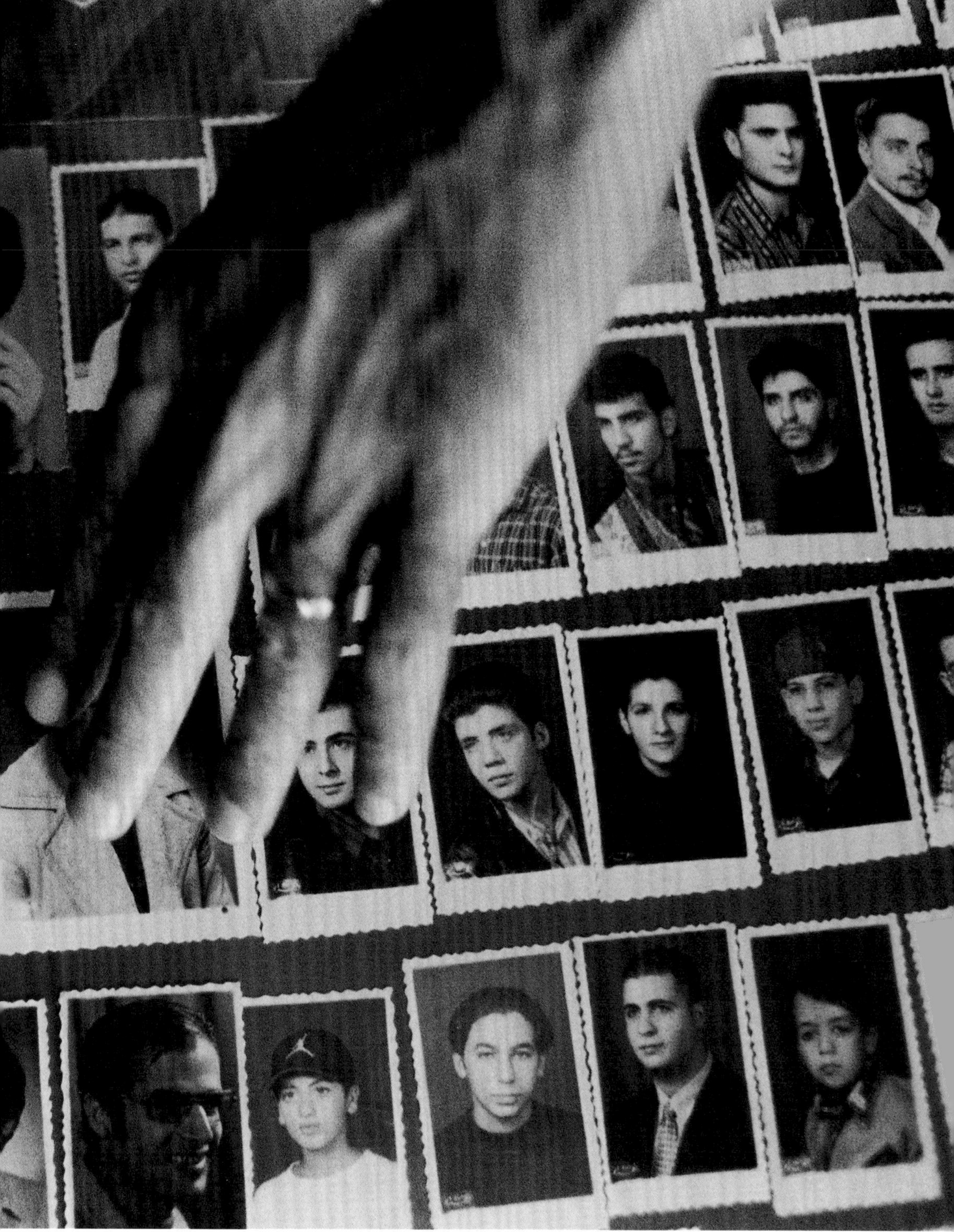

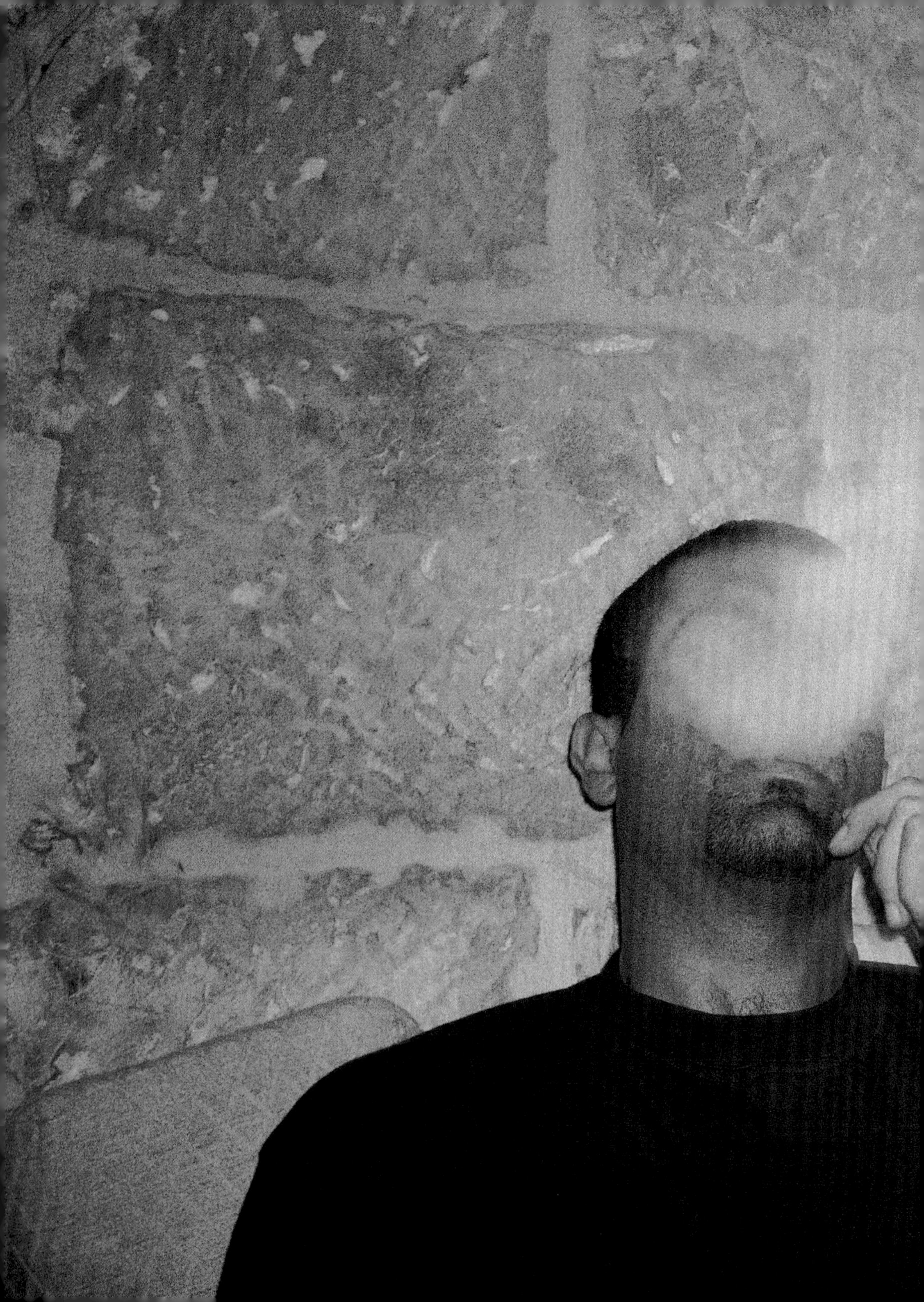

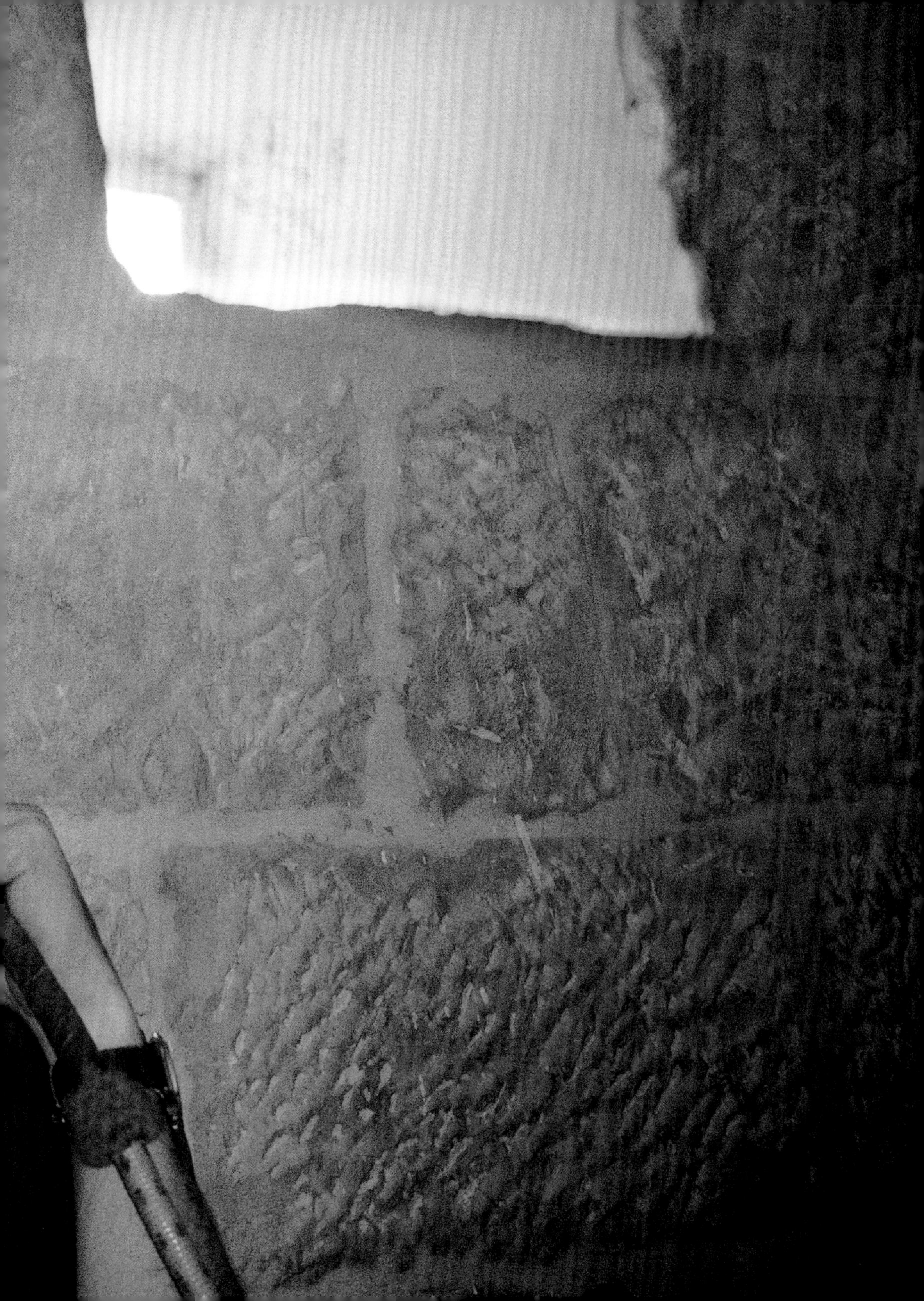

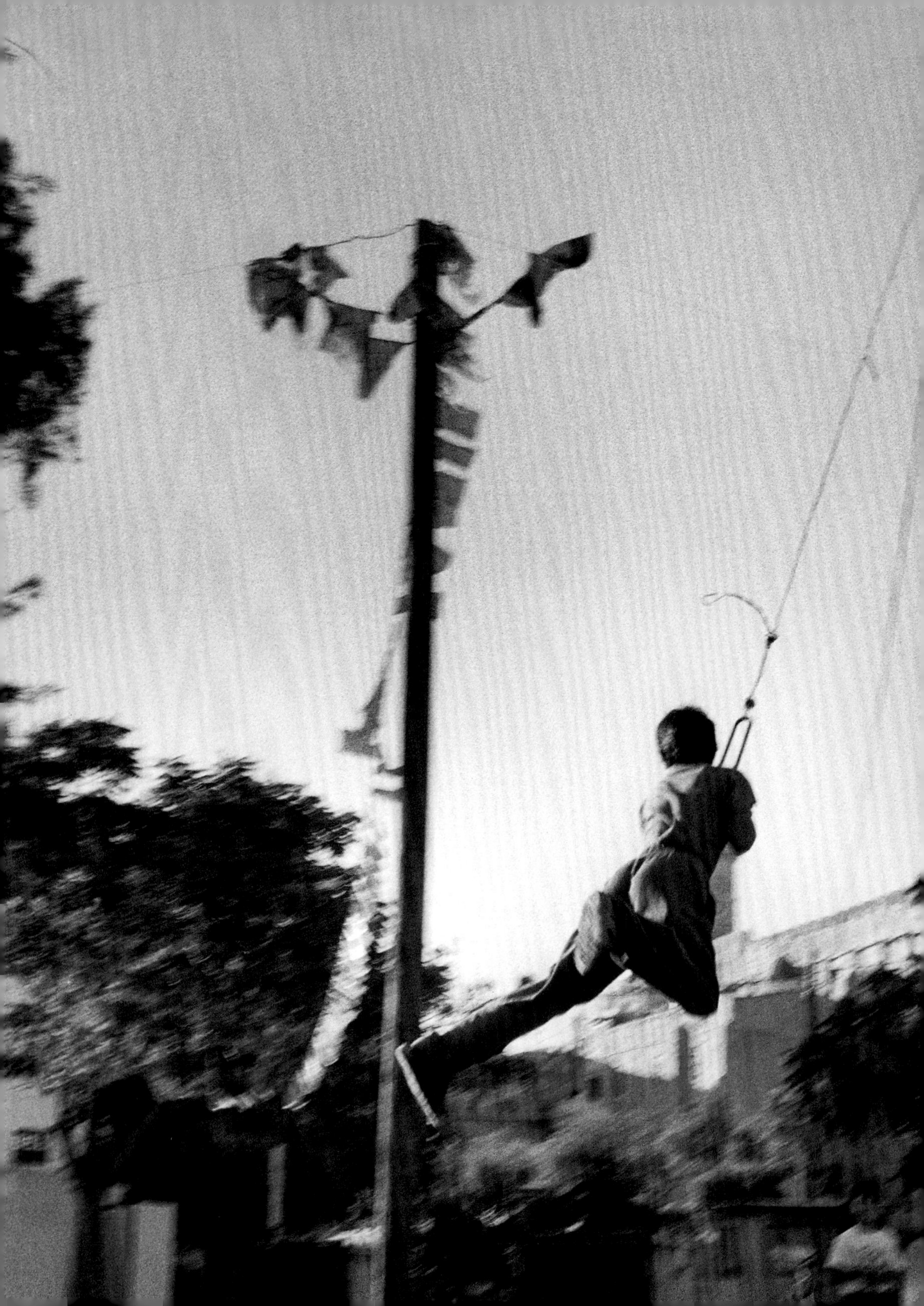

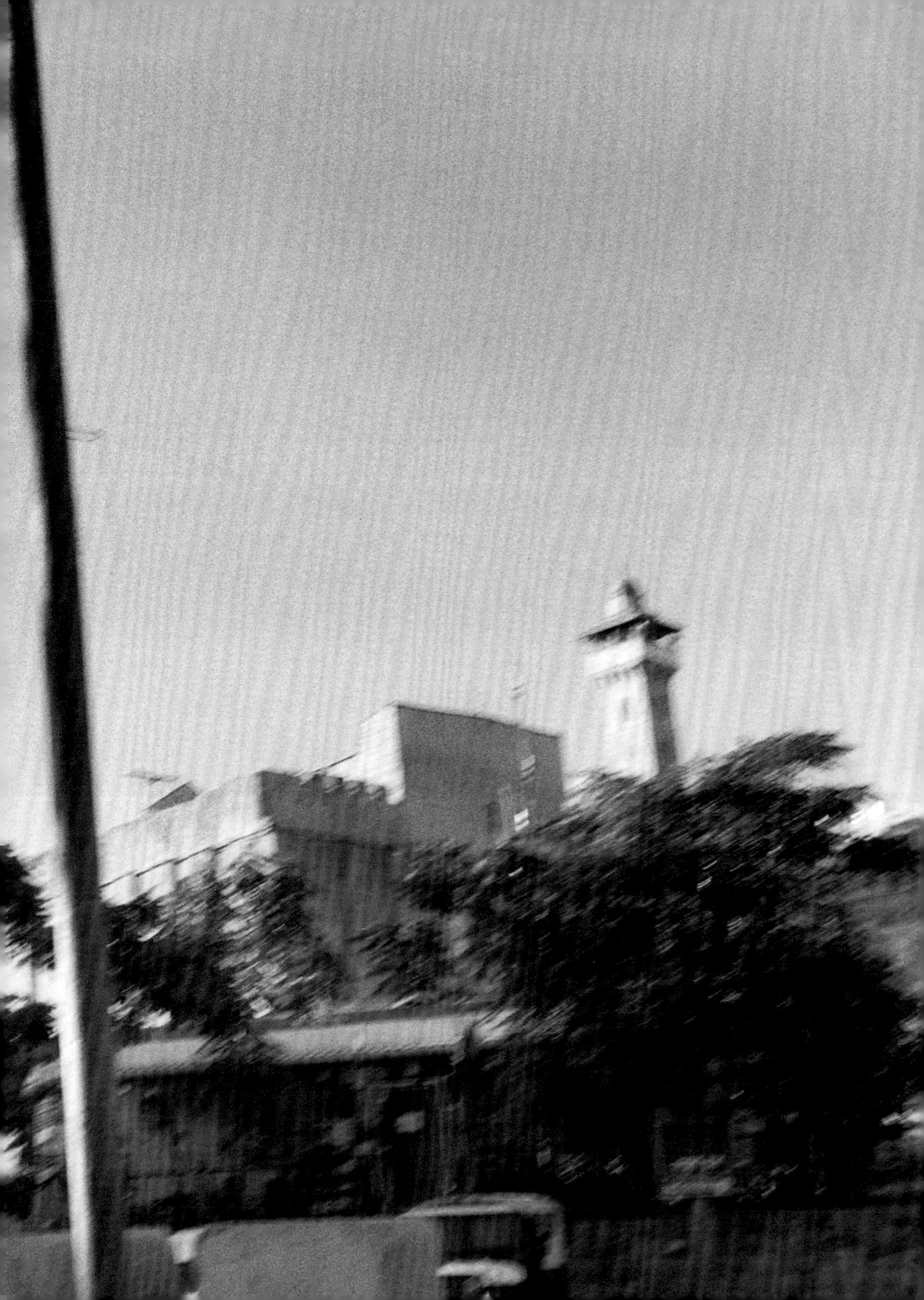

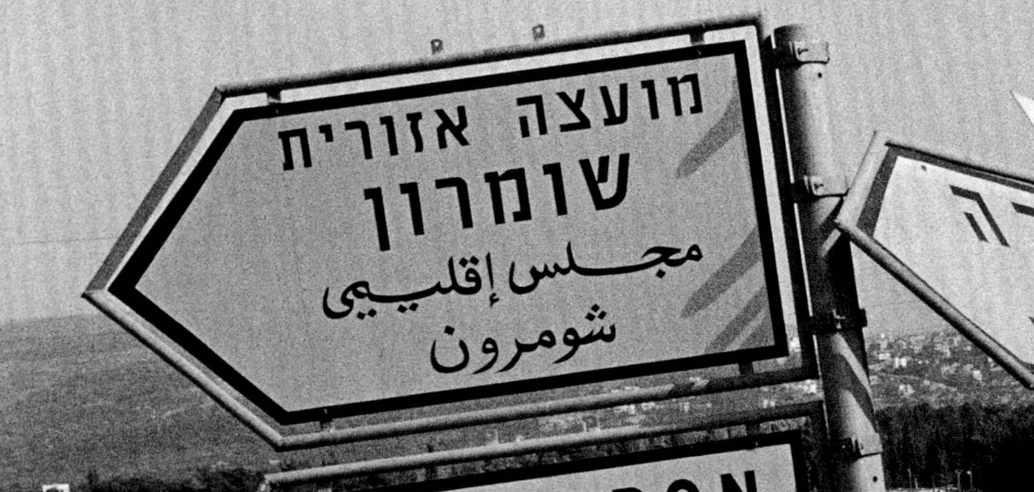
מועצה אזורית
שומרון
مجلس إقليمي
شومرون
SHOMERON
REGIONAL
COUNCIL
60
הדרך
برك
BERA

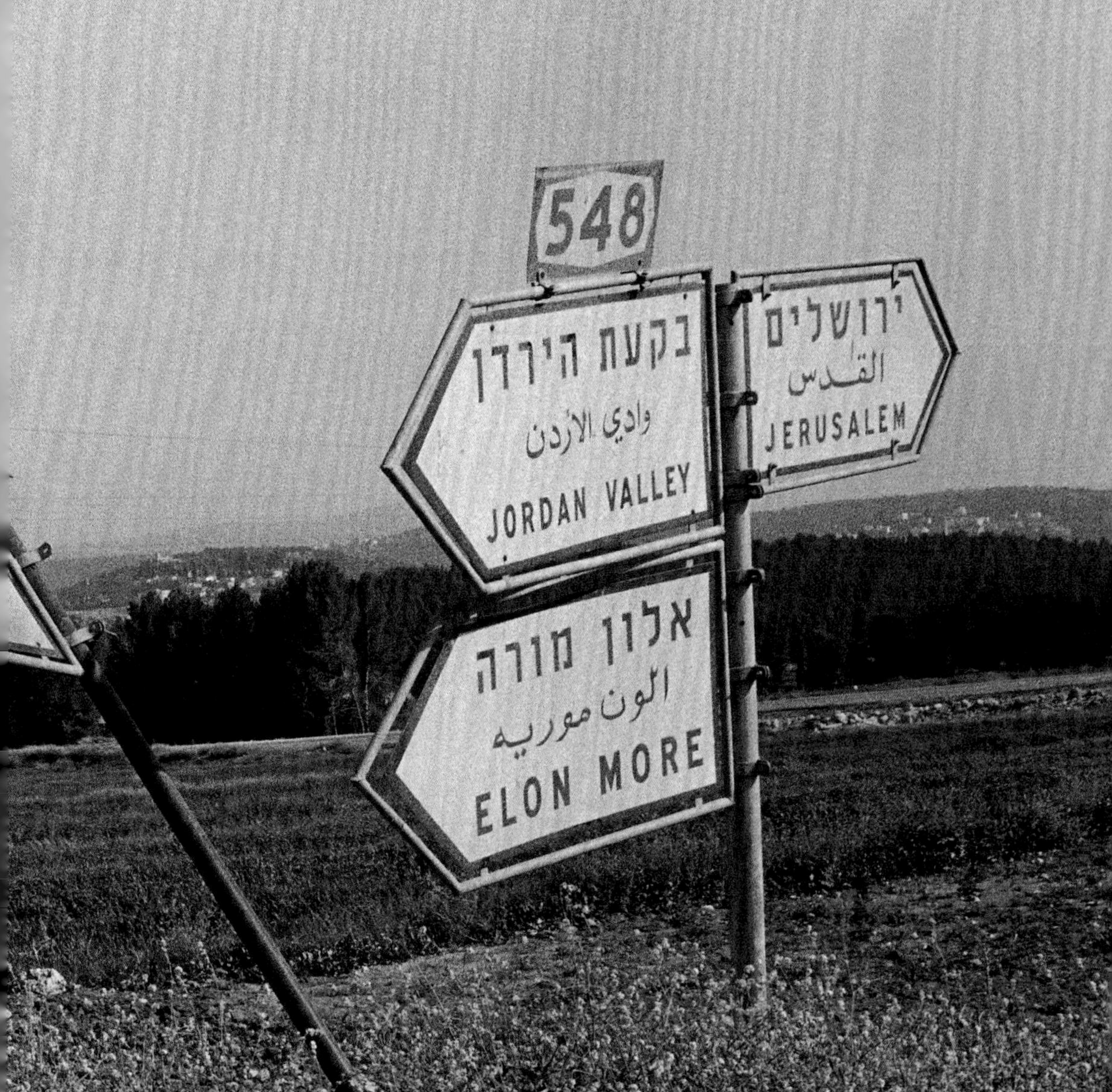
548
בקעת הירדן
وادي الأردن
JORDAN VALLEY
ירושלים
القدس
JERUSALEM
אלון מורה
الون موريه
ELON MORE

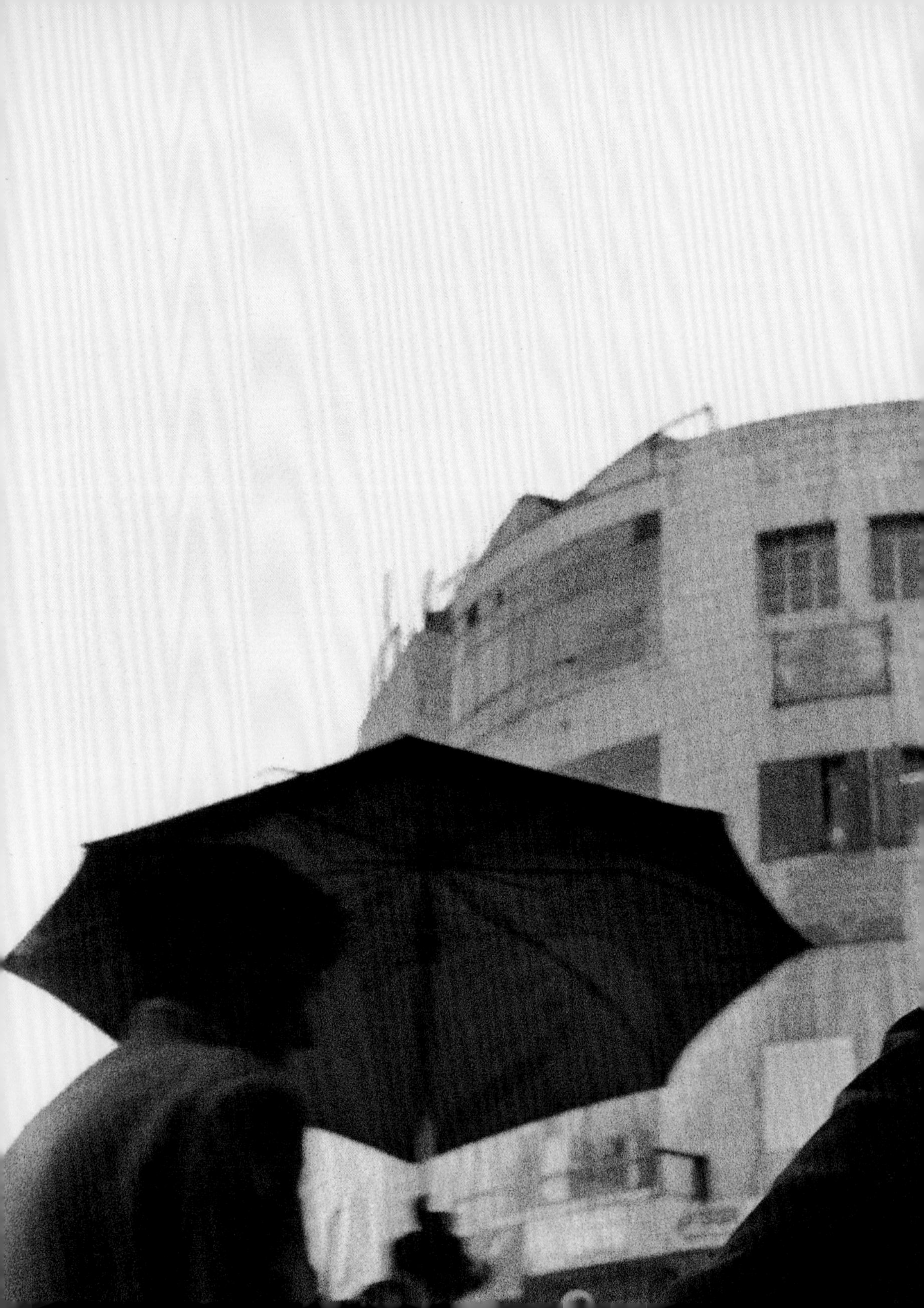

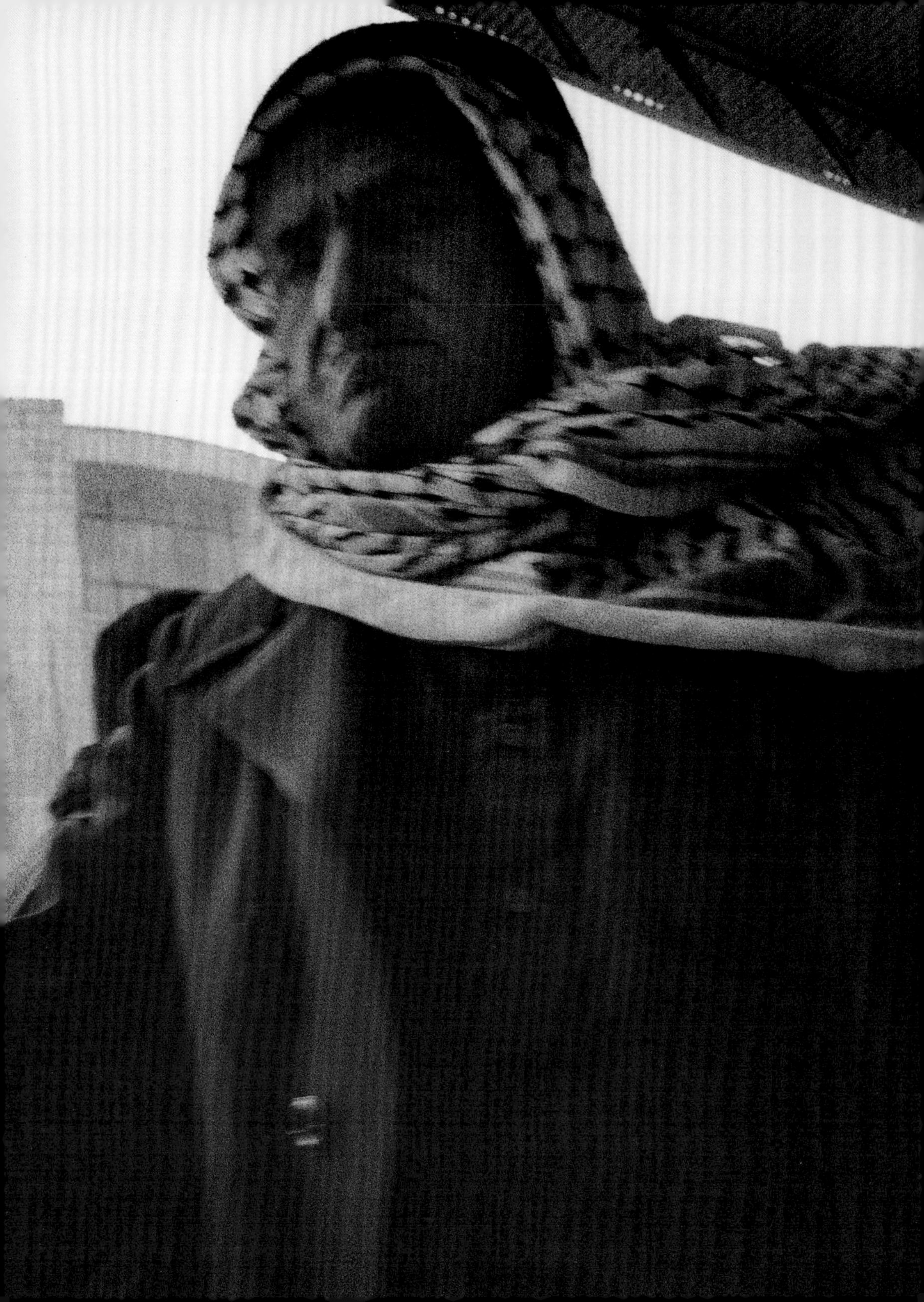

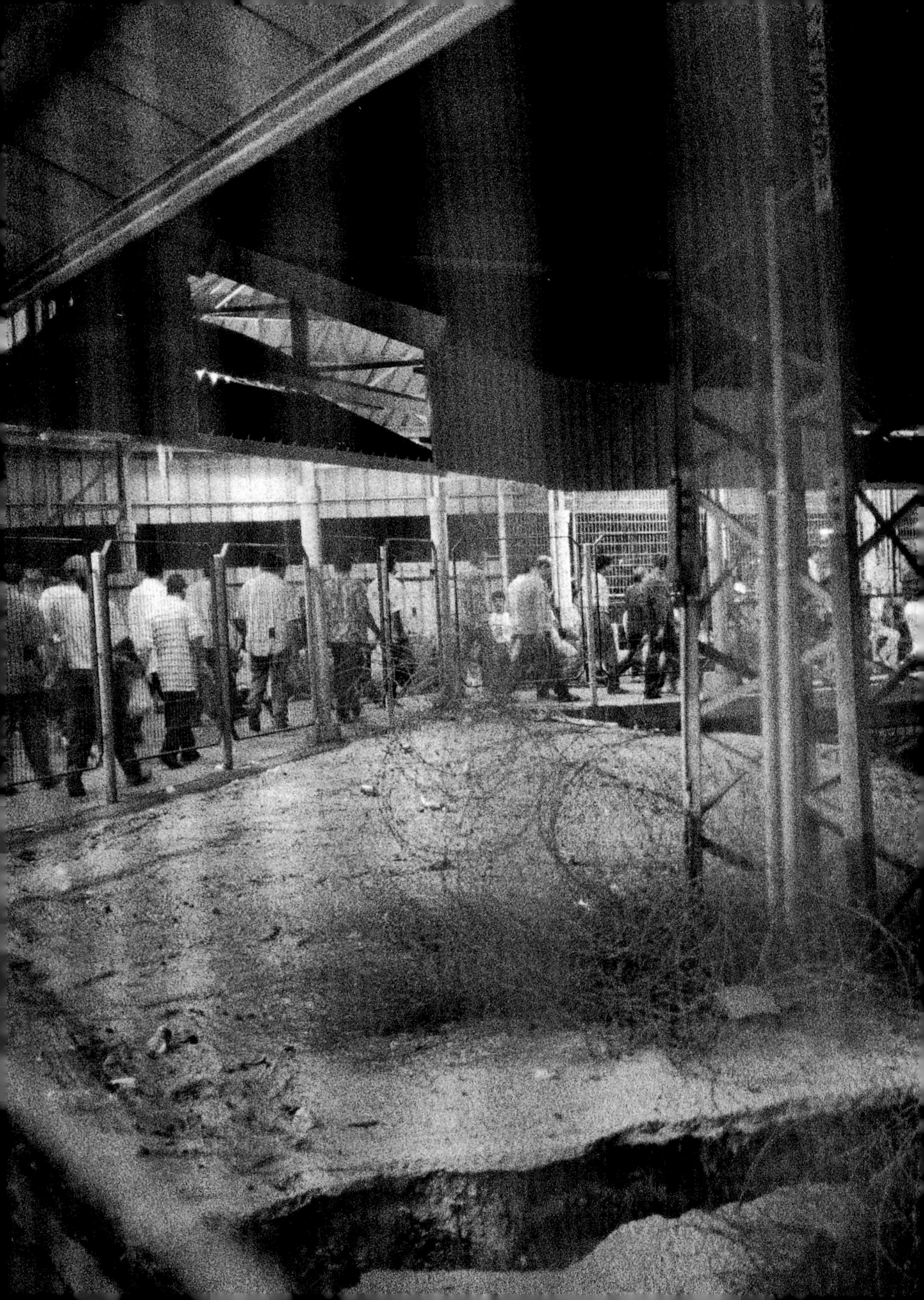

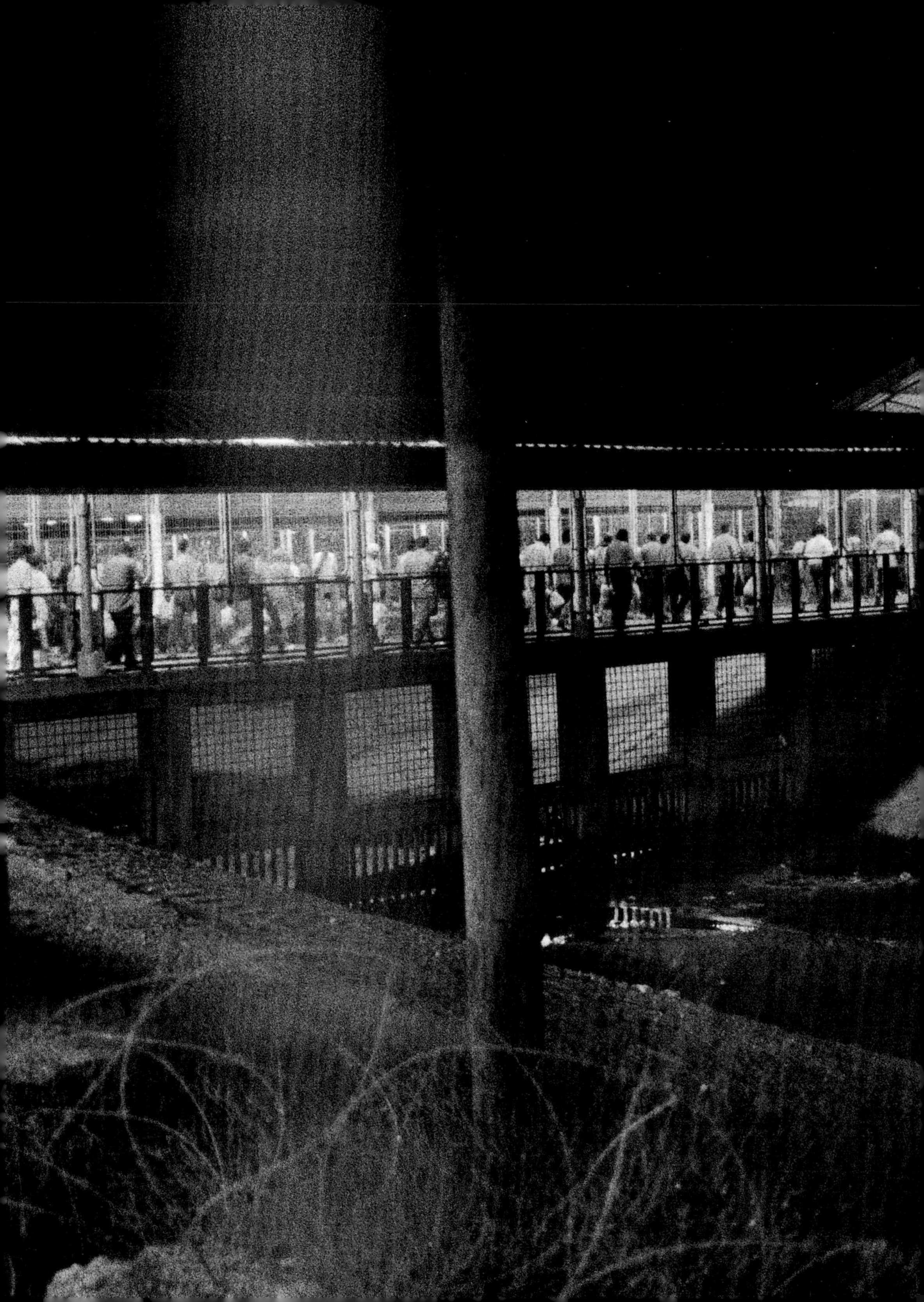

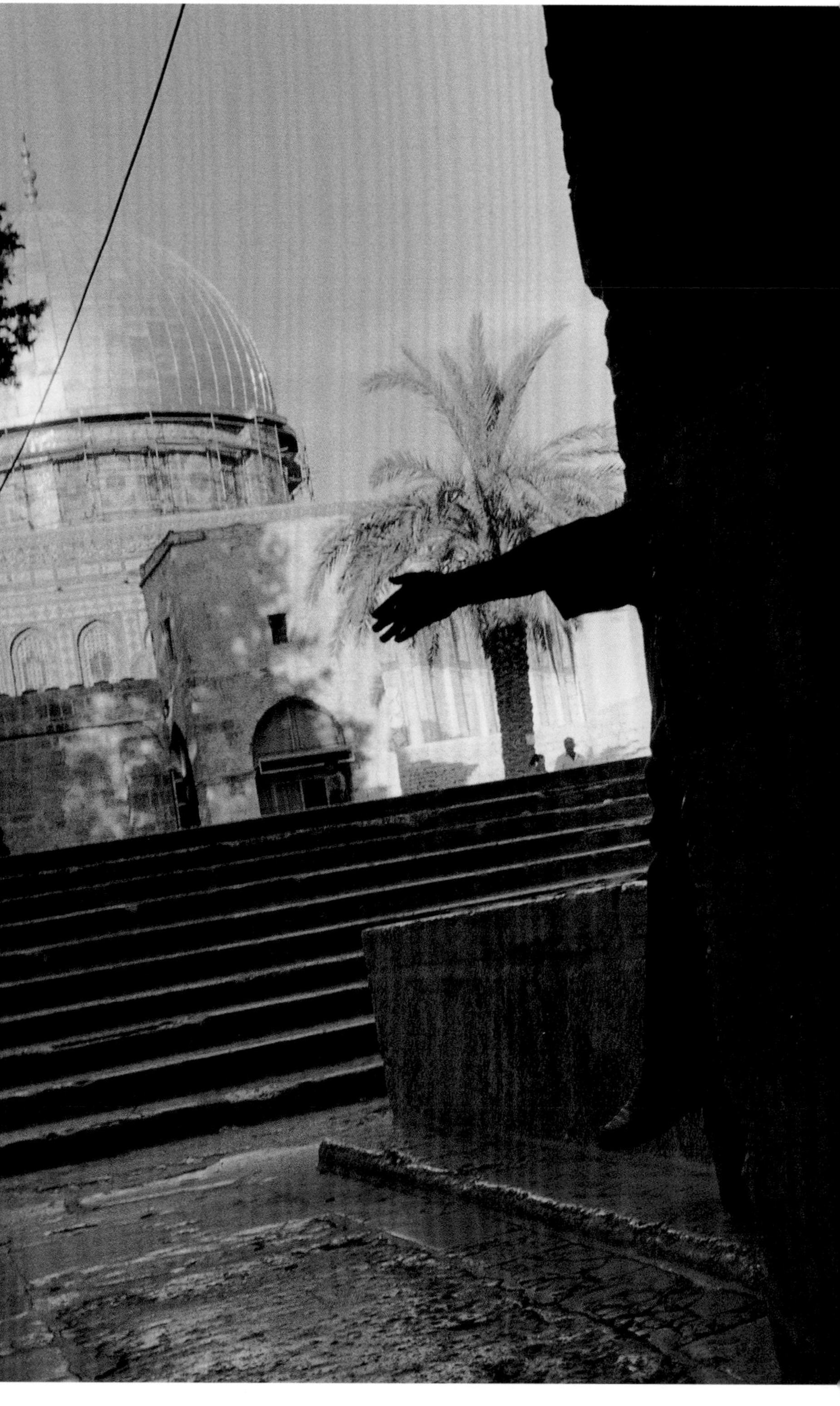

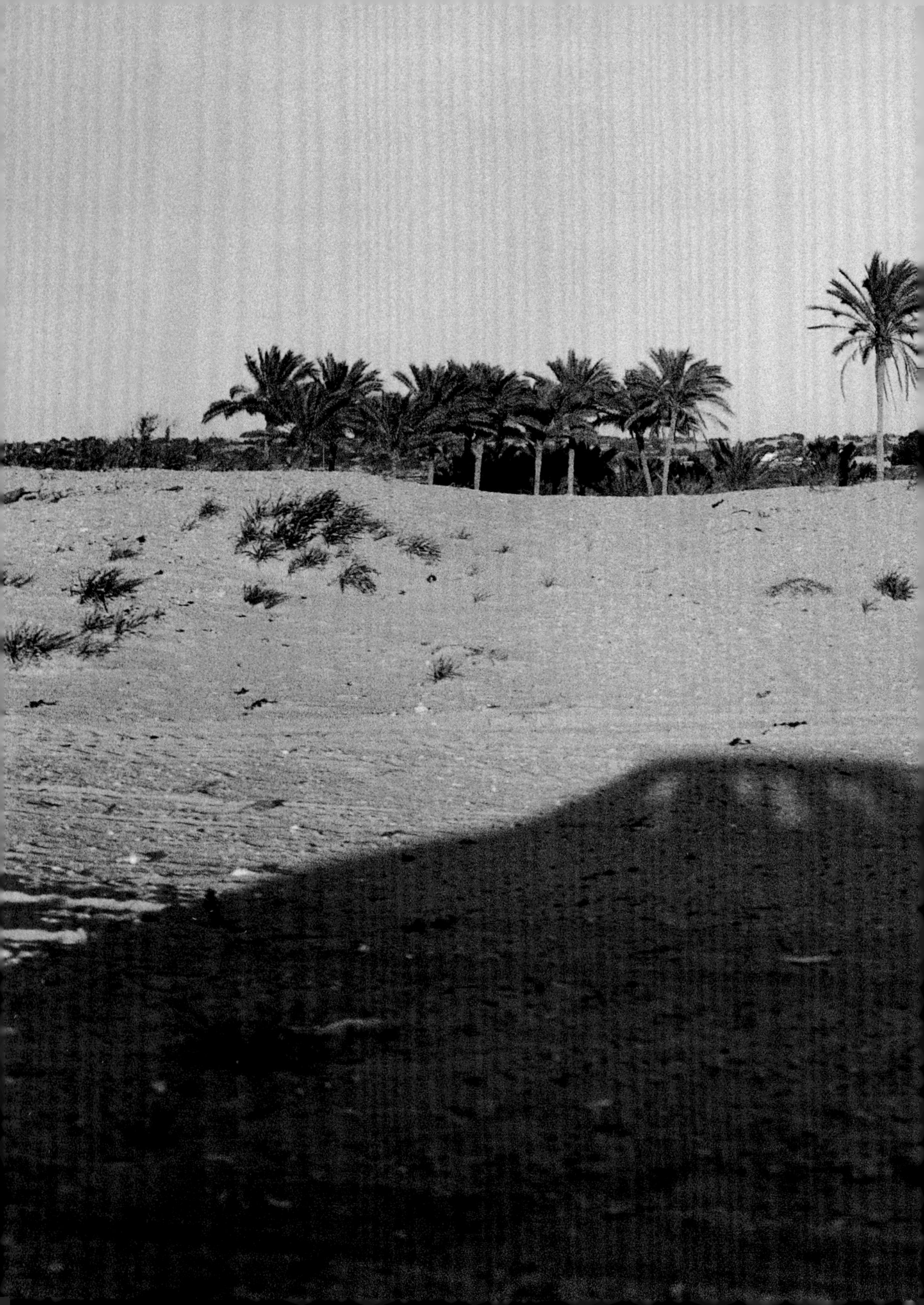

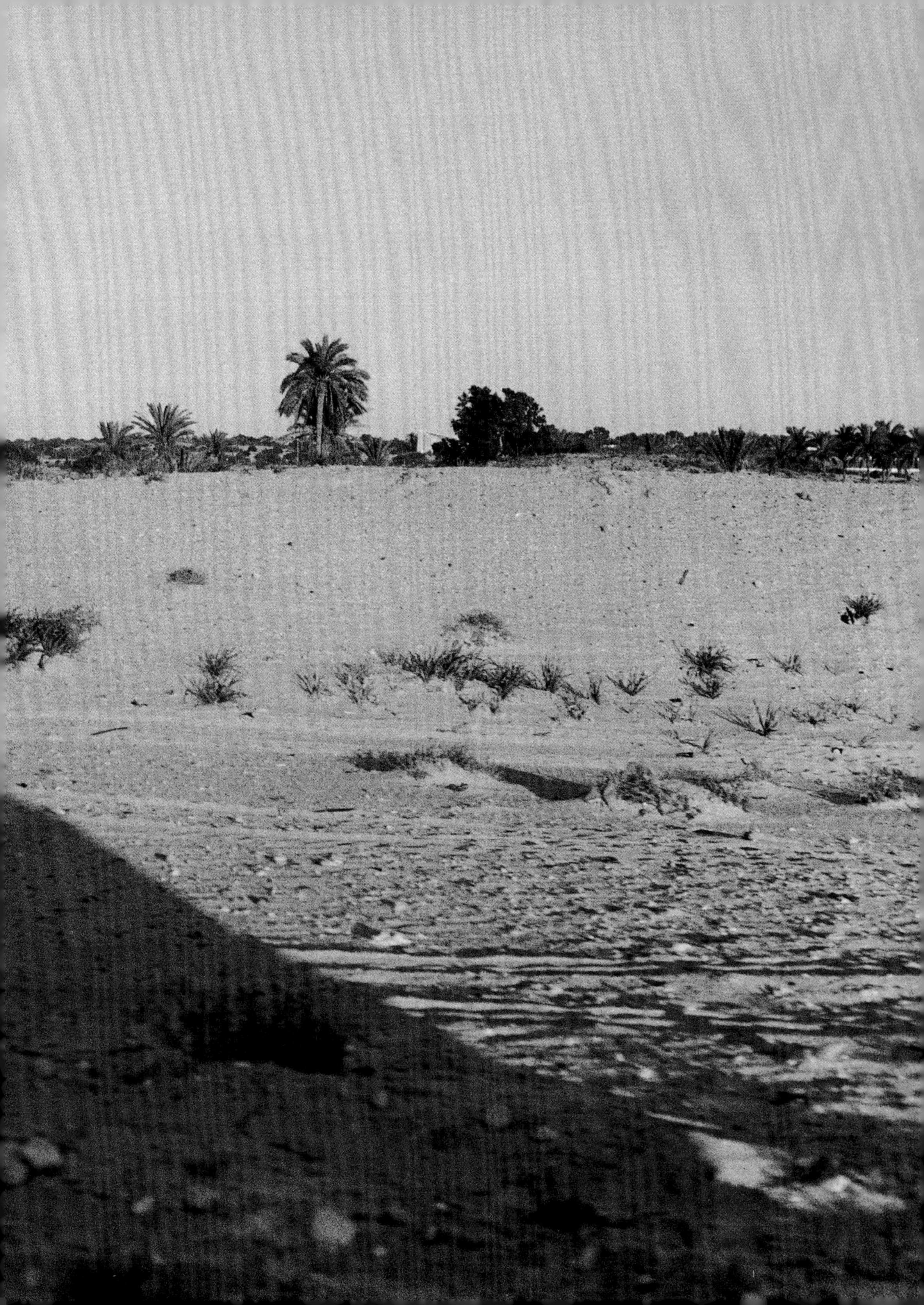

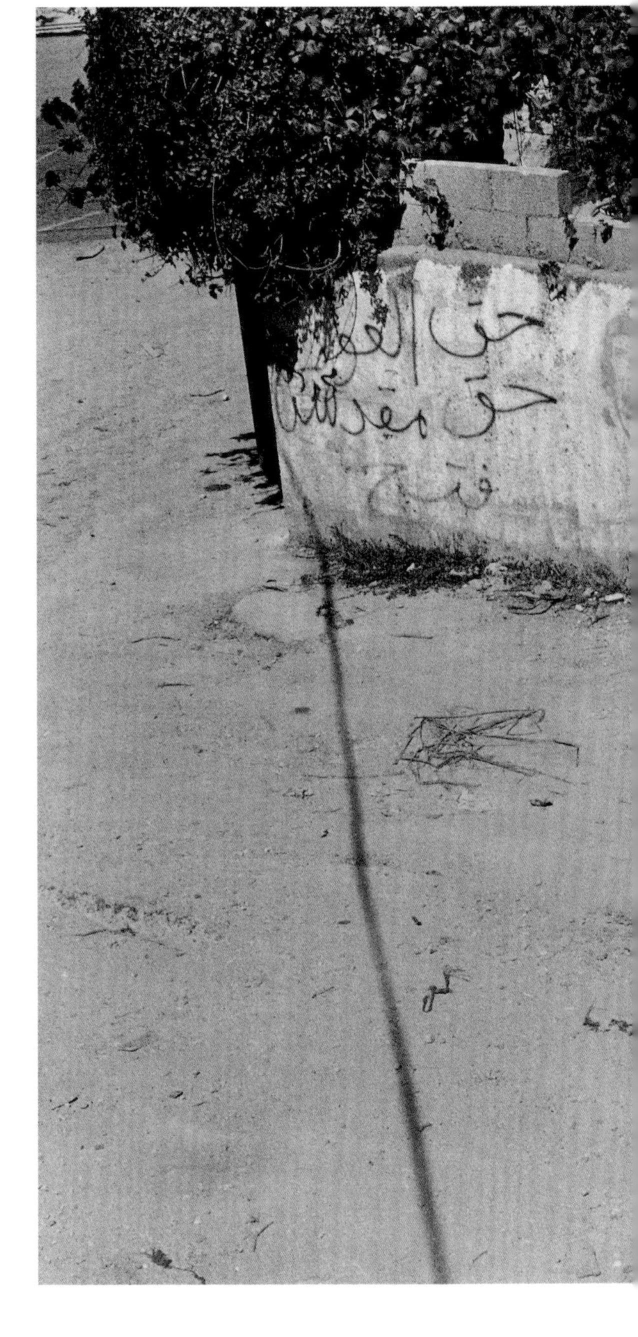

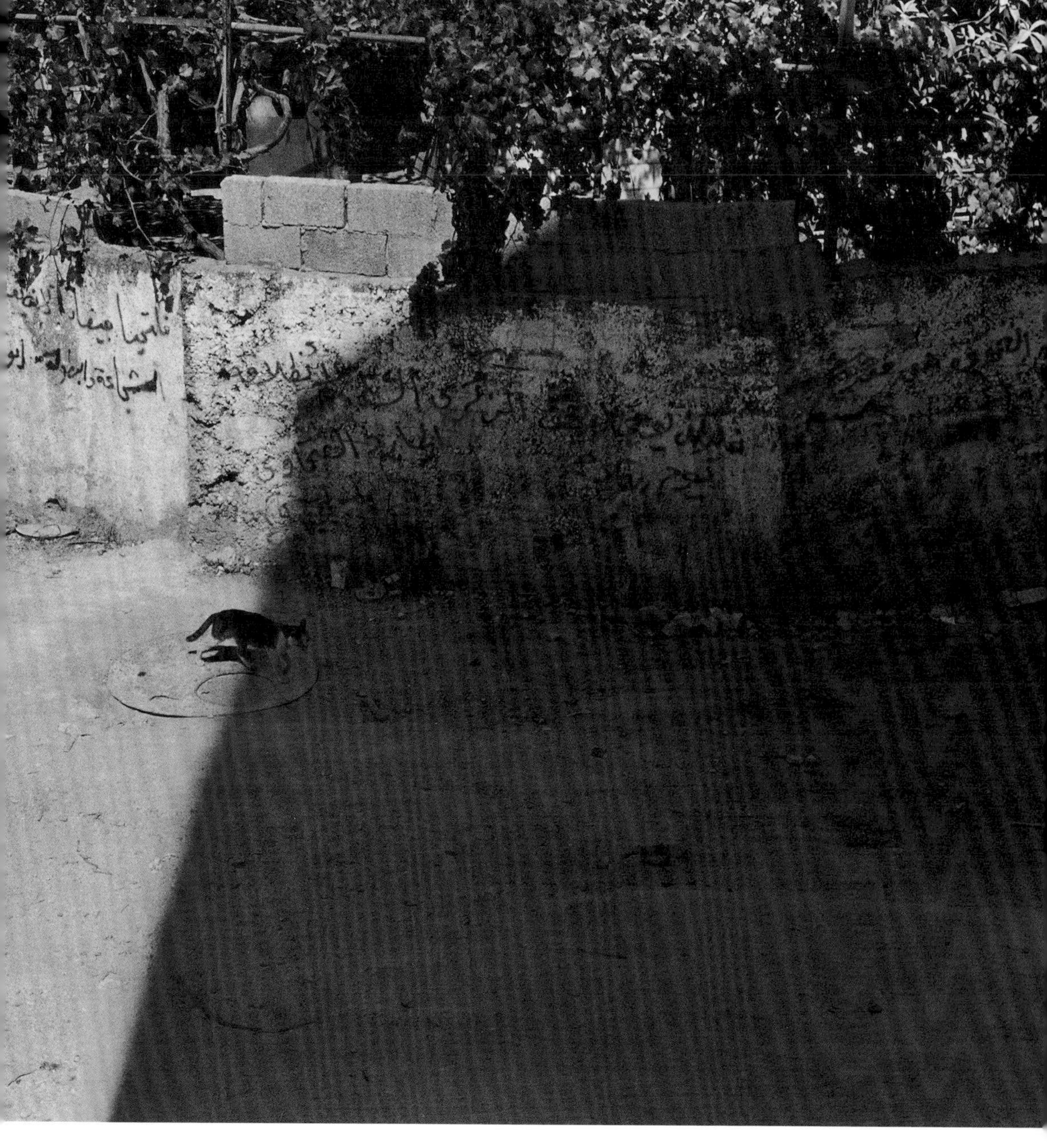

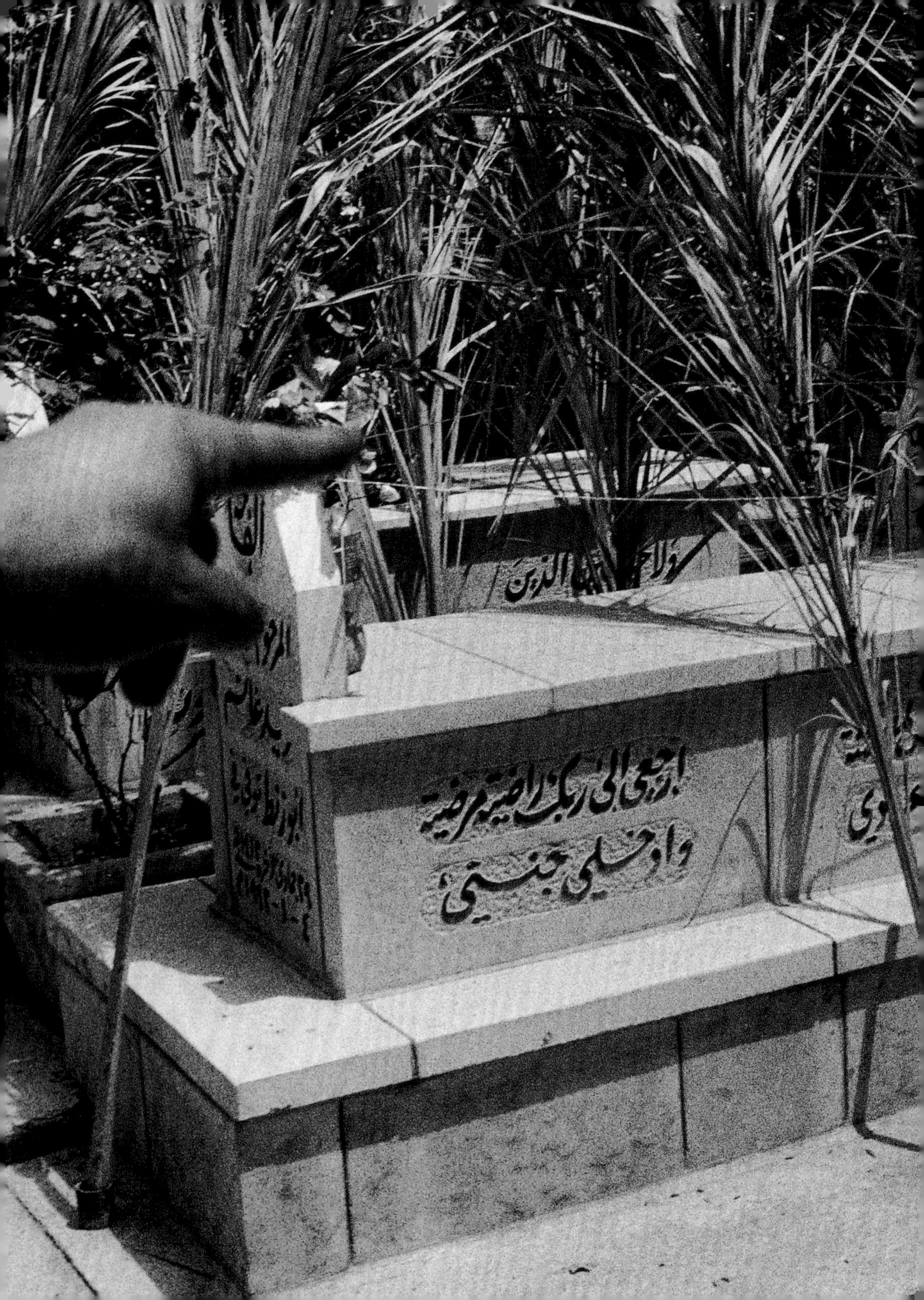

ارجعى الى ربك راضية مرضية
وادخلى جنتى

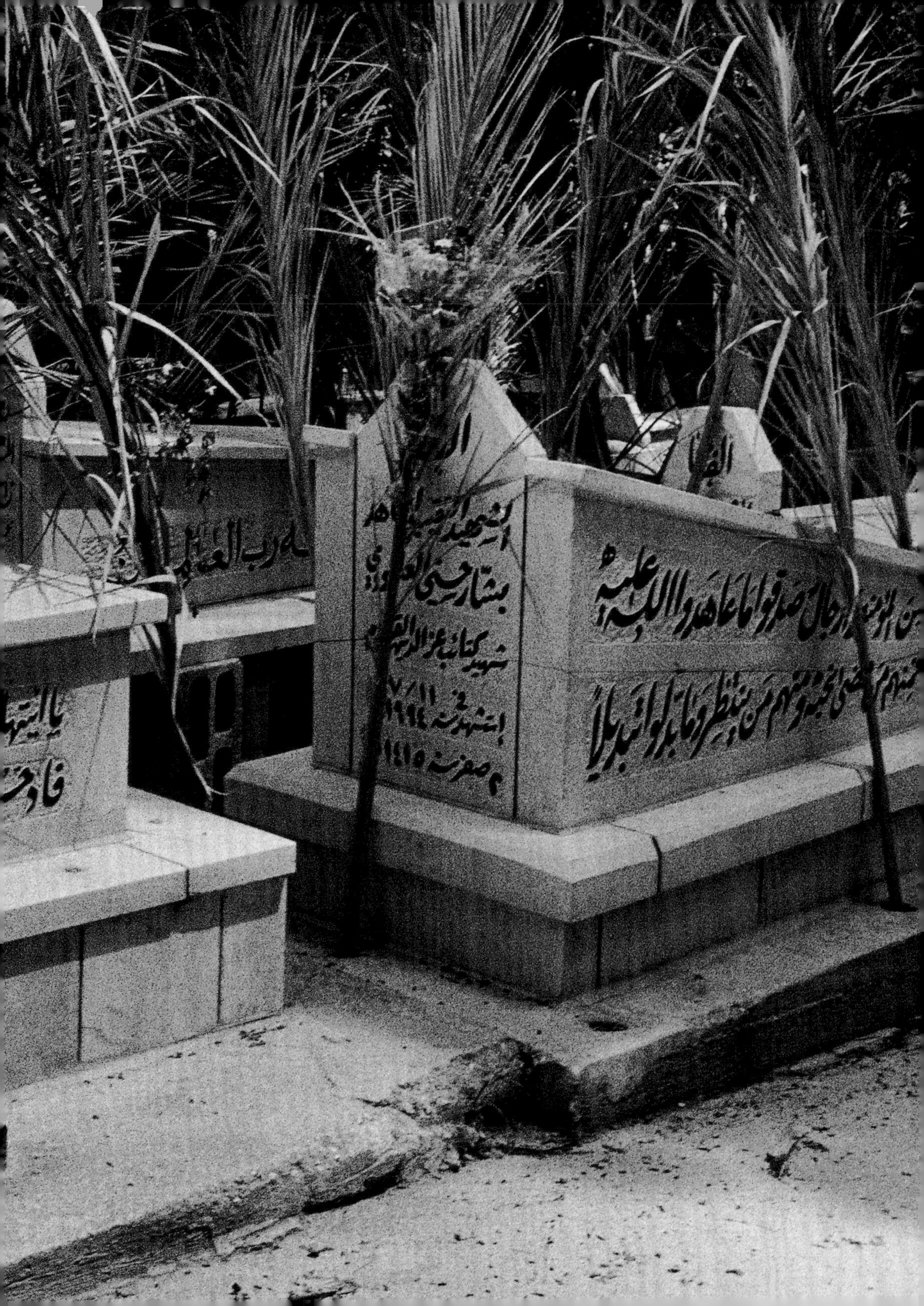
من المؤمنين رجال صدقوا ما عاهدوا الله عليه
فمنهم من قضى نحبه ومنهم من ينتظر وما بدلوا تبديلا
الشهيد
بشار فهمي العمودي
شهيد كتائب عز الدين القسام
٨١/٧
بتشرين ١٩٩٤
صفر ١٤١٥
الله رب العالمين

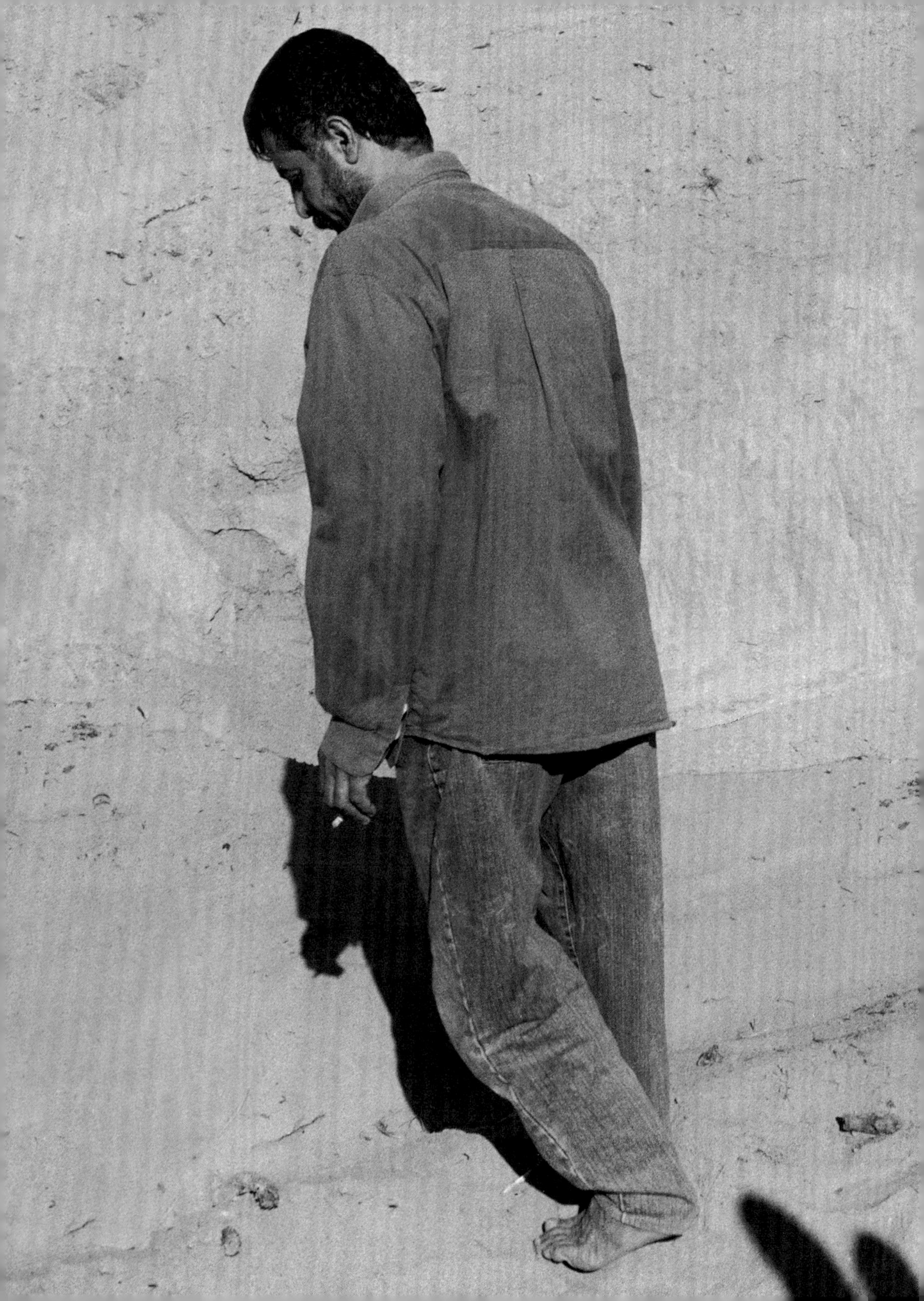

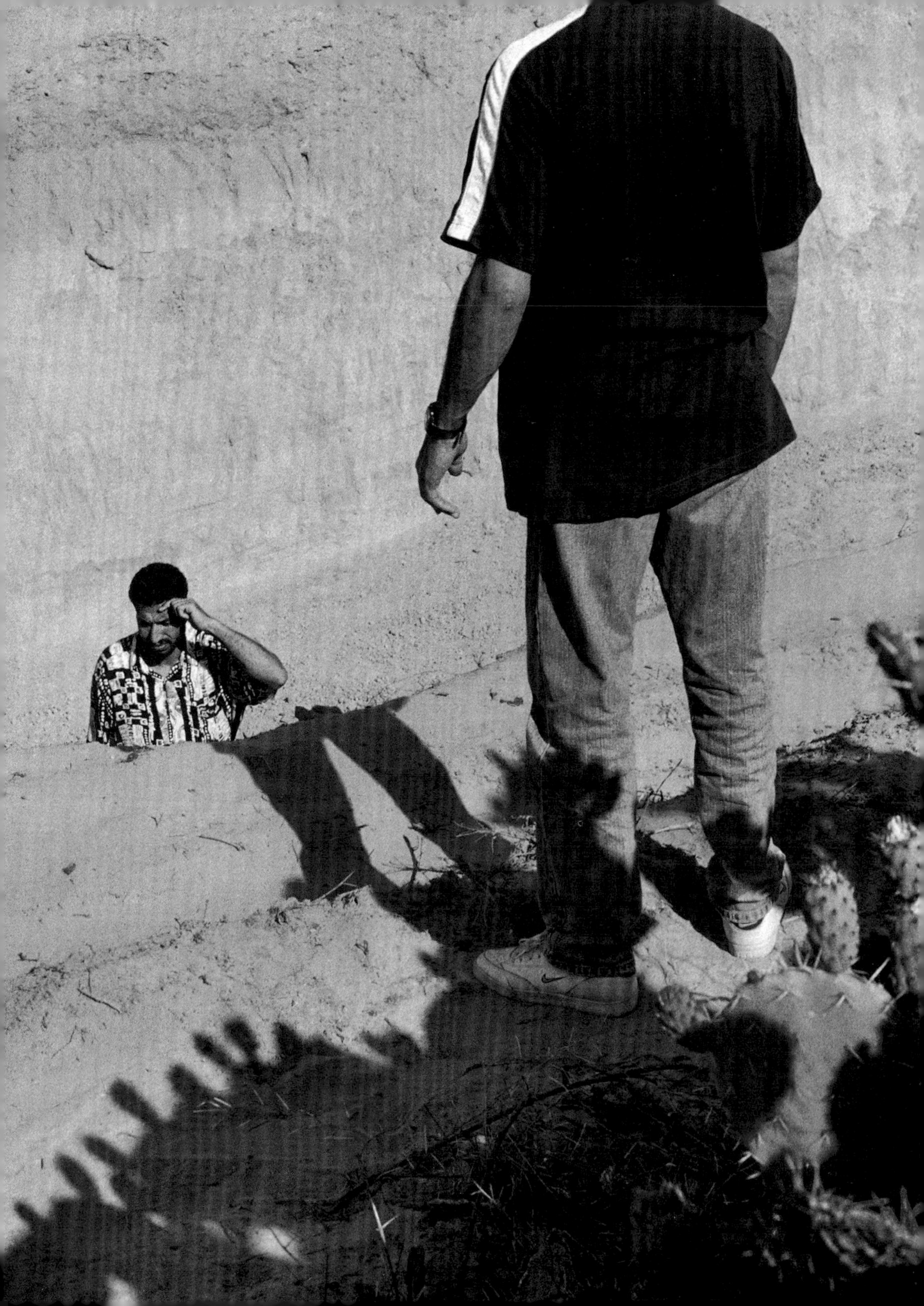

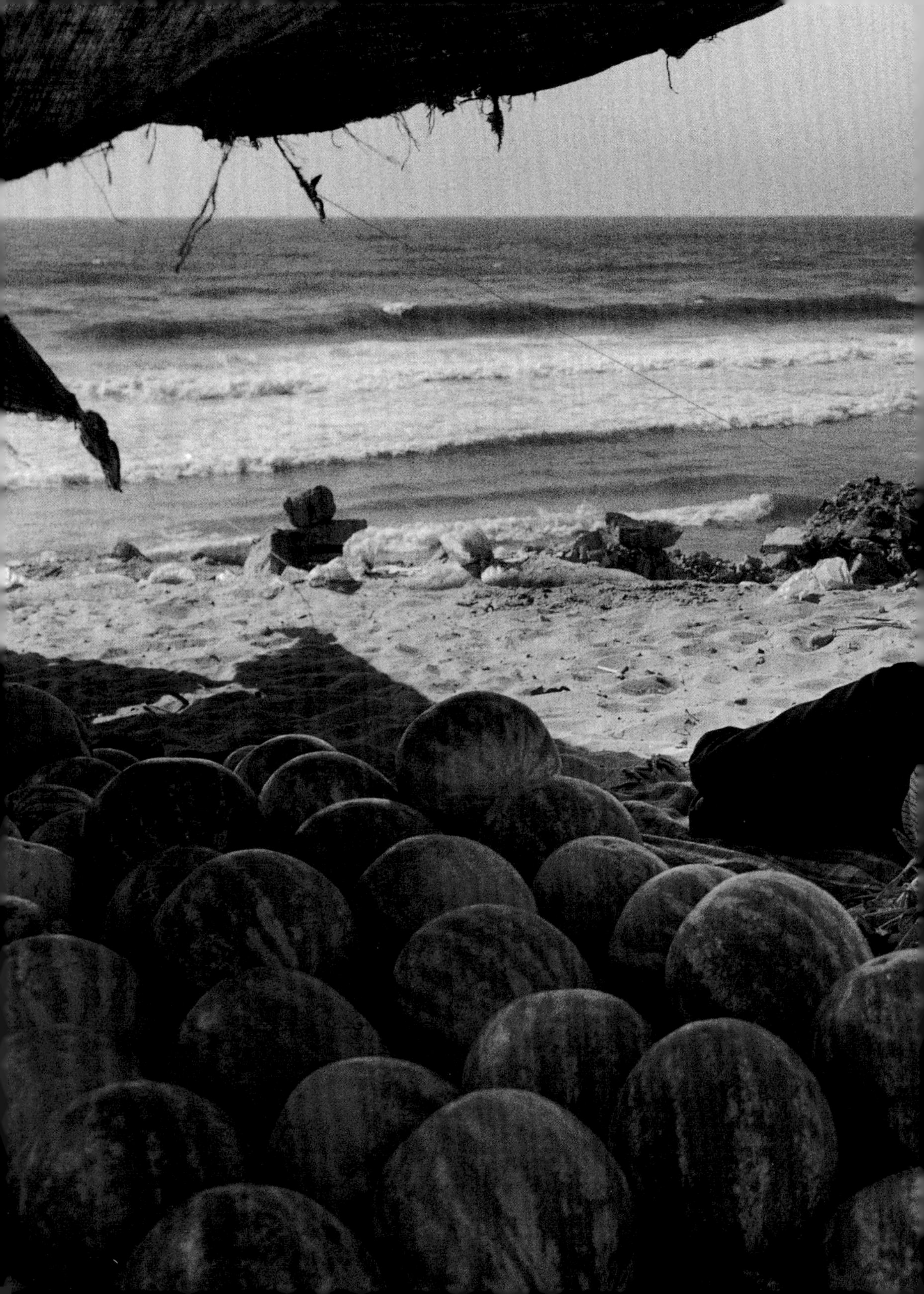

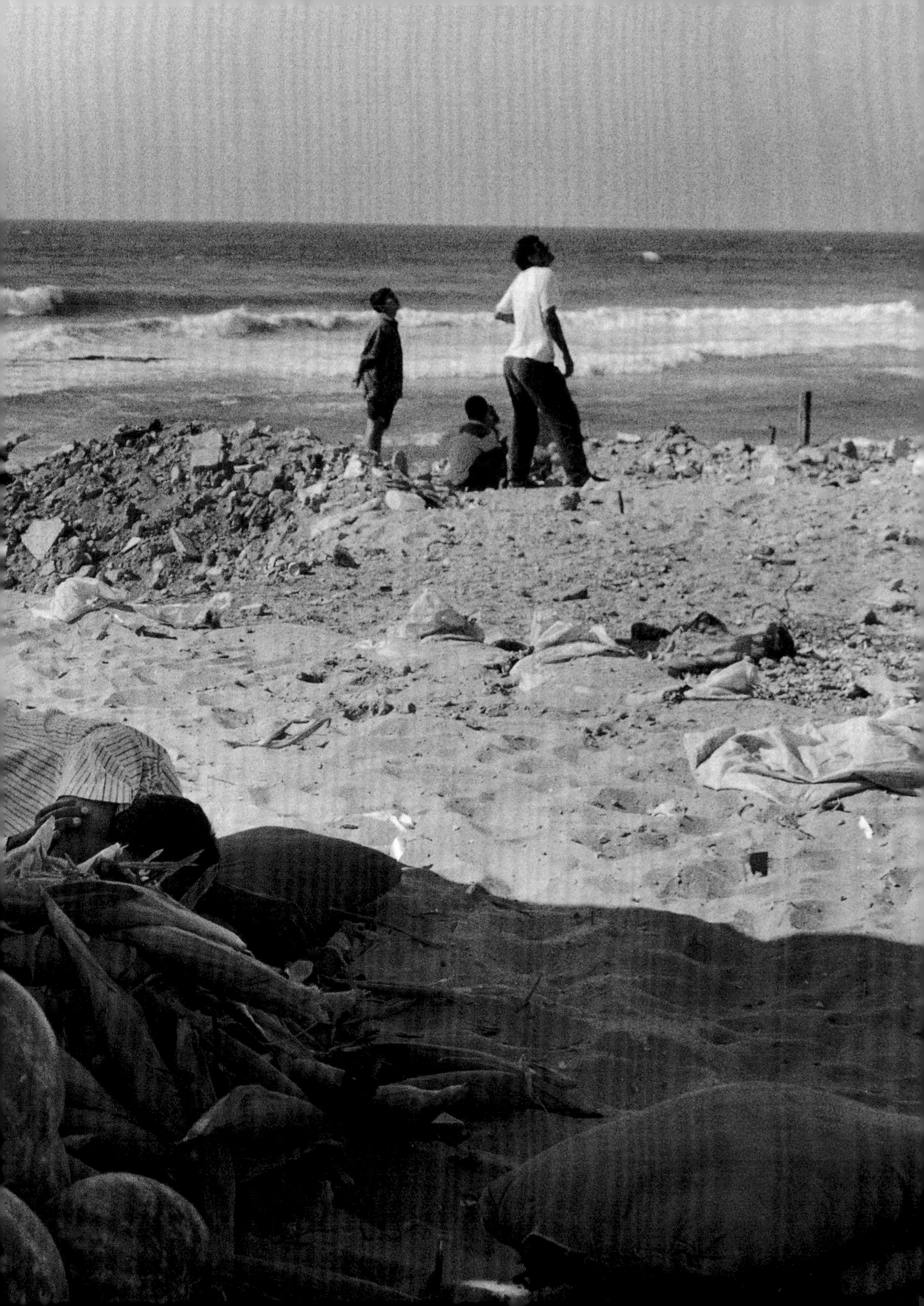

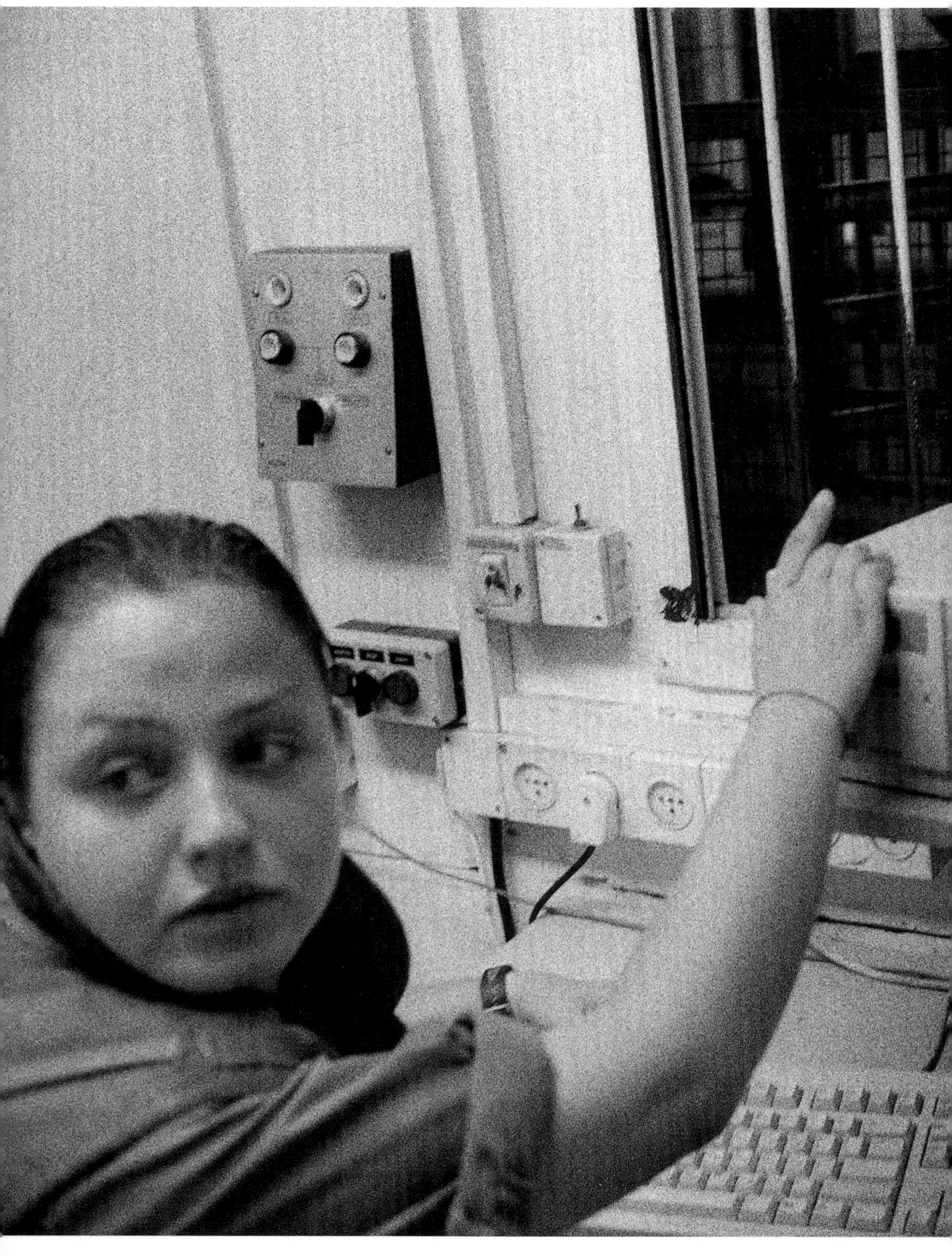

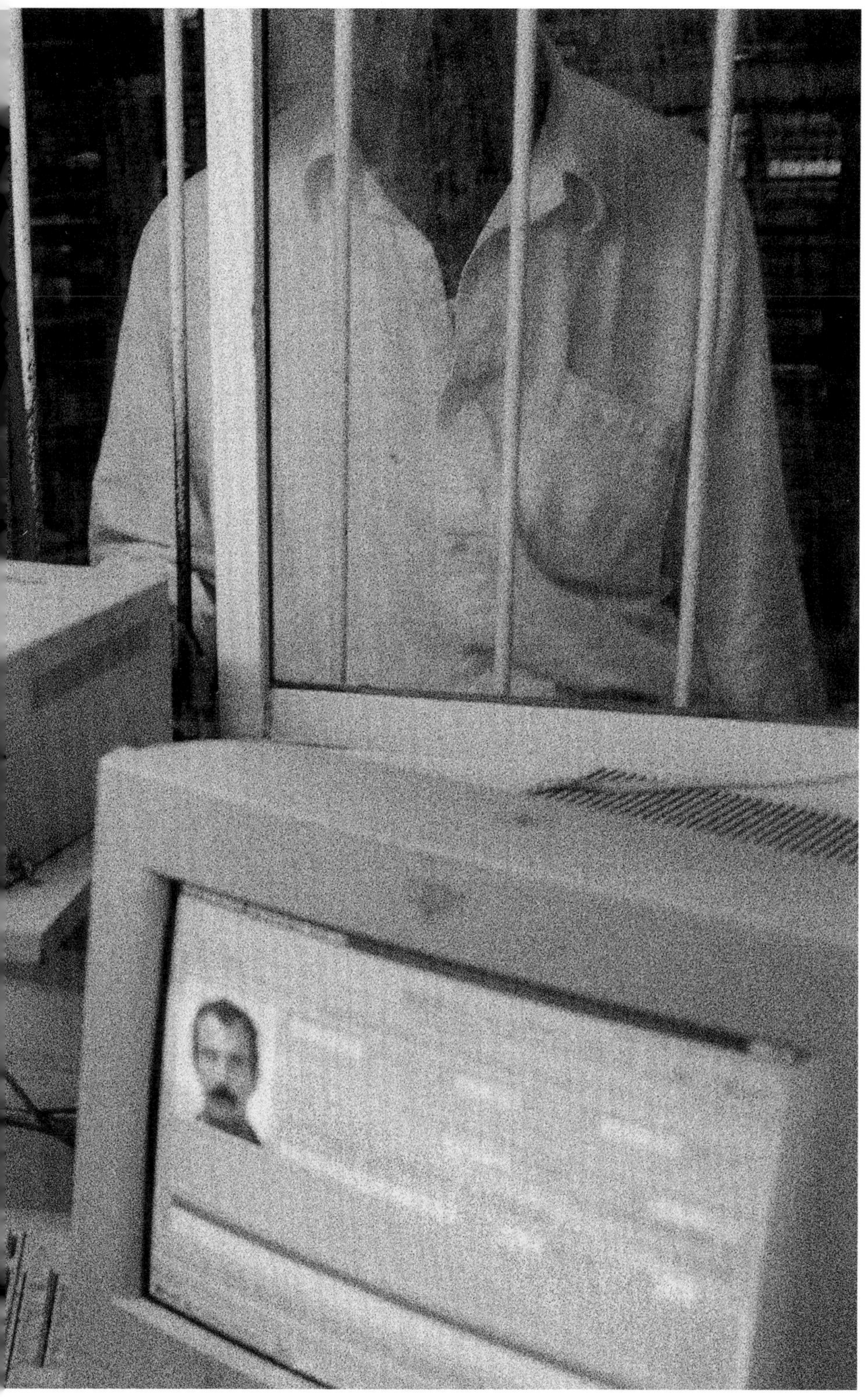

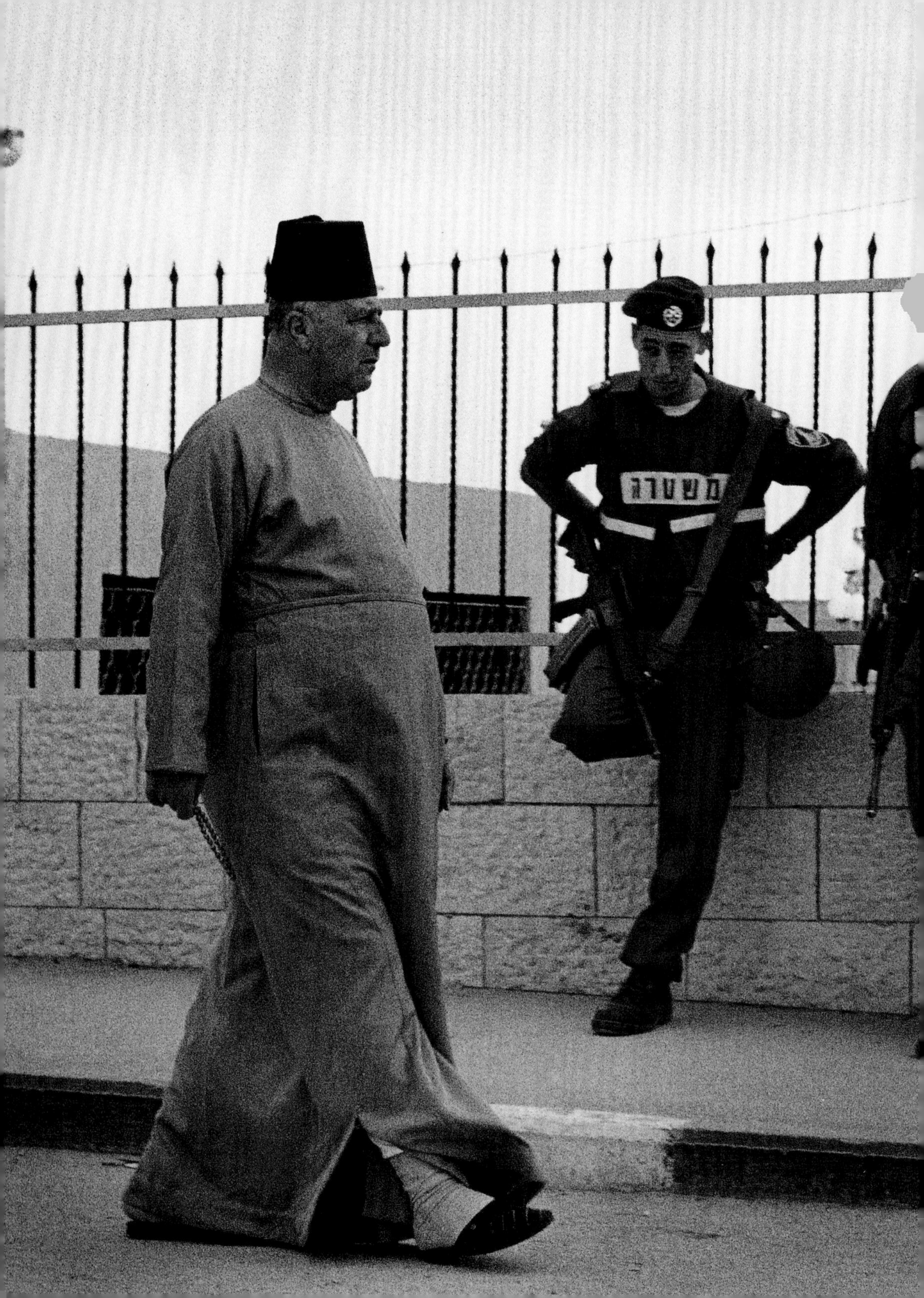
משטרה

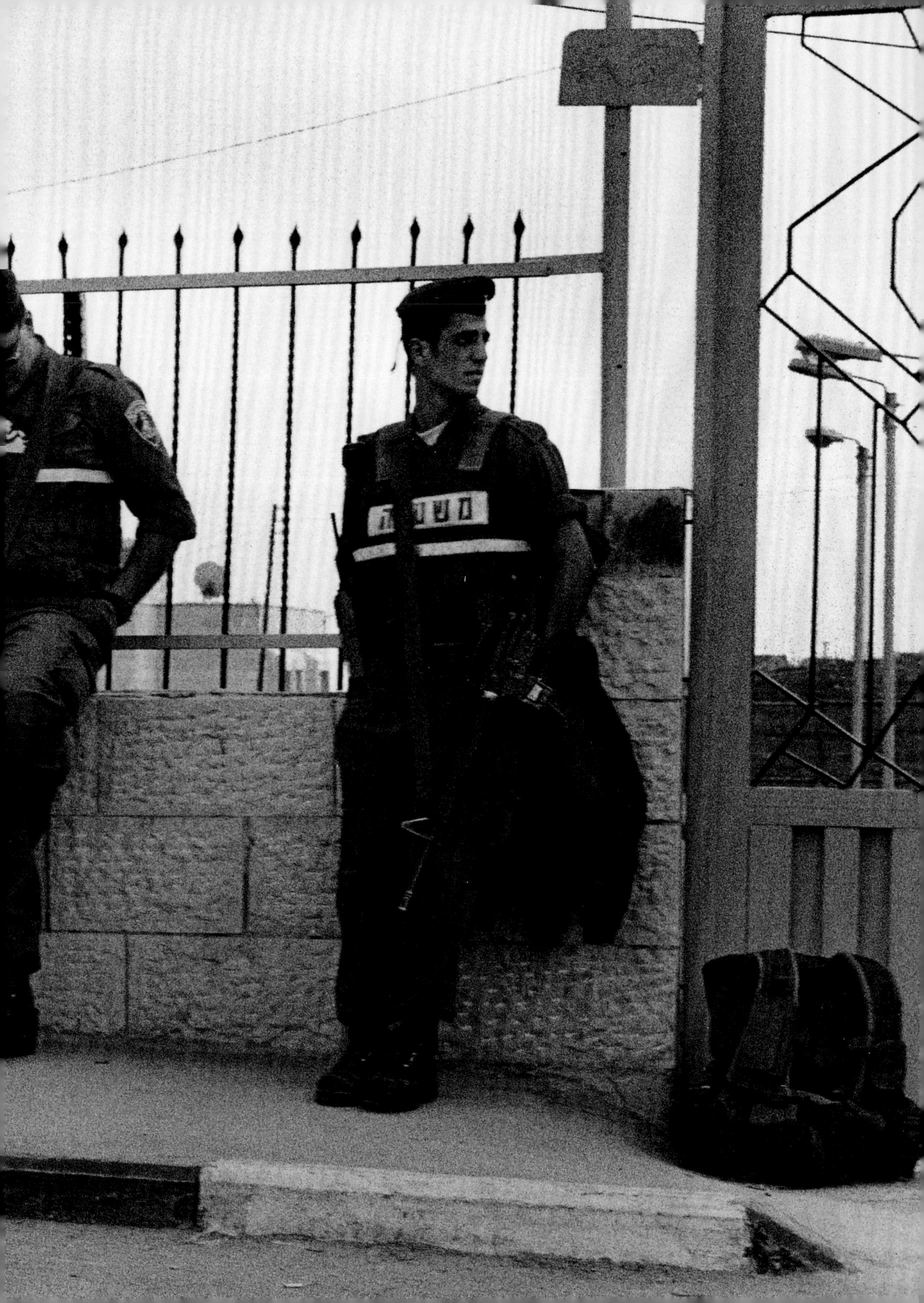
משטרה

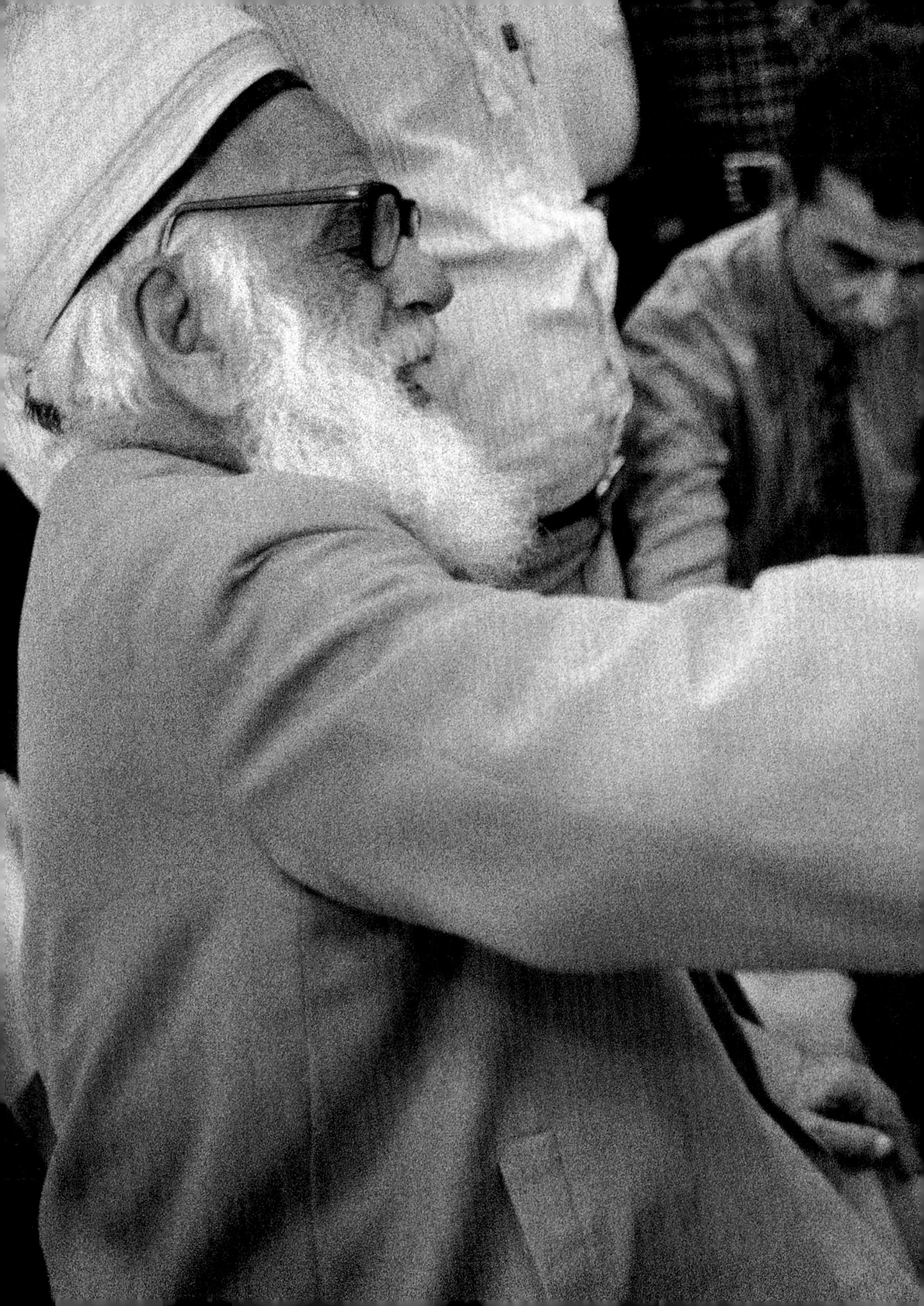

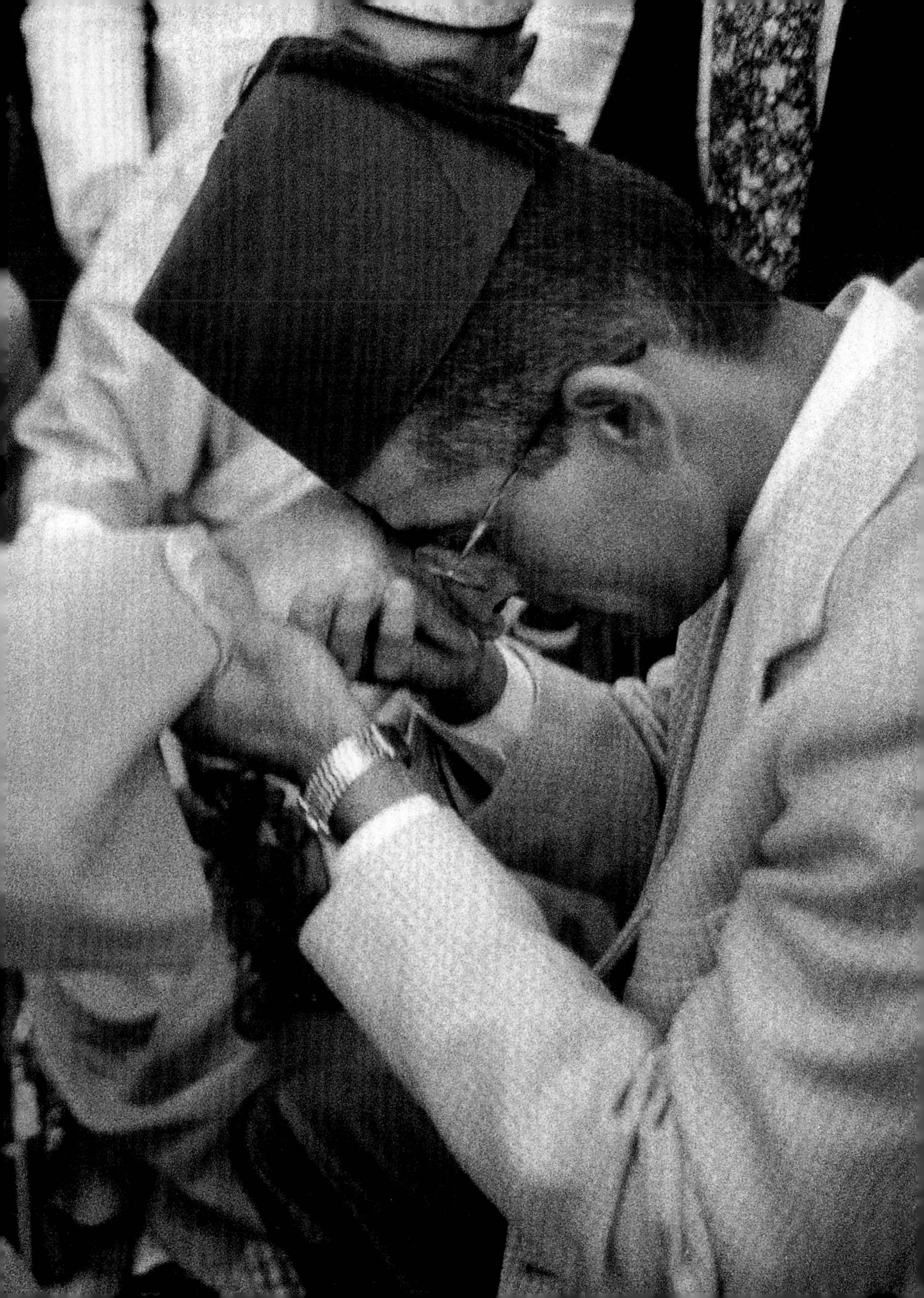

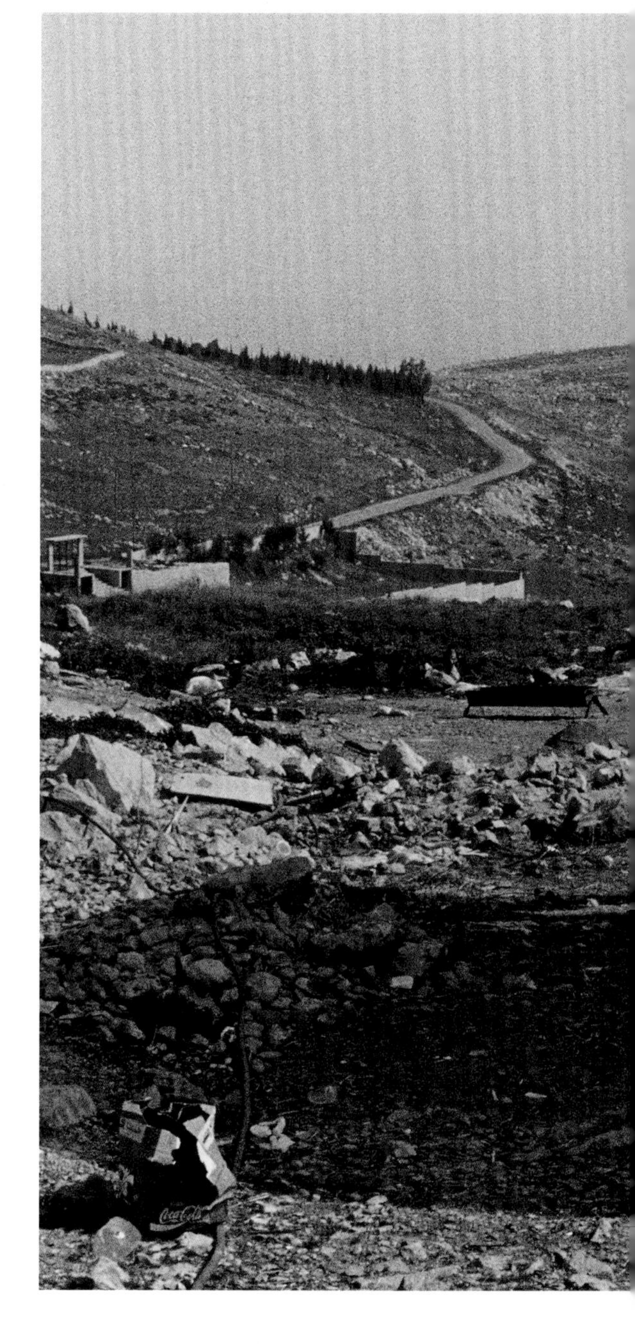

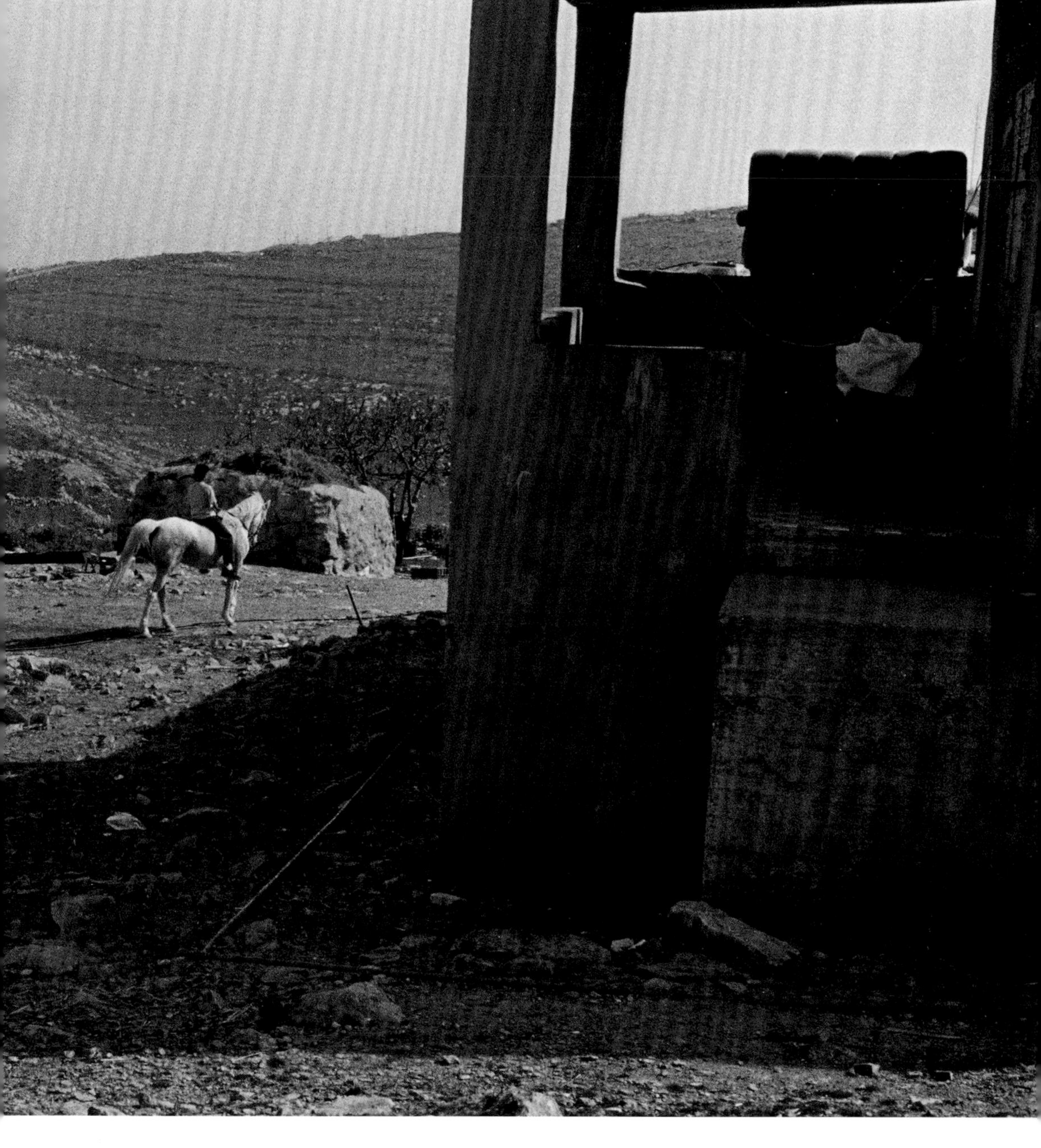

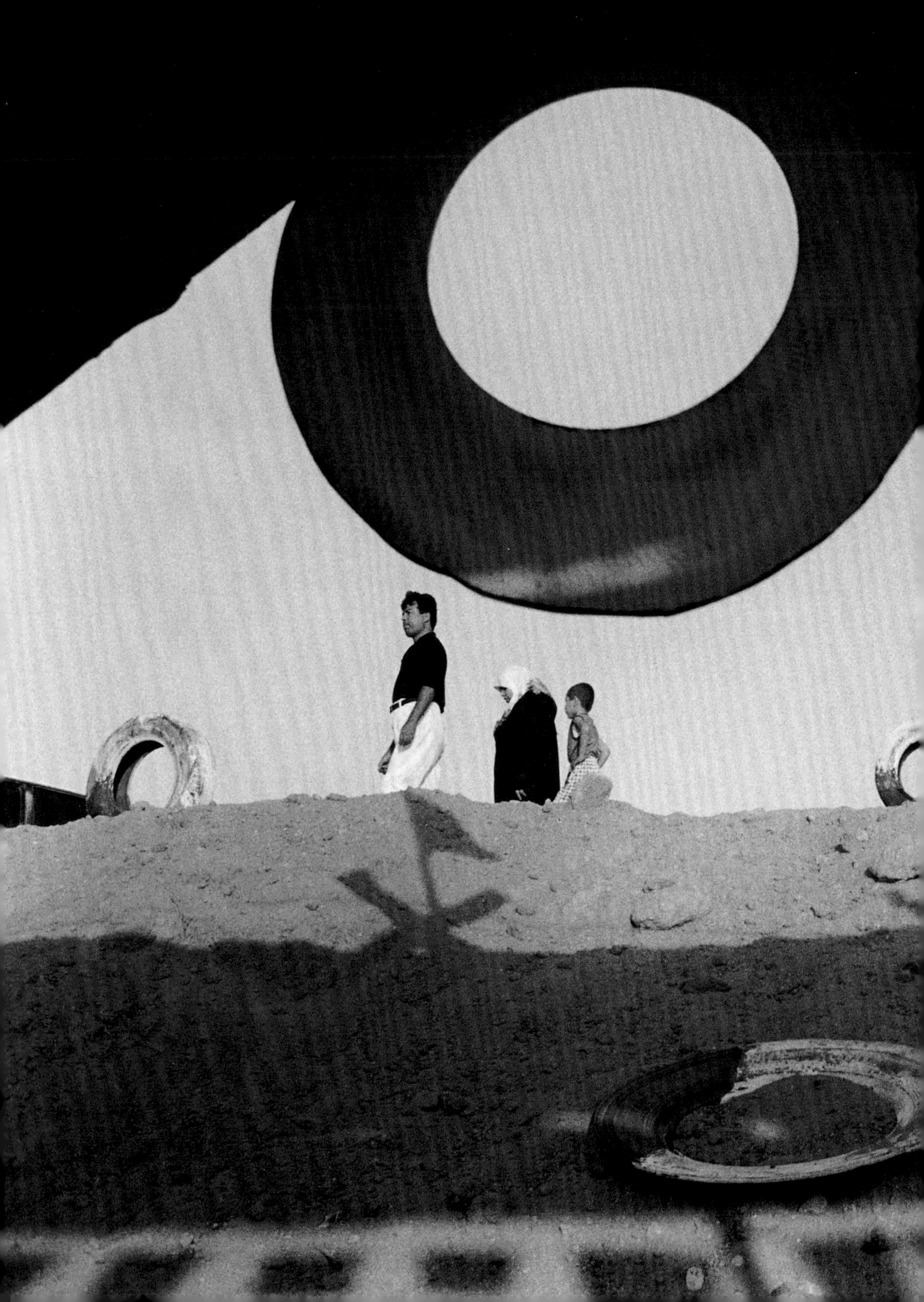

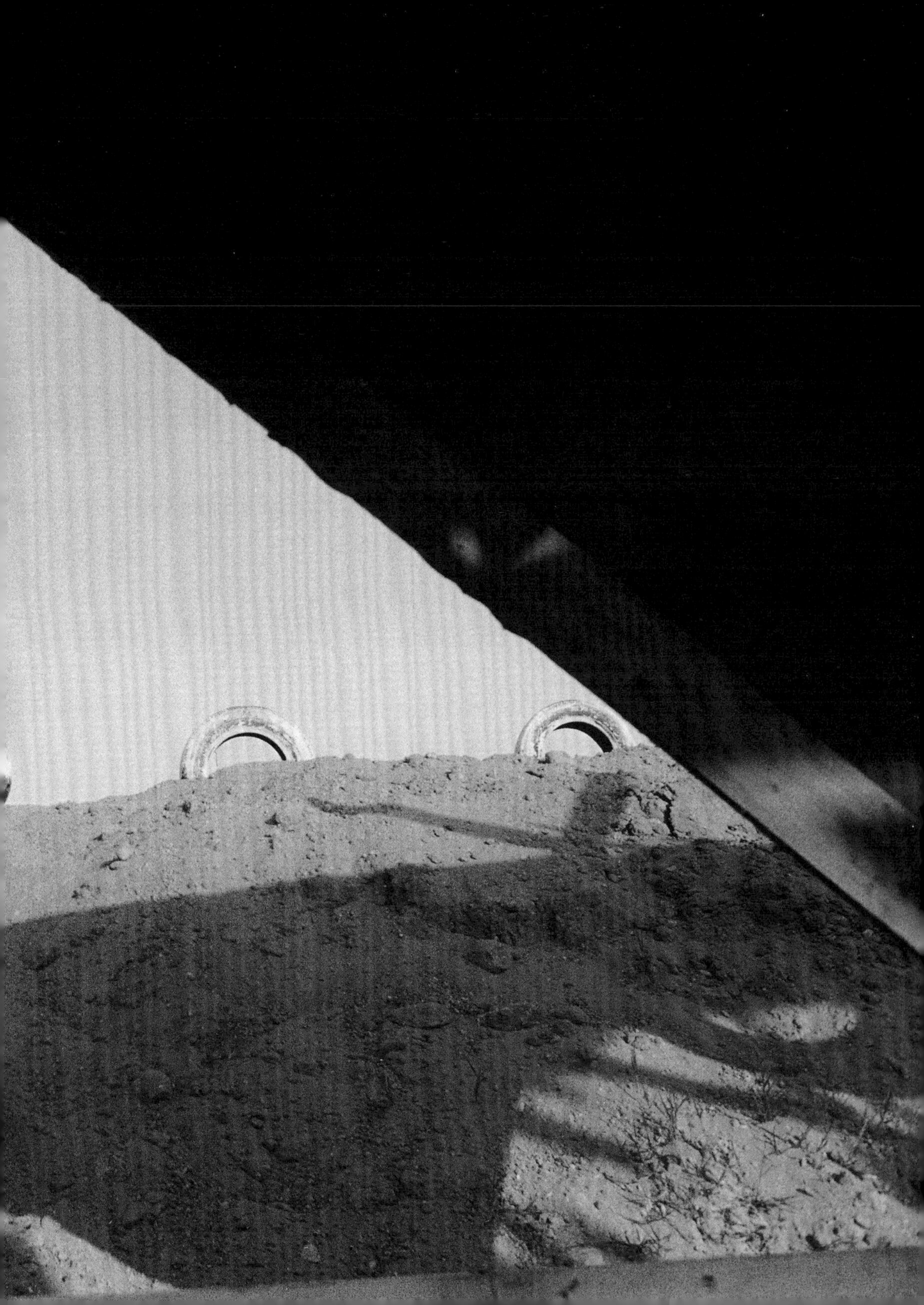

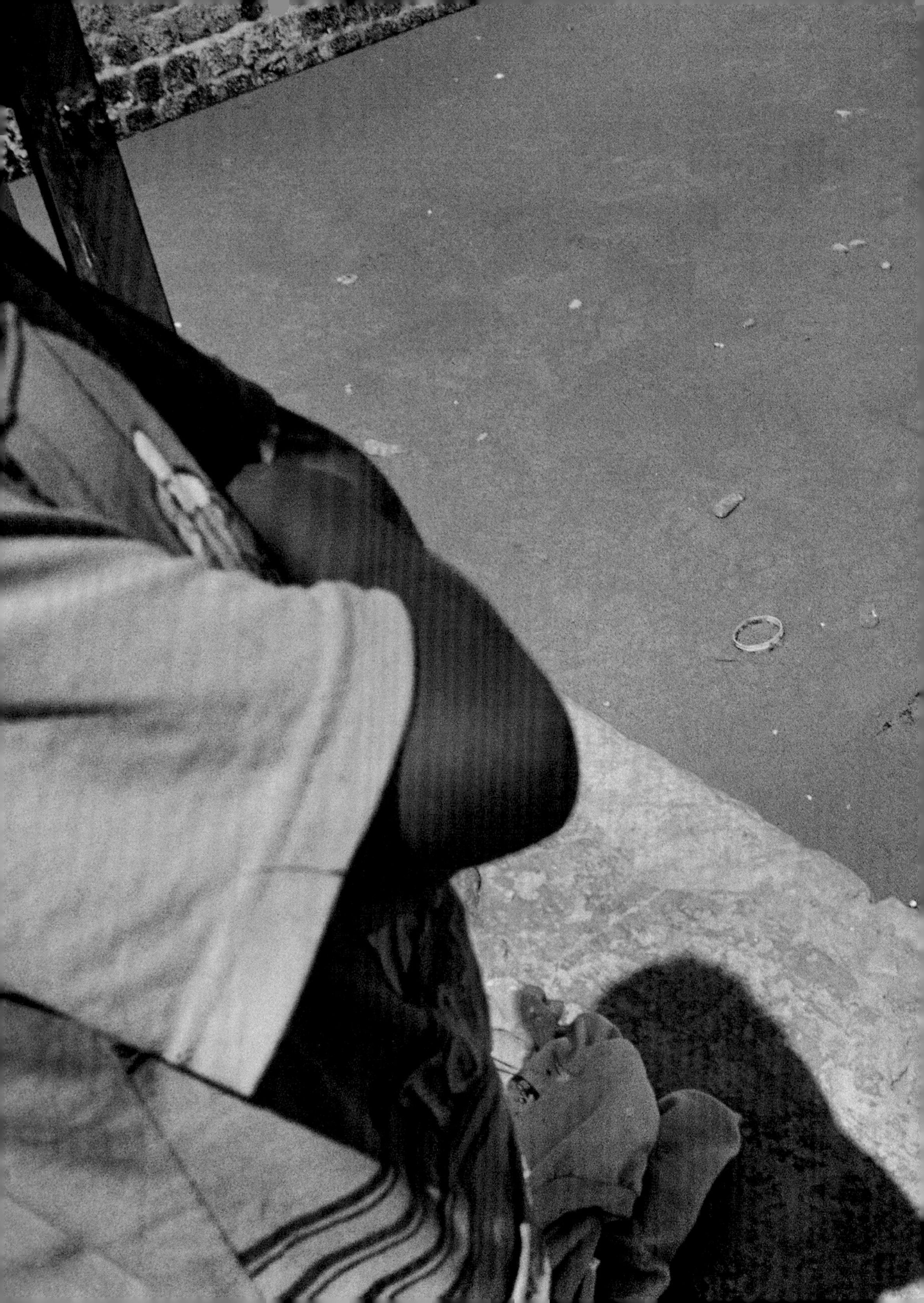

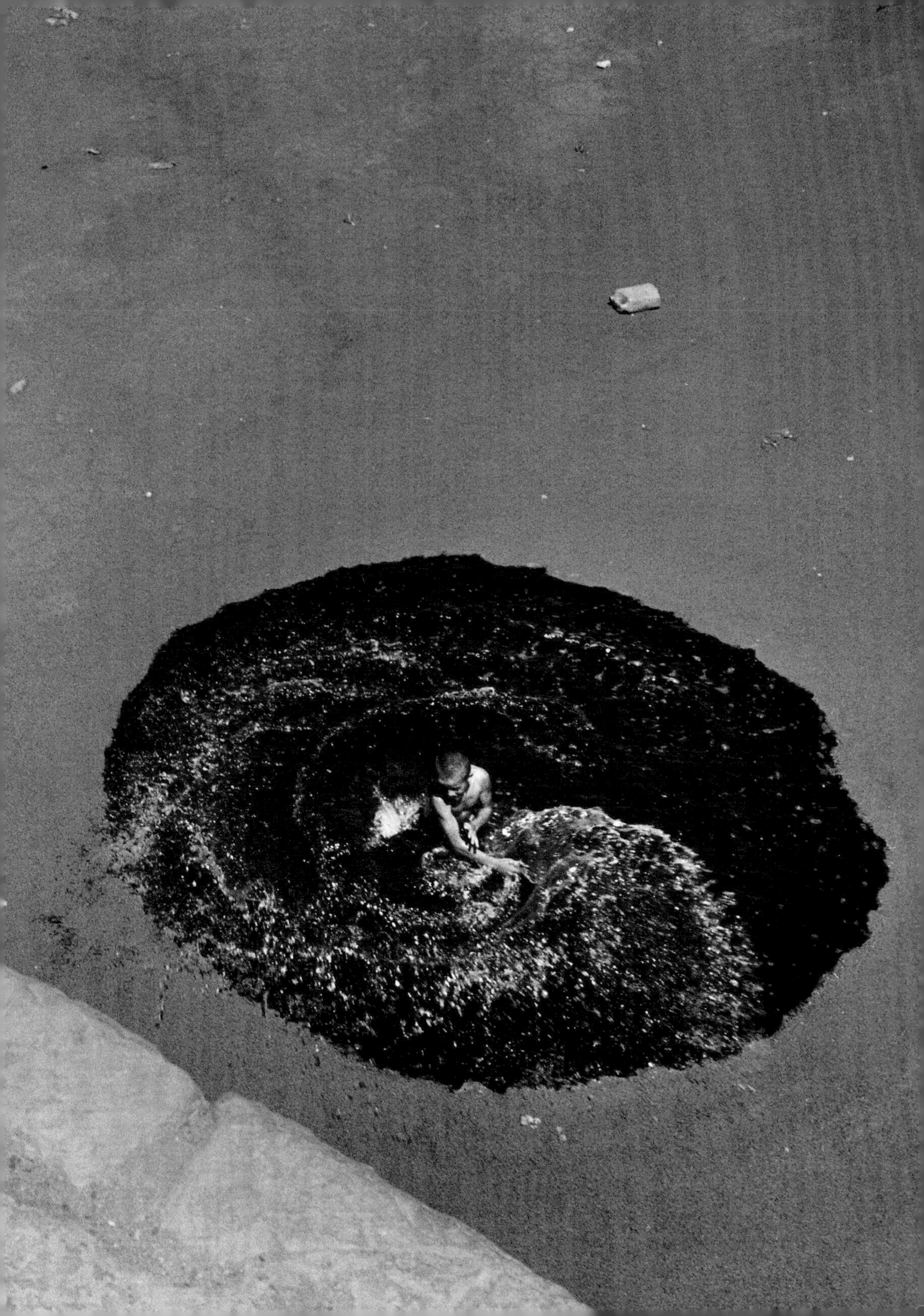

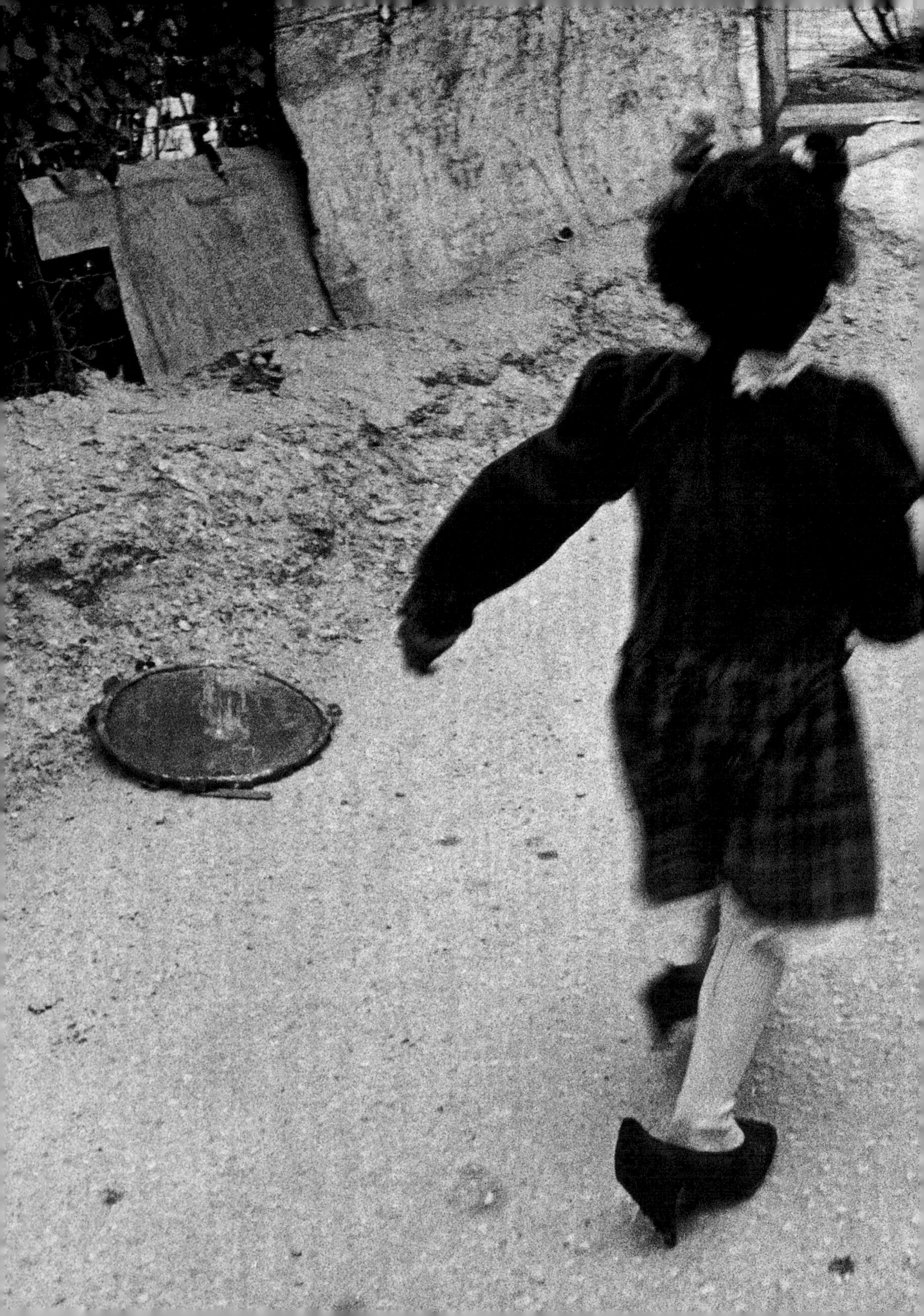

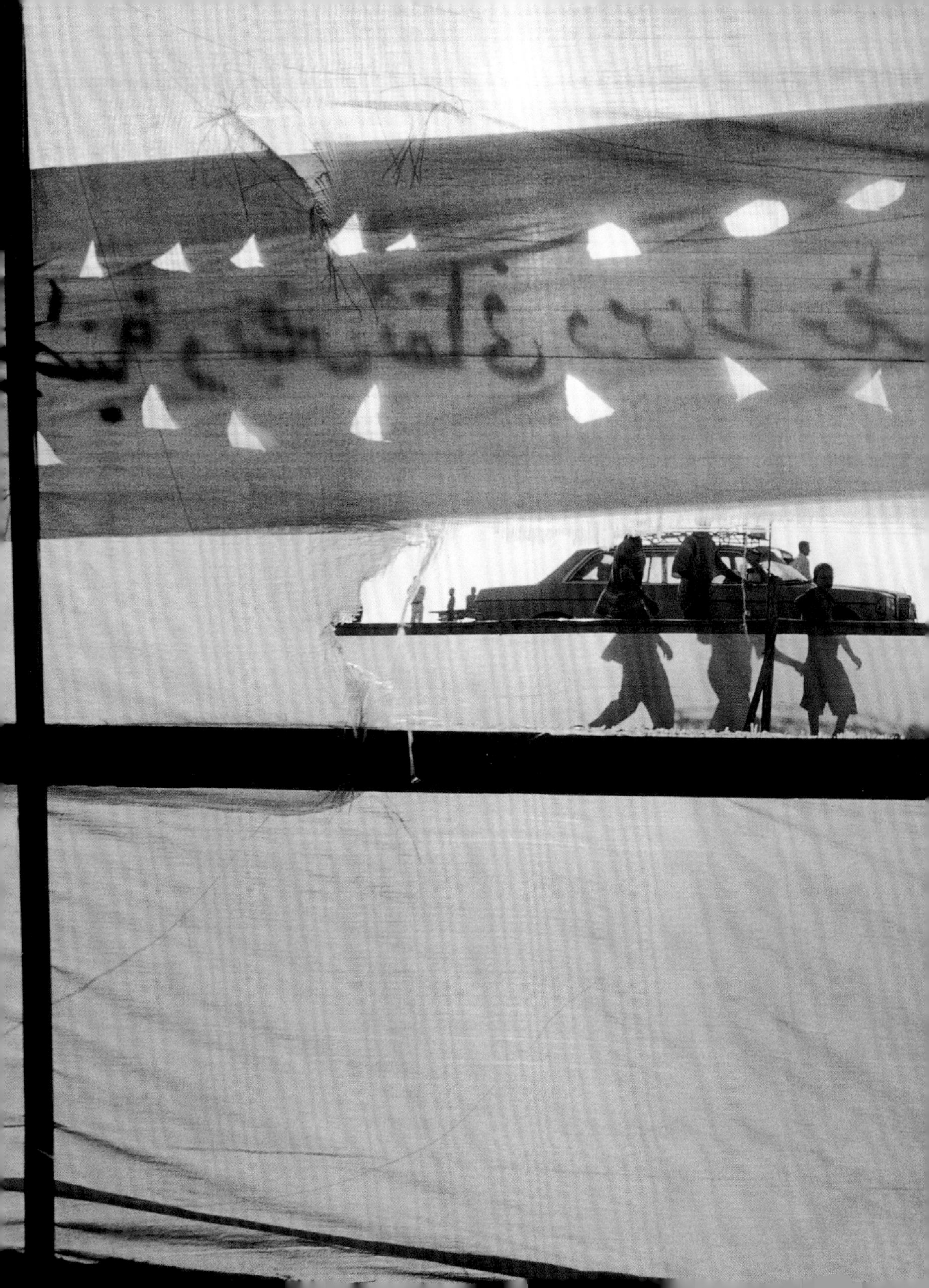

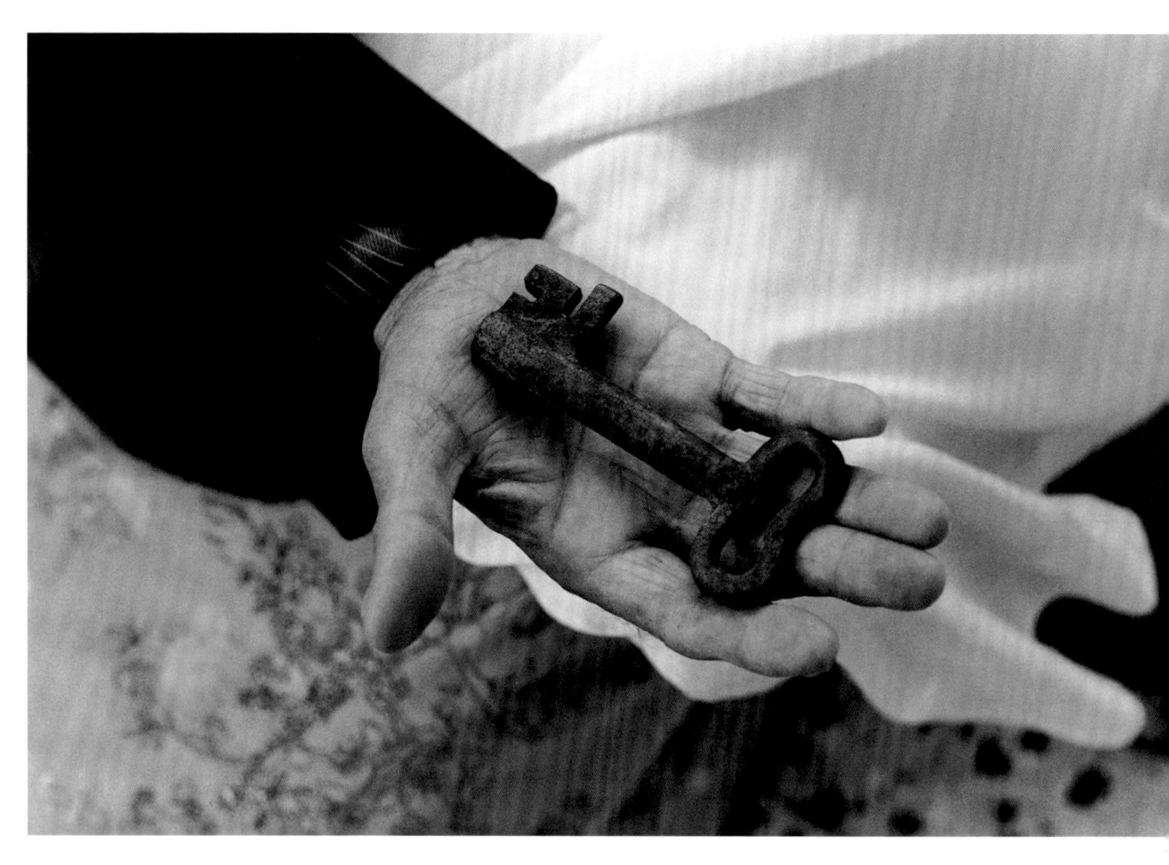

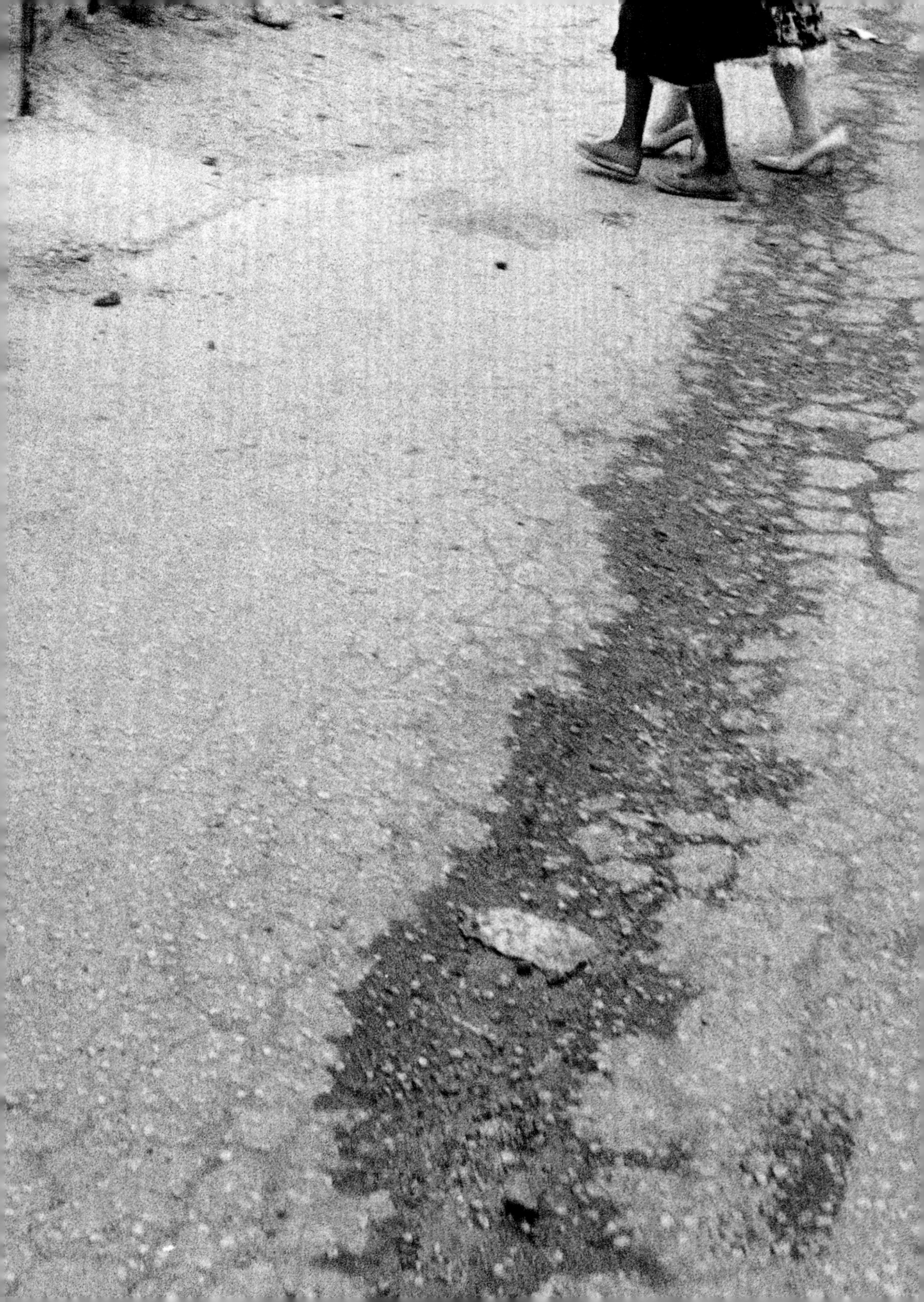

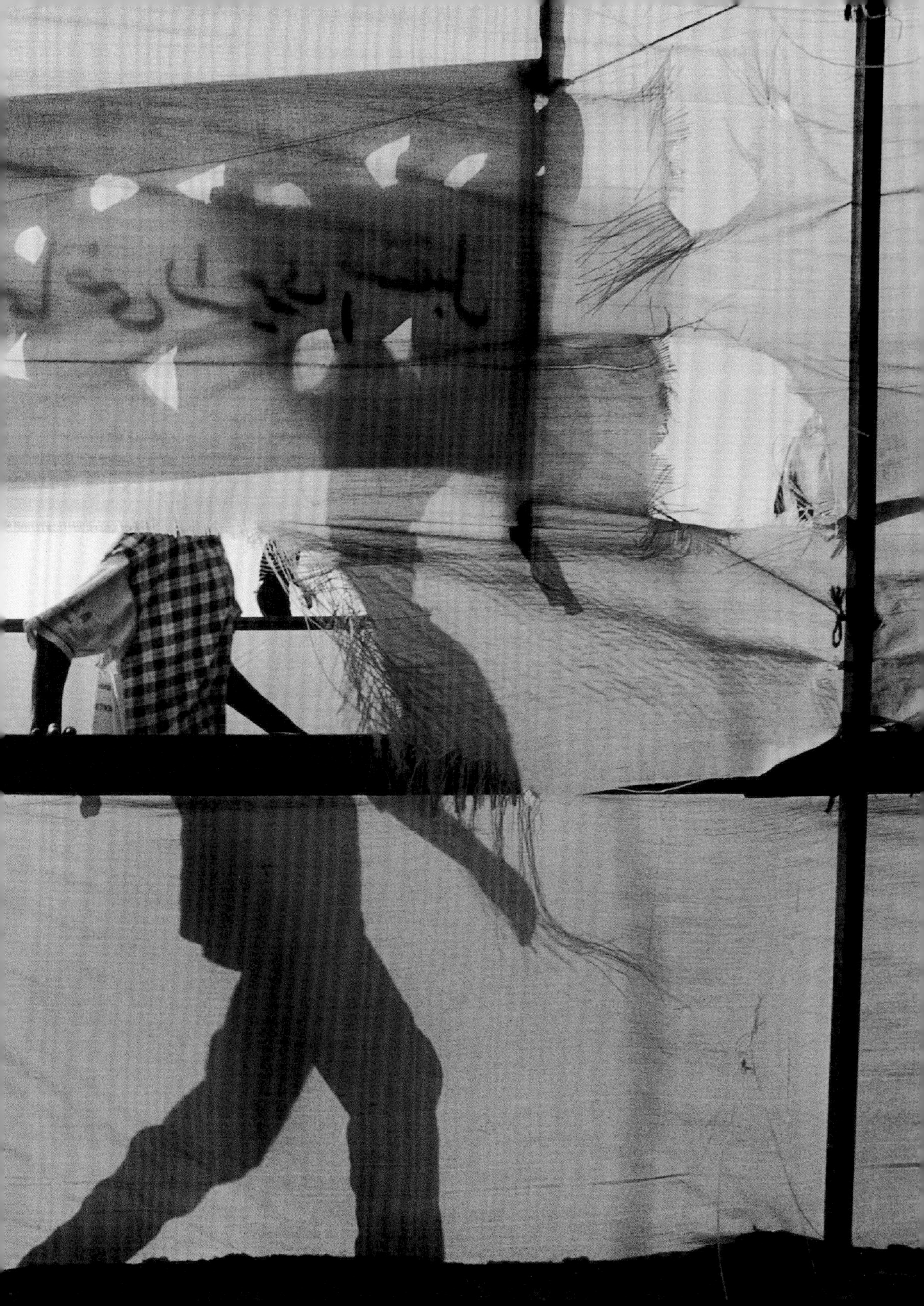

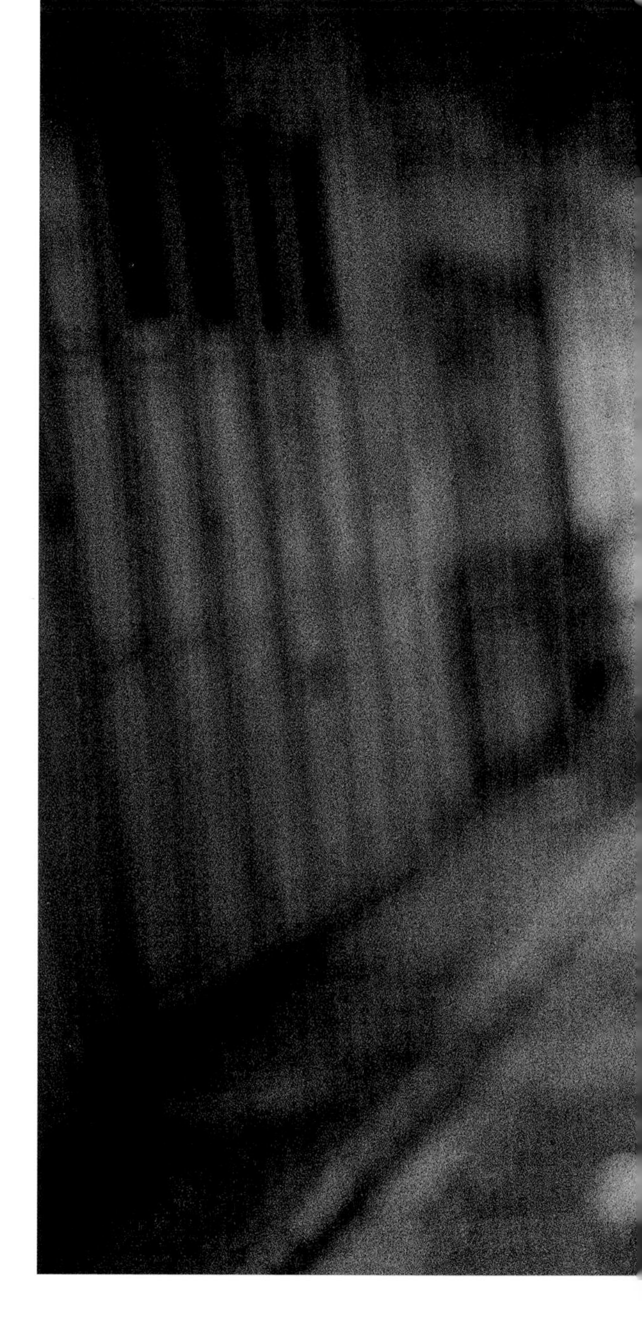

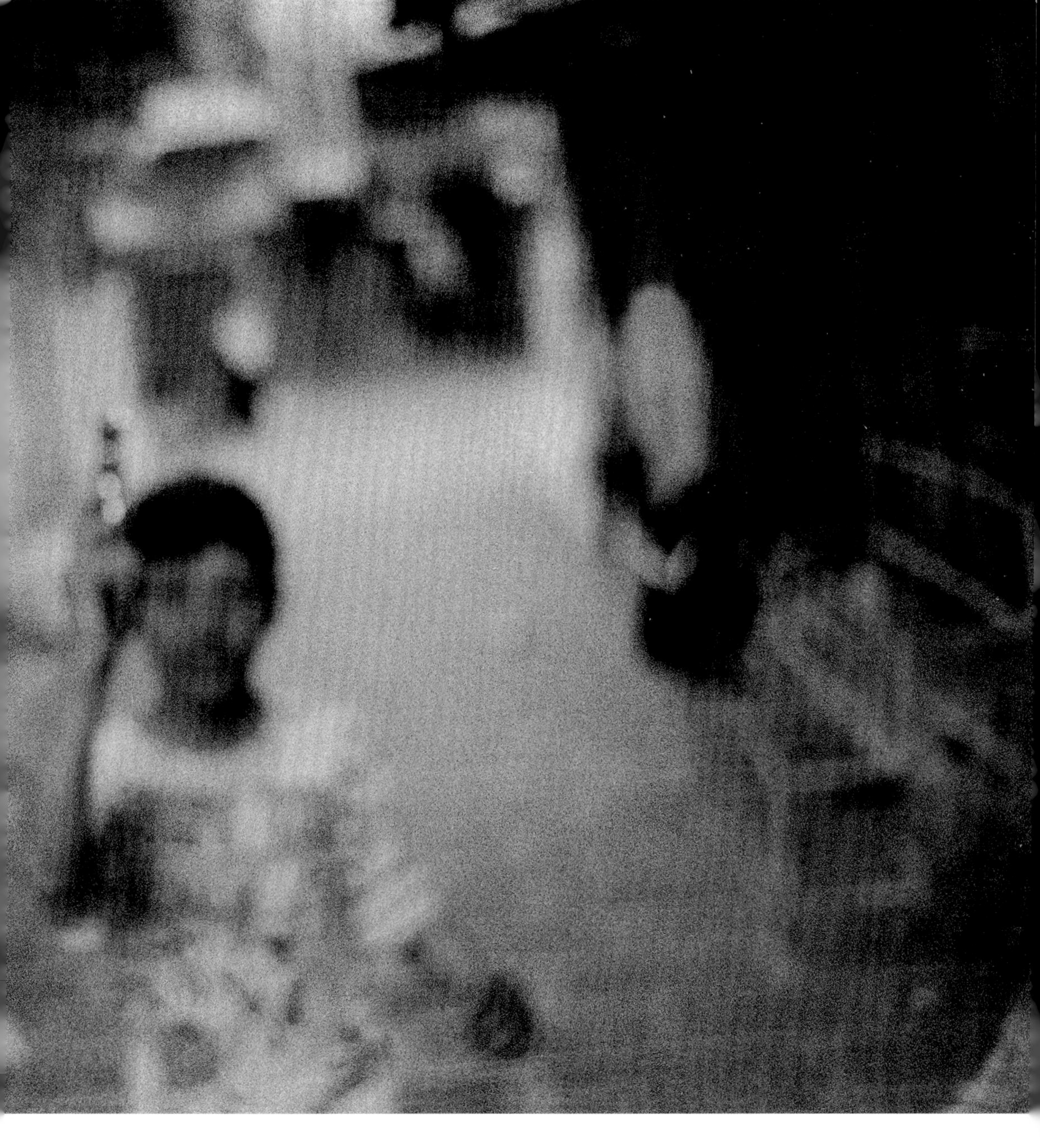

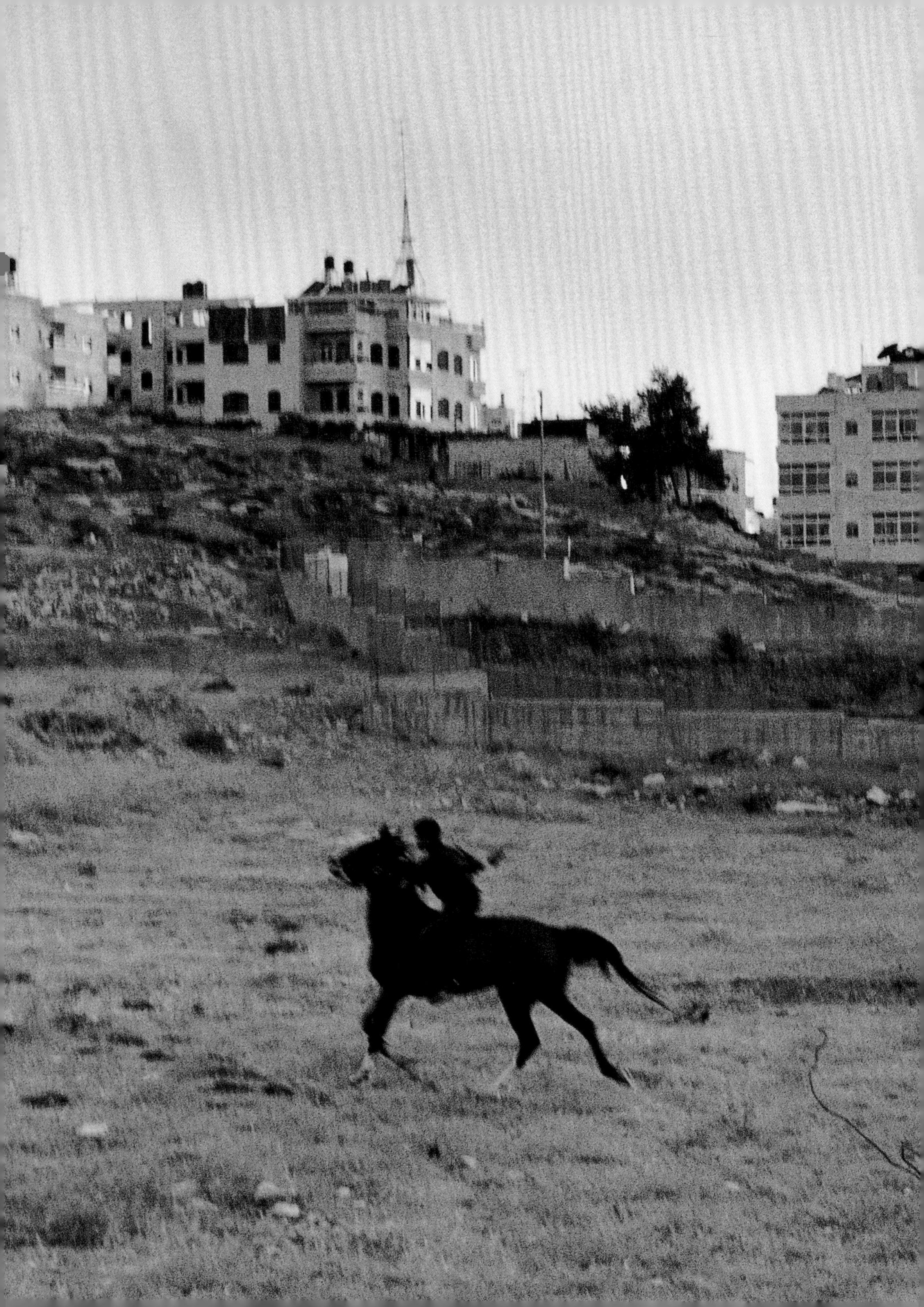

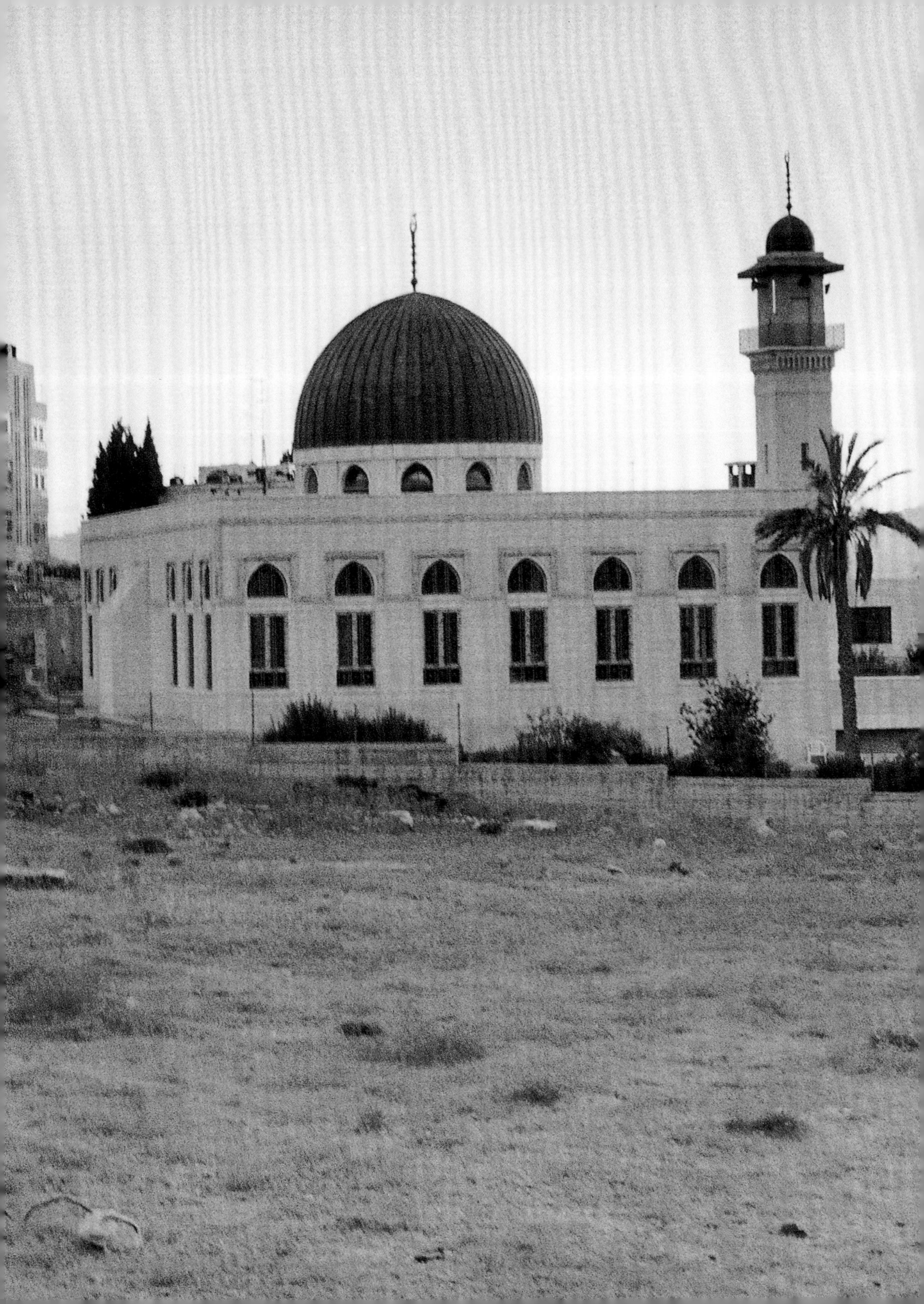

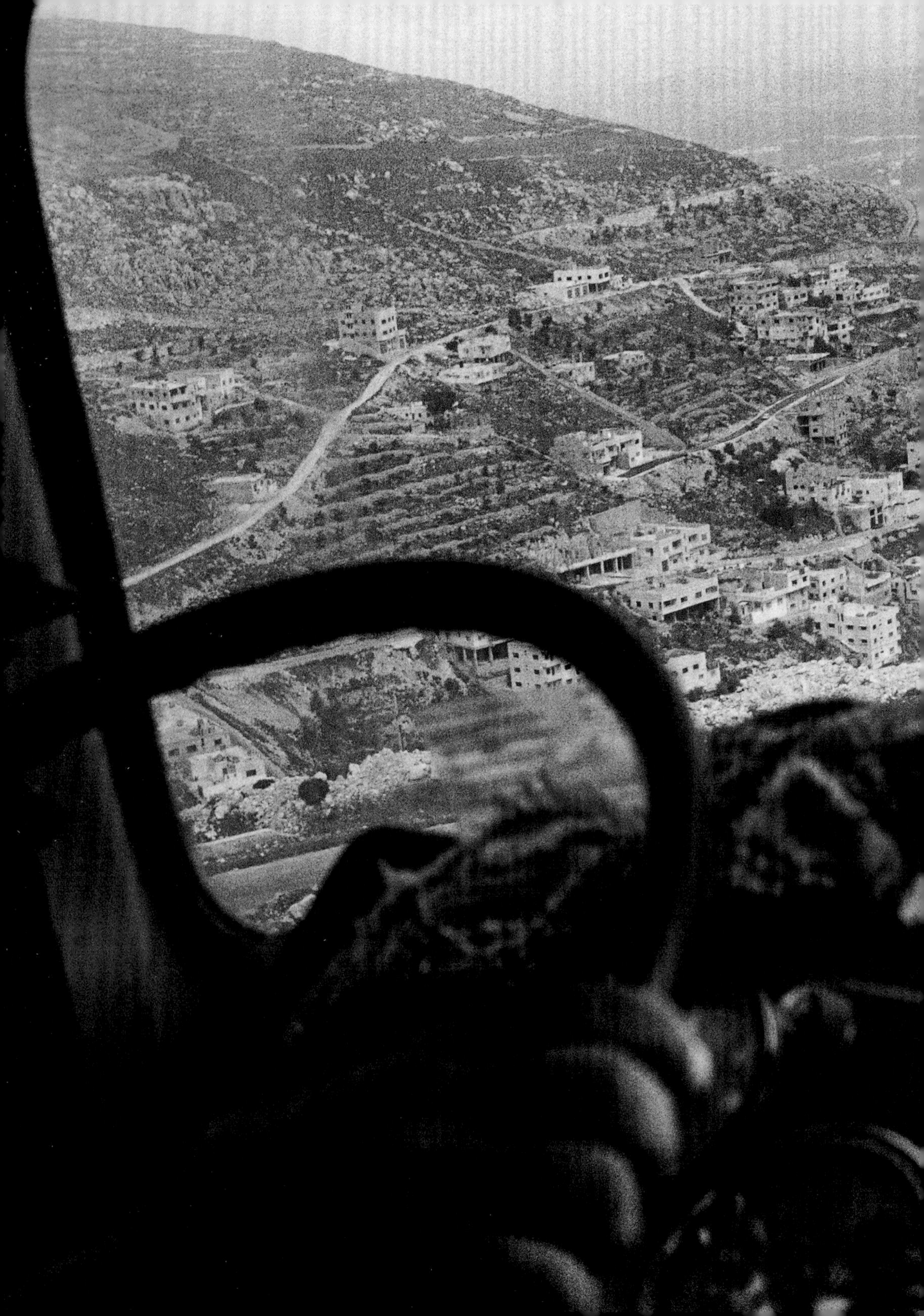

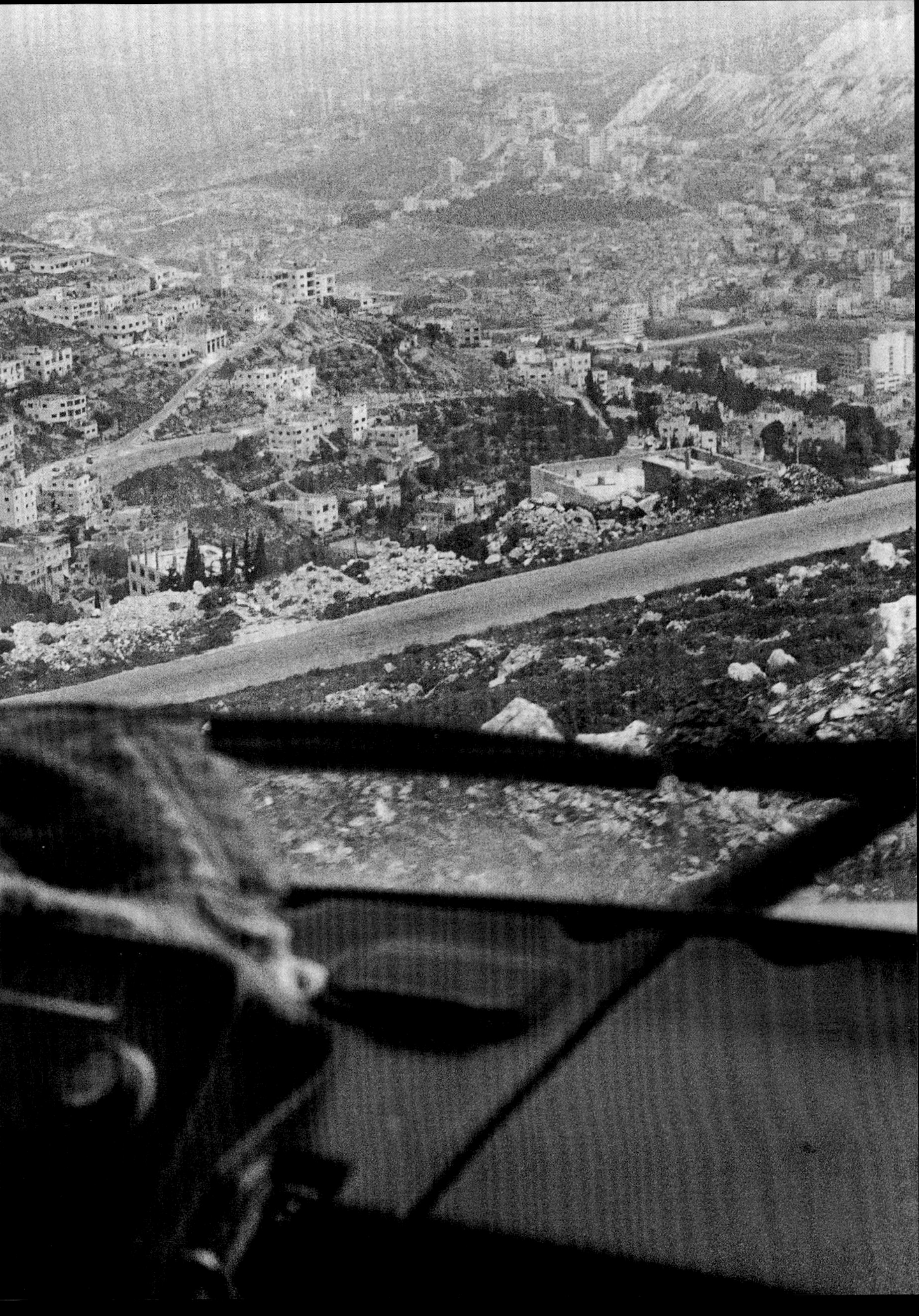

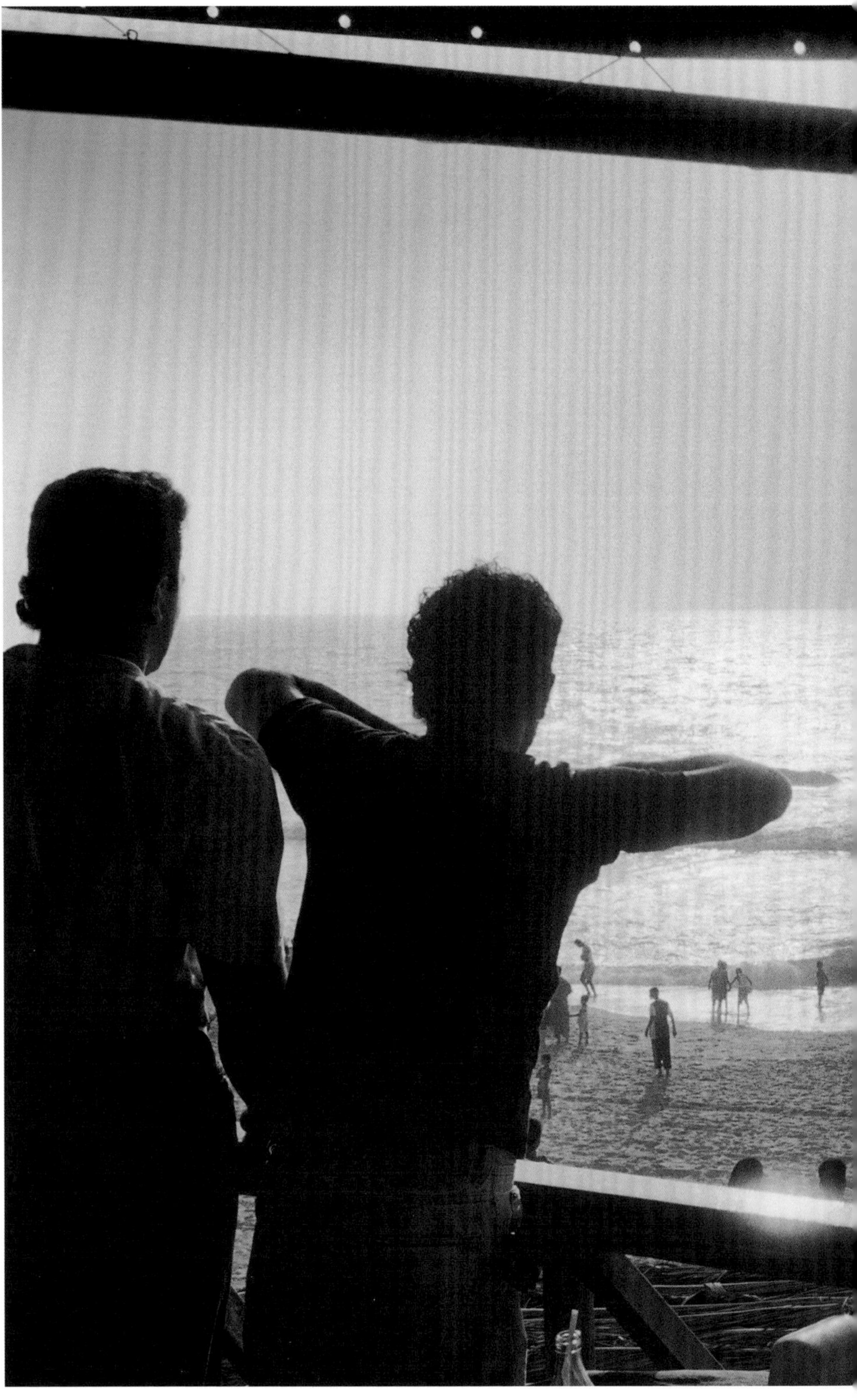

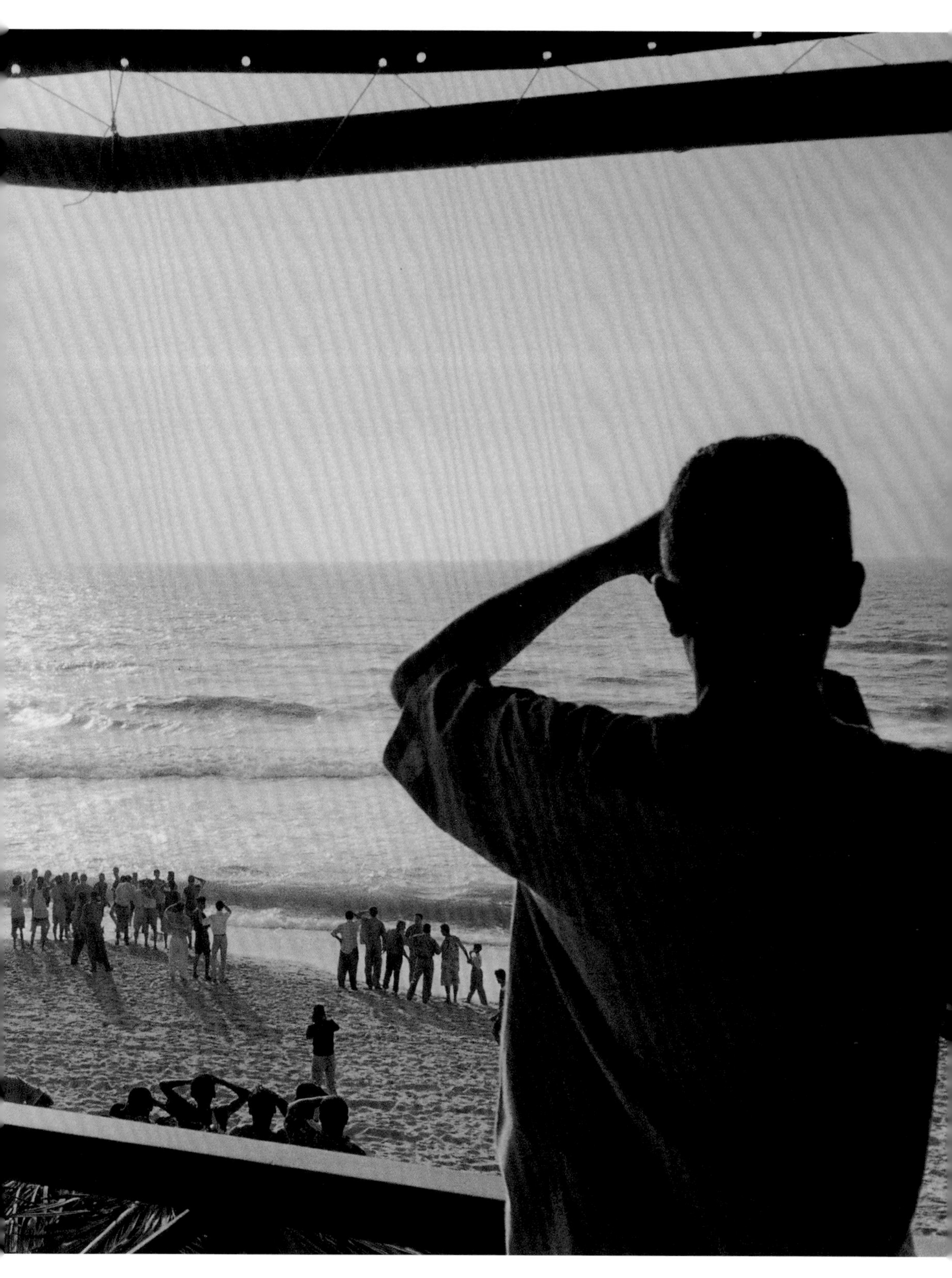

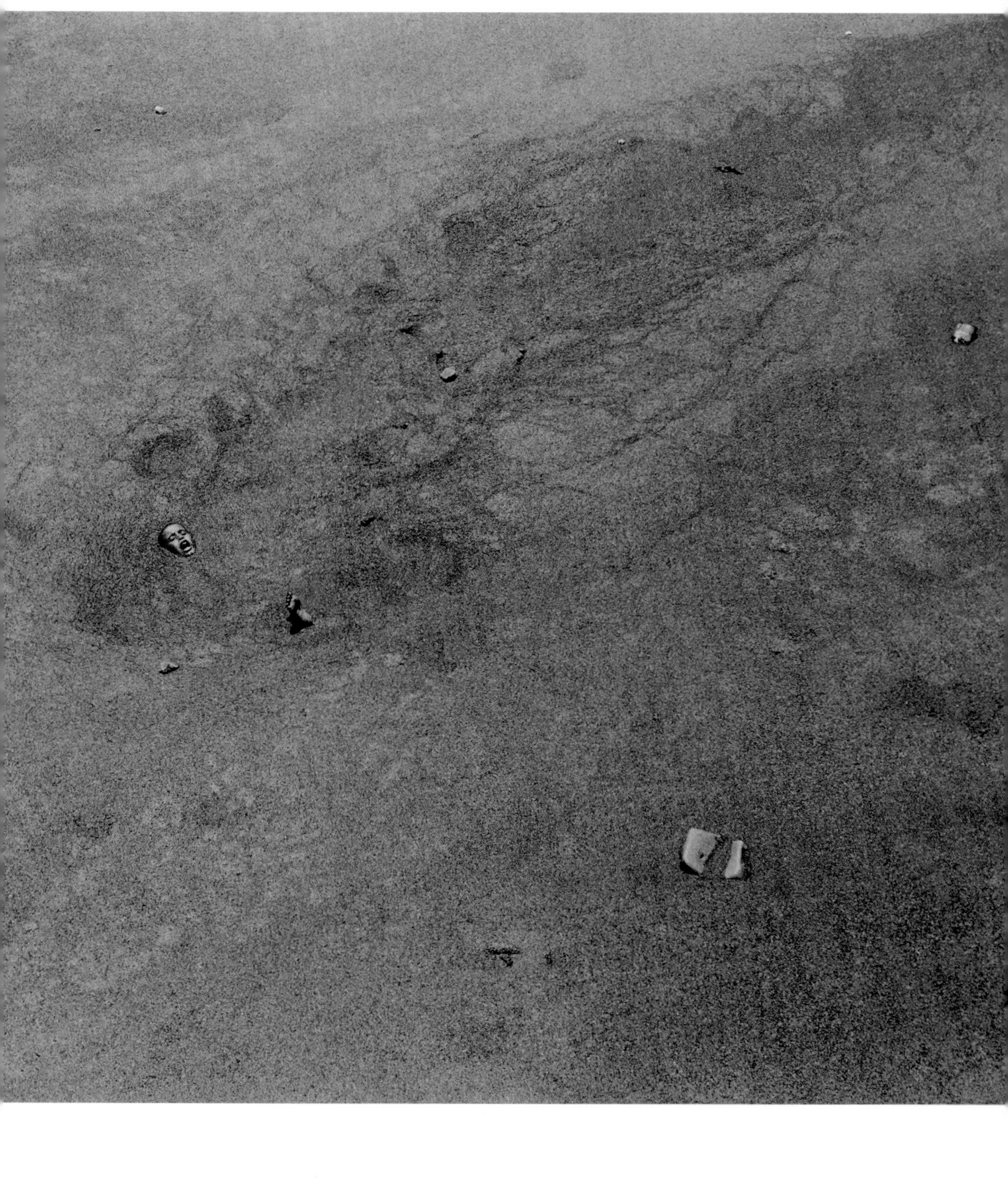

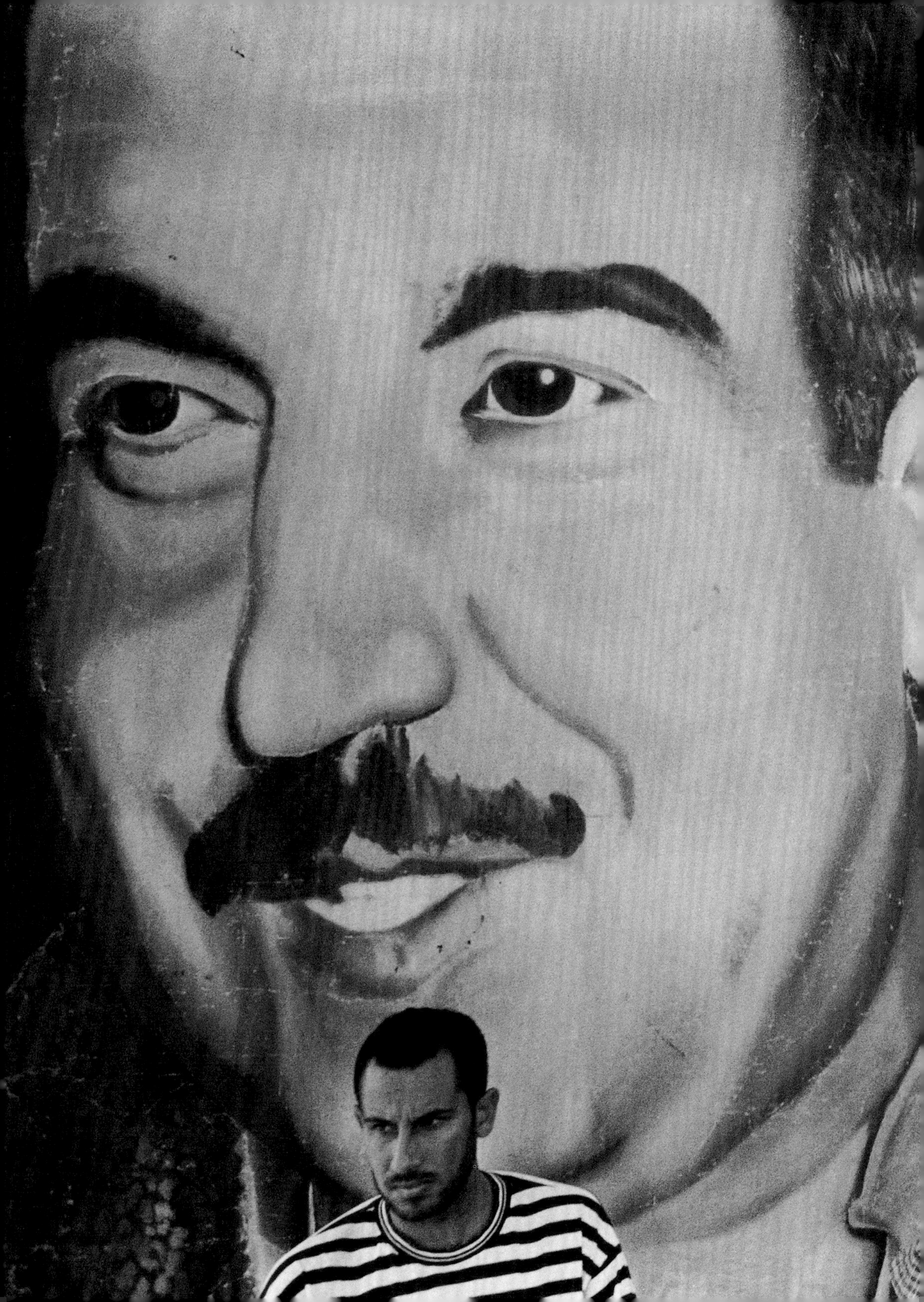

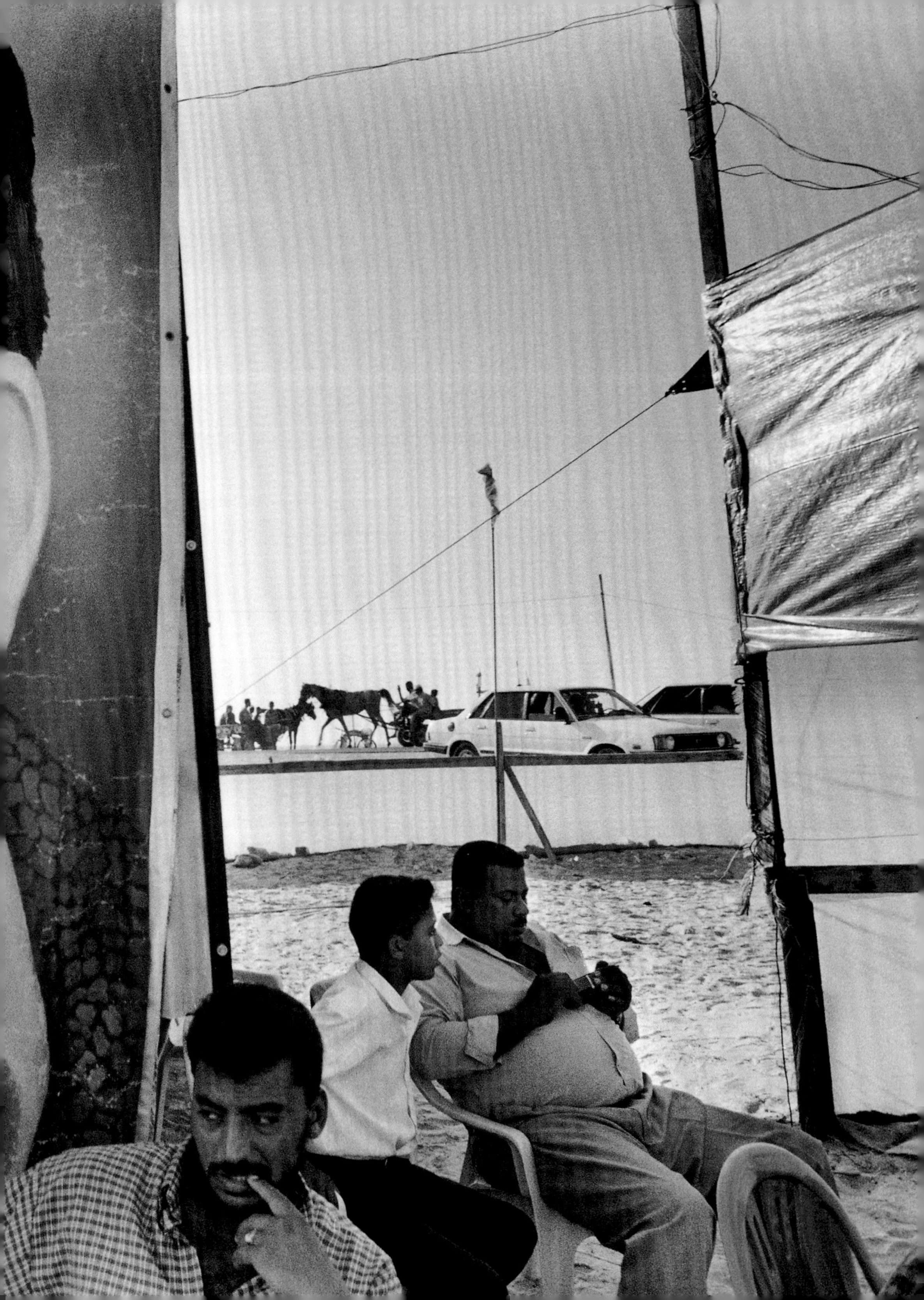

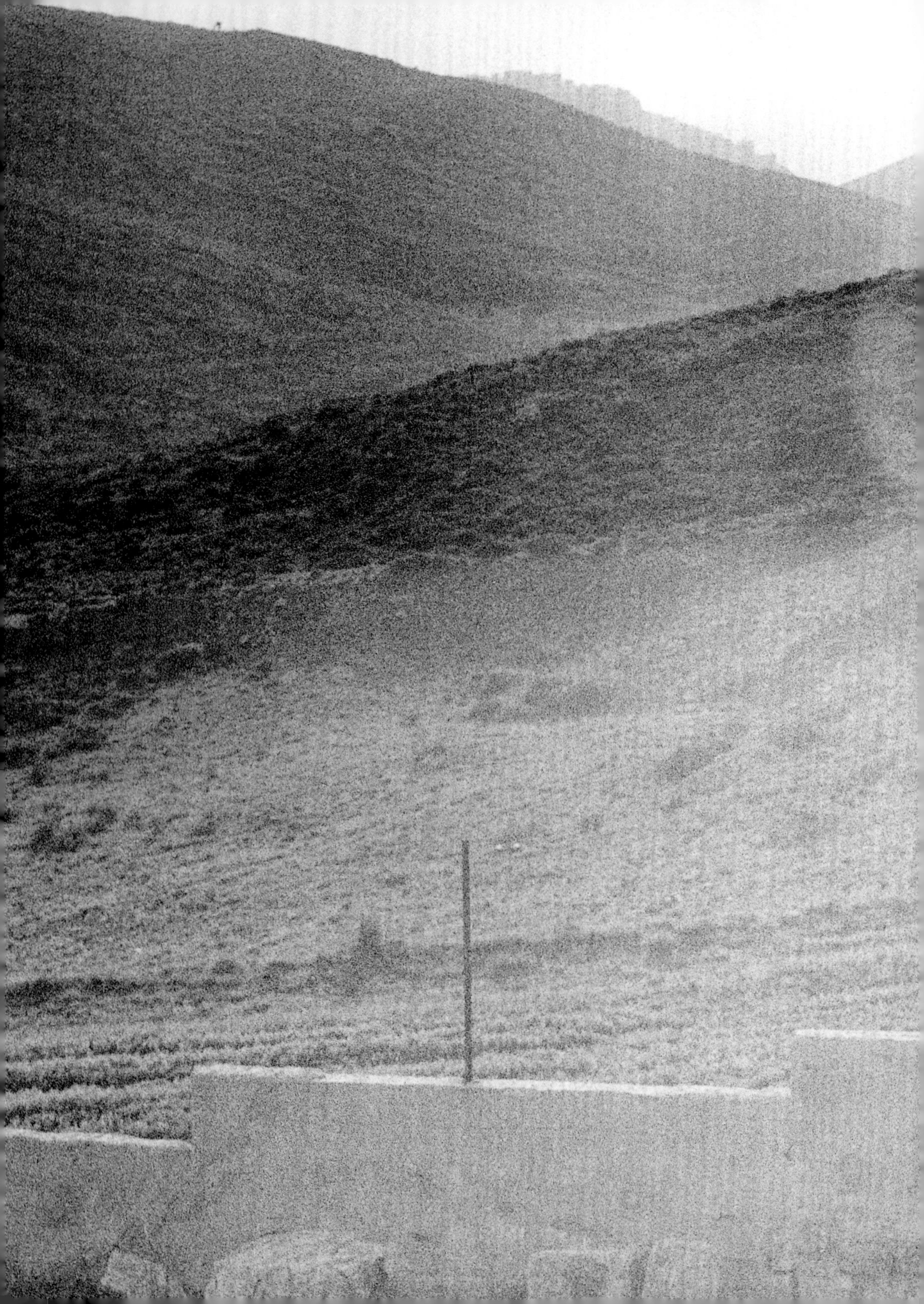

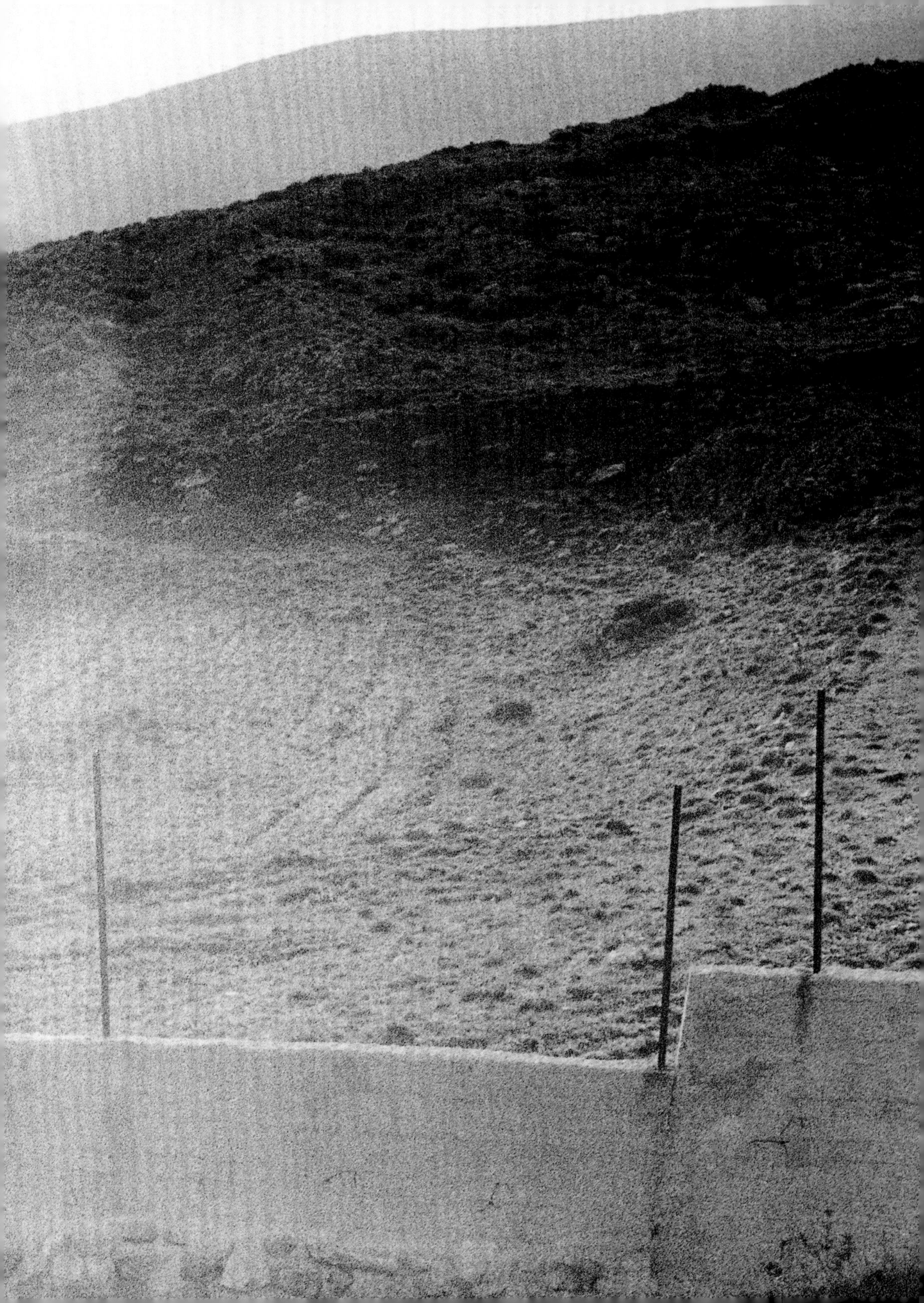

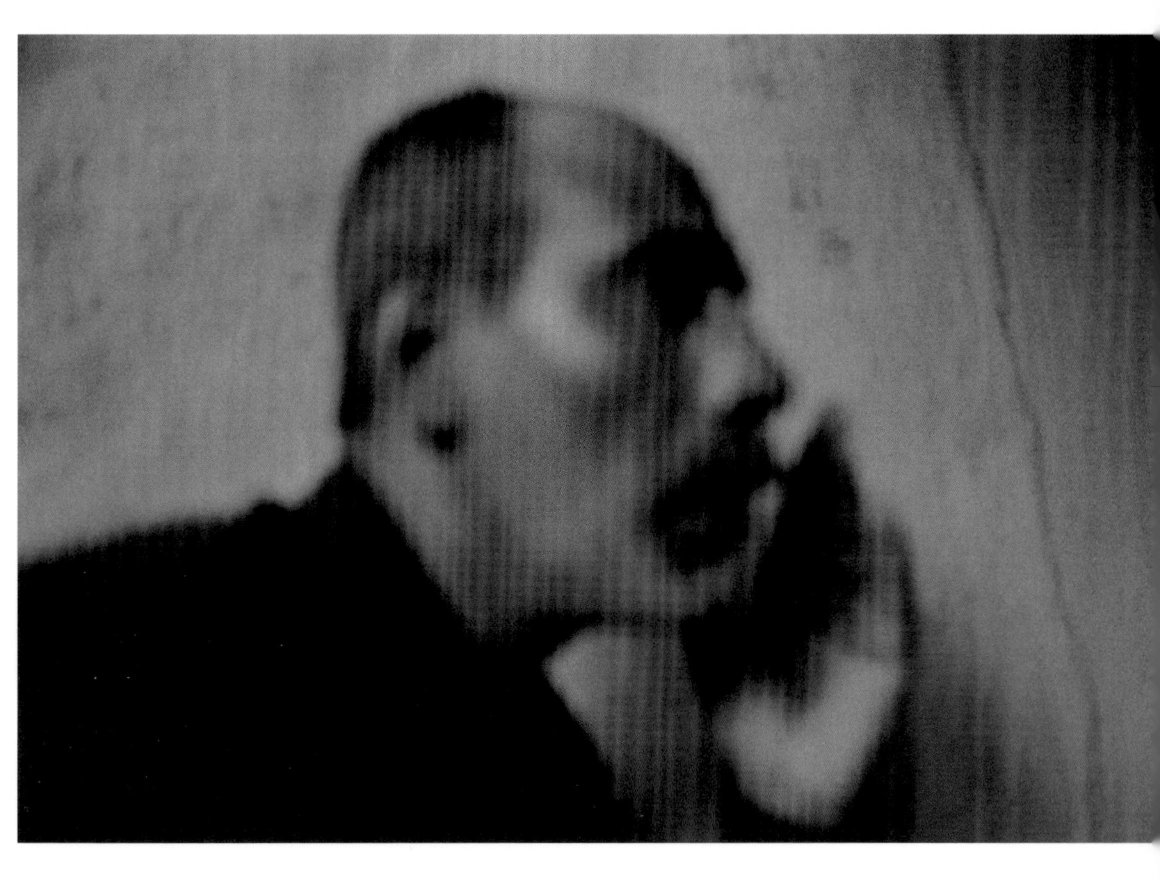

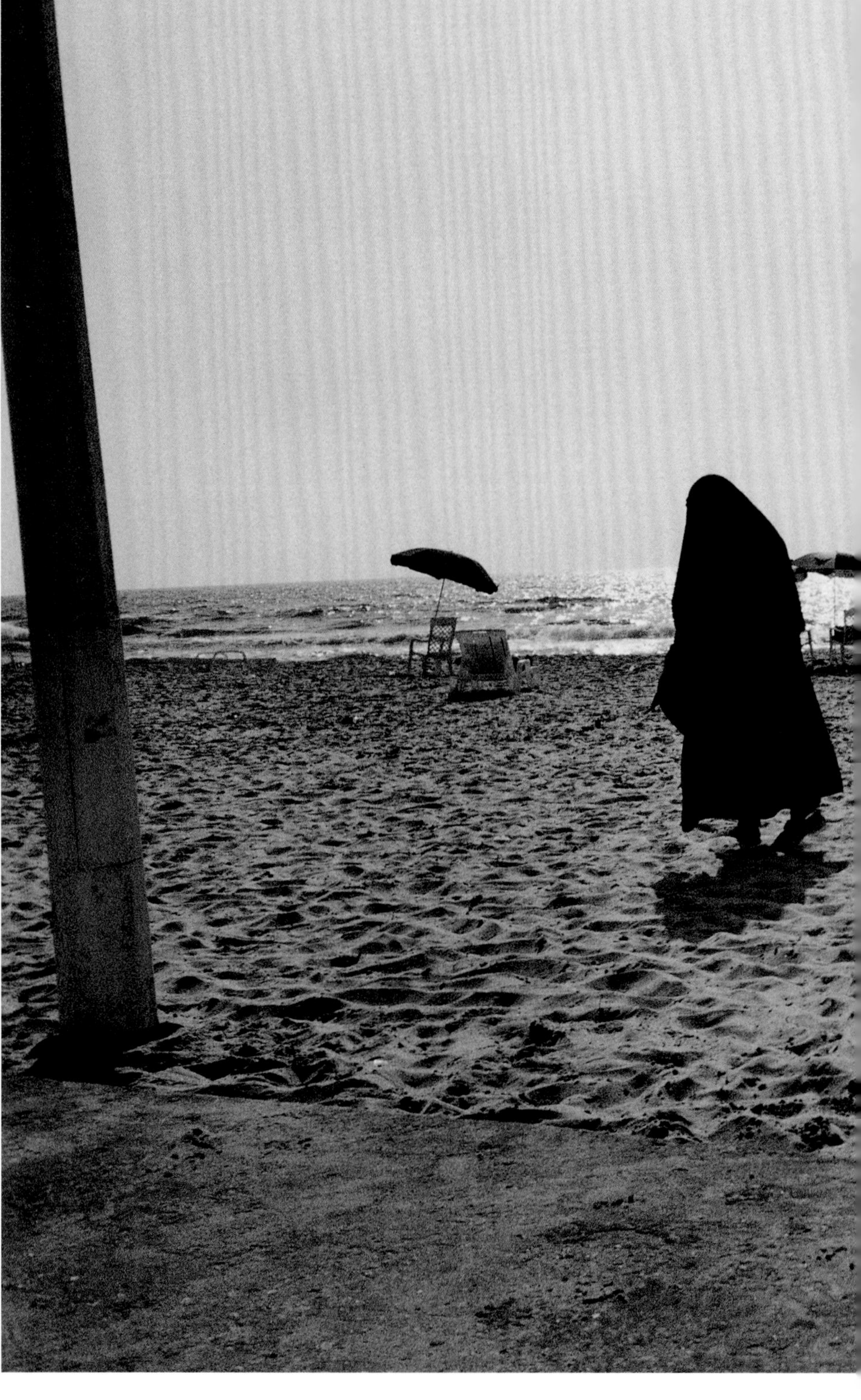

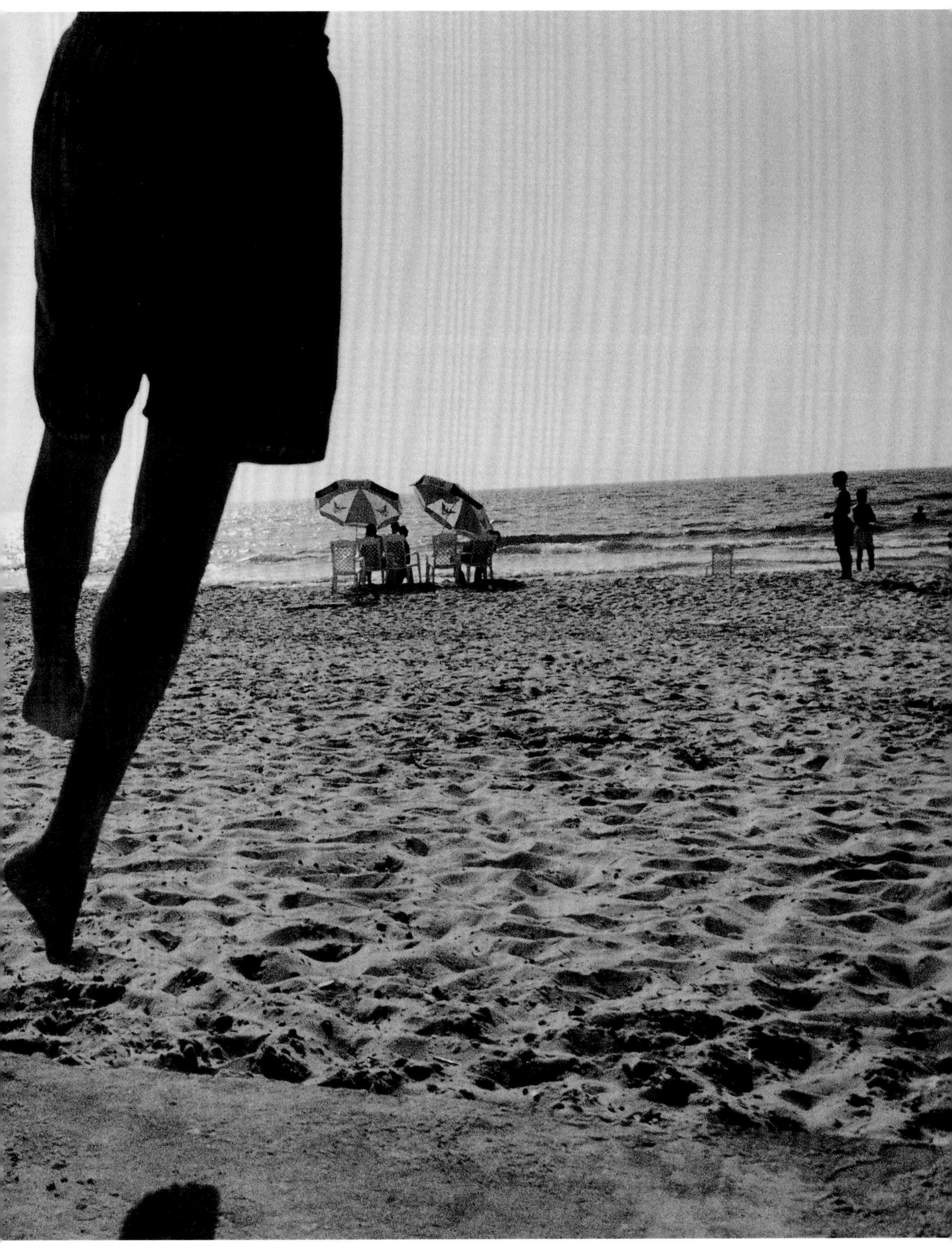

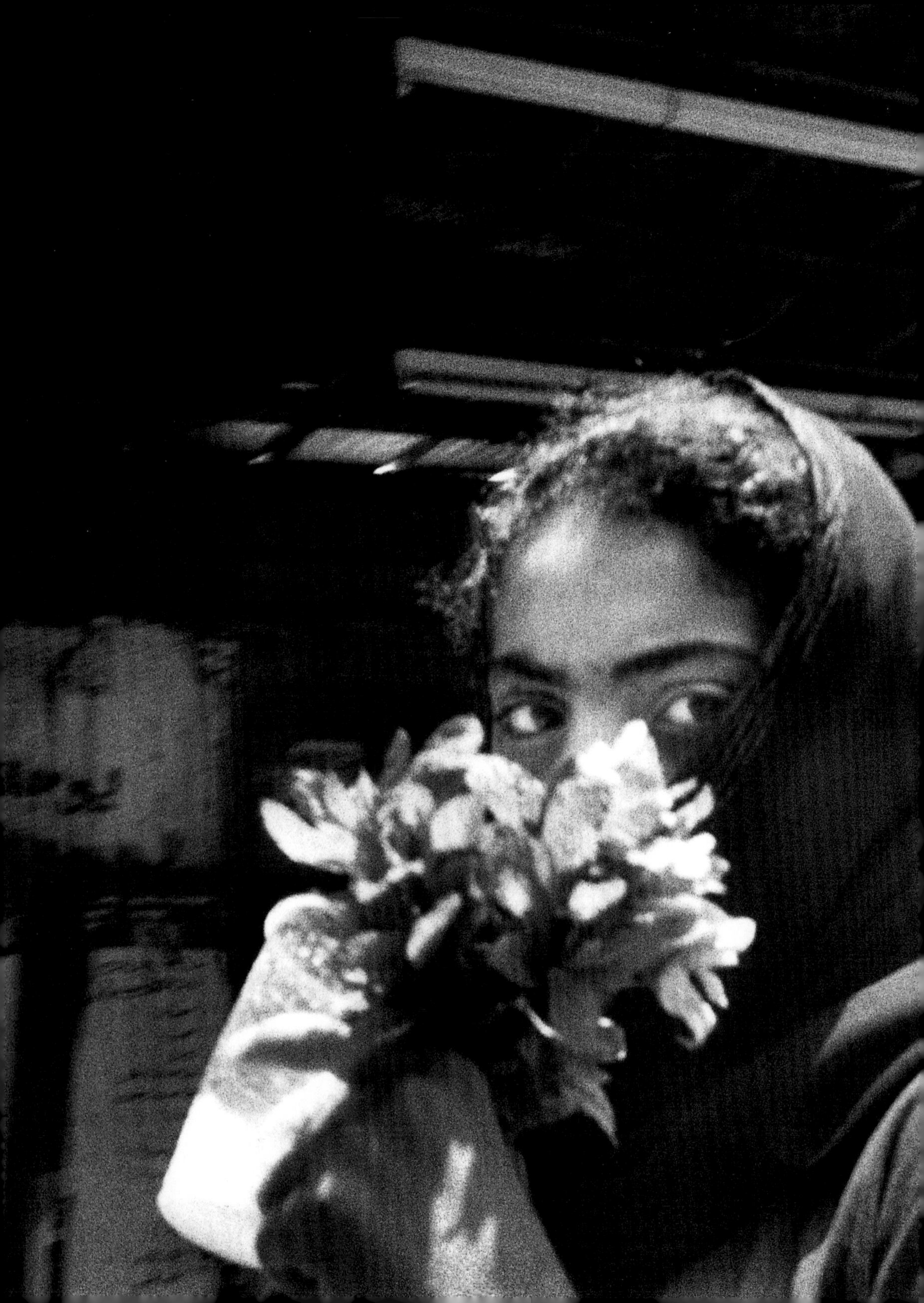

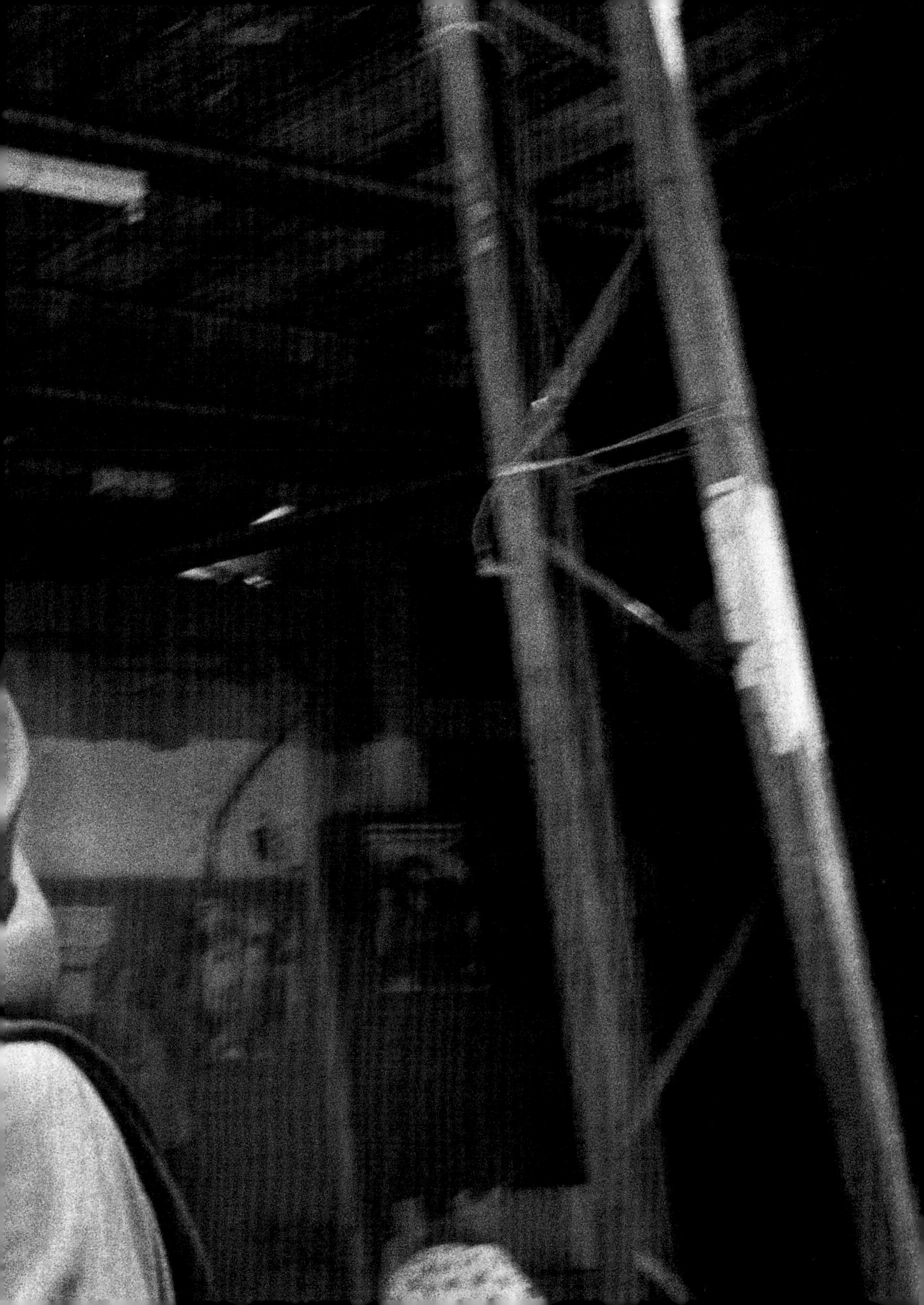

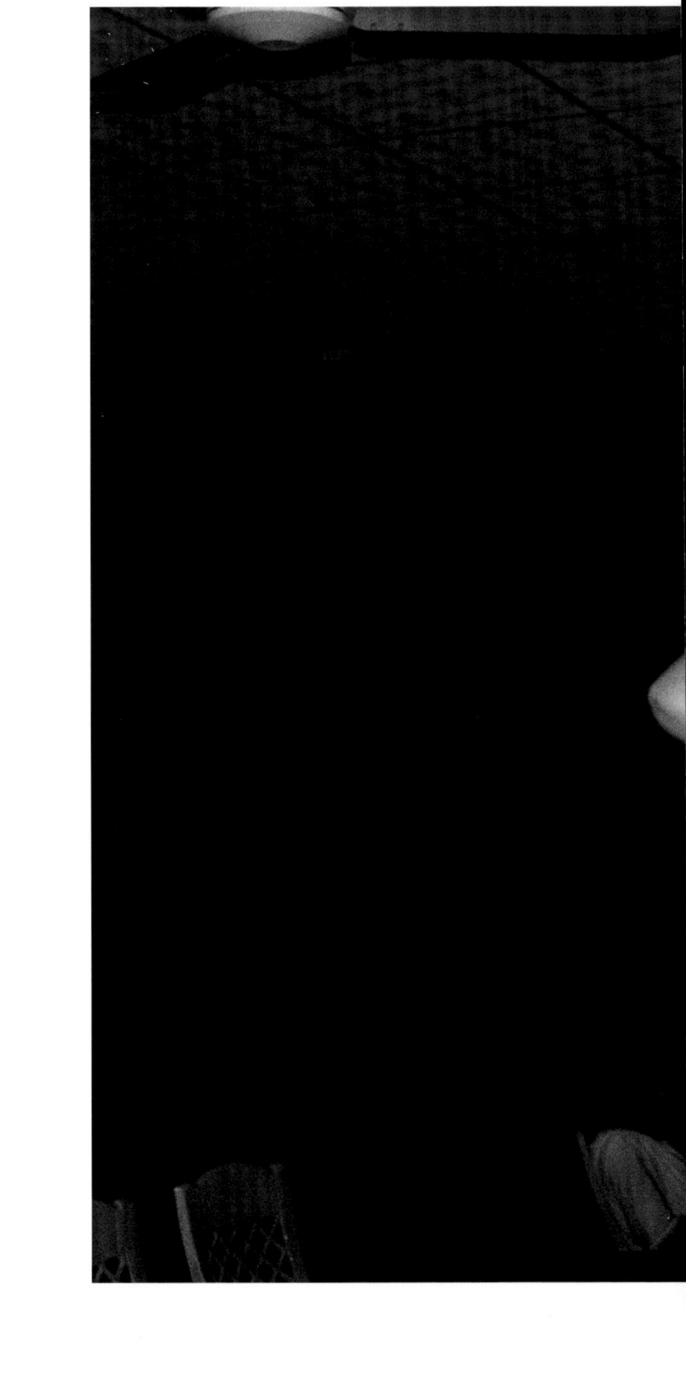

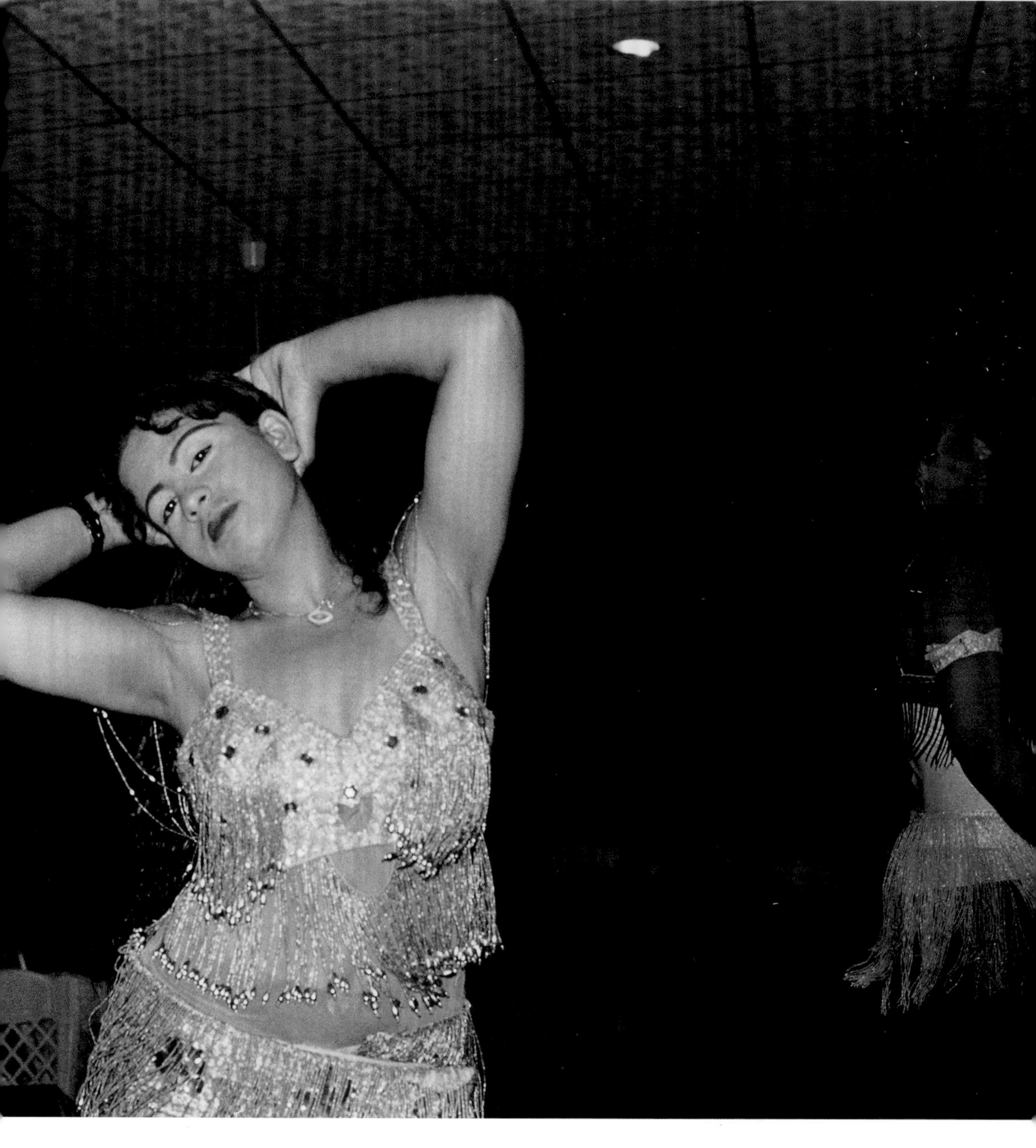

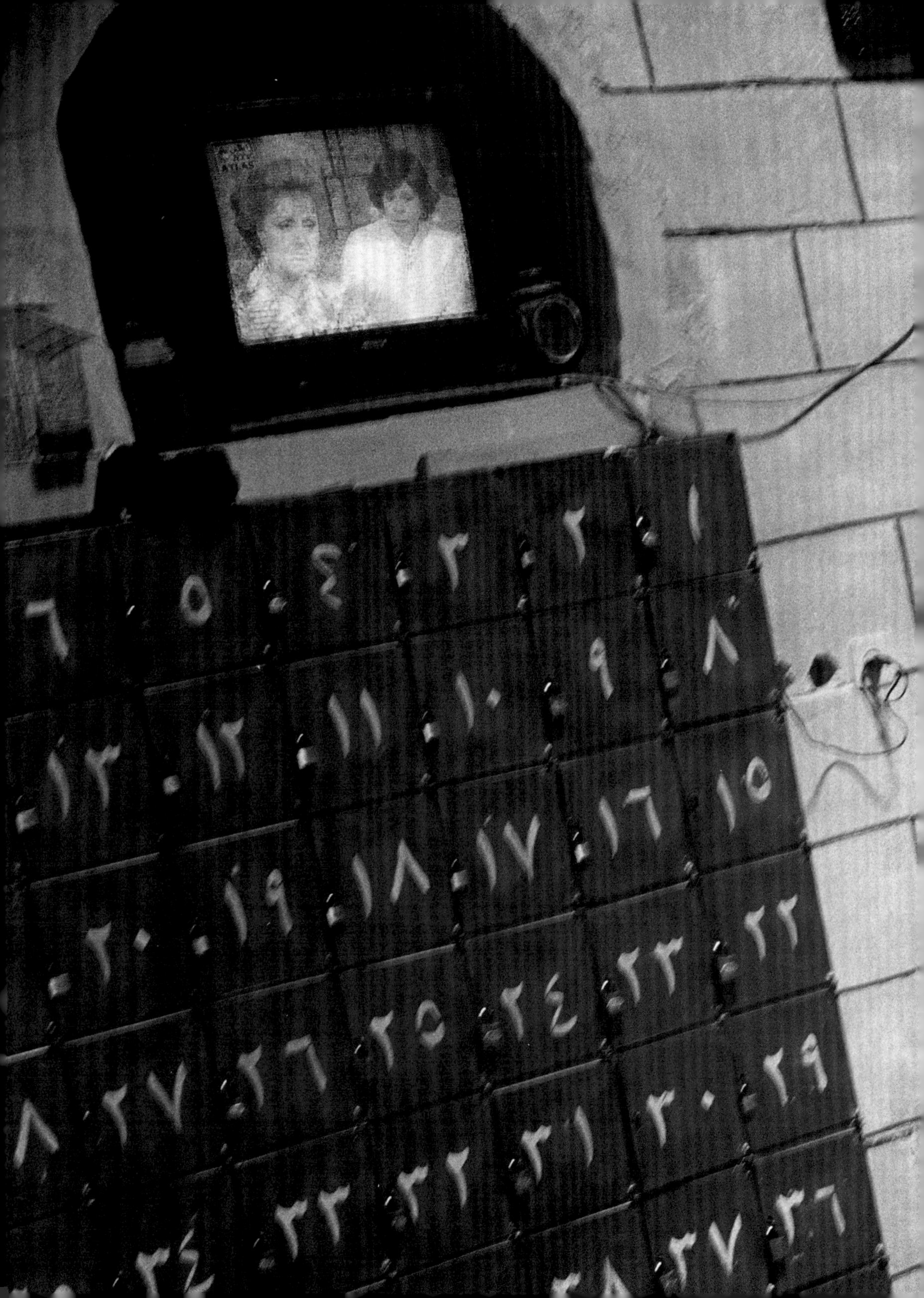

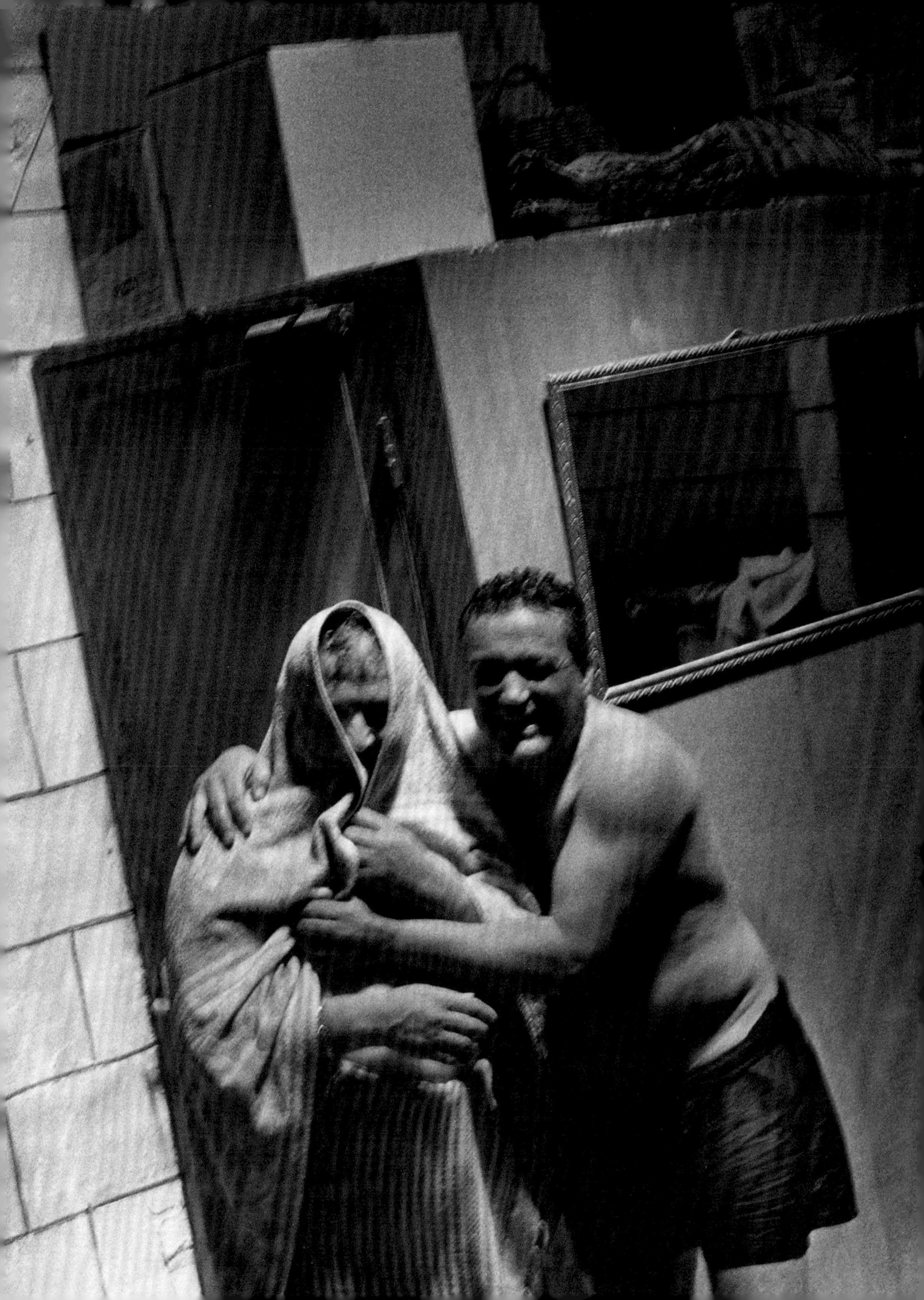

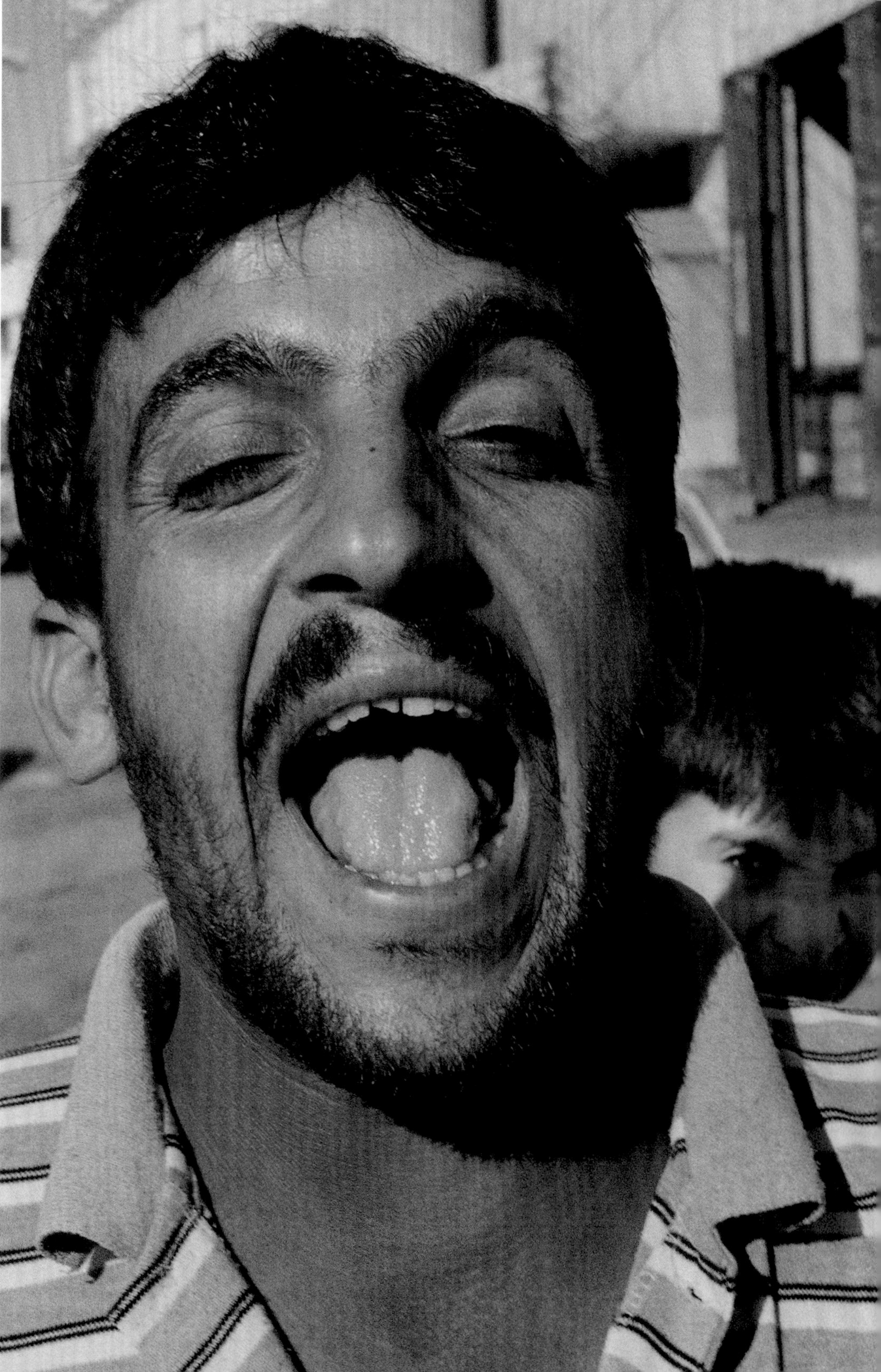

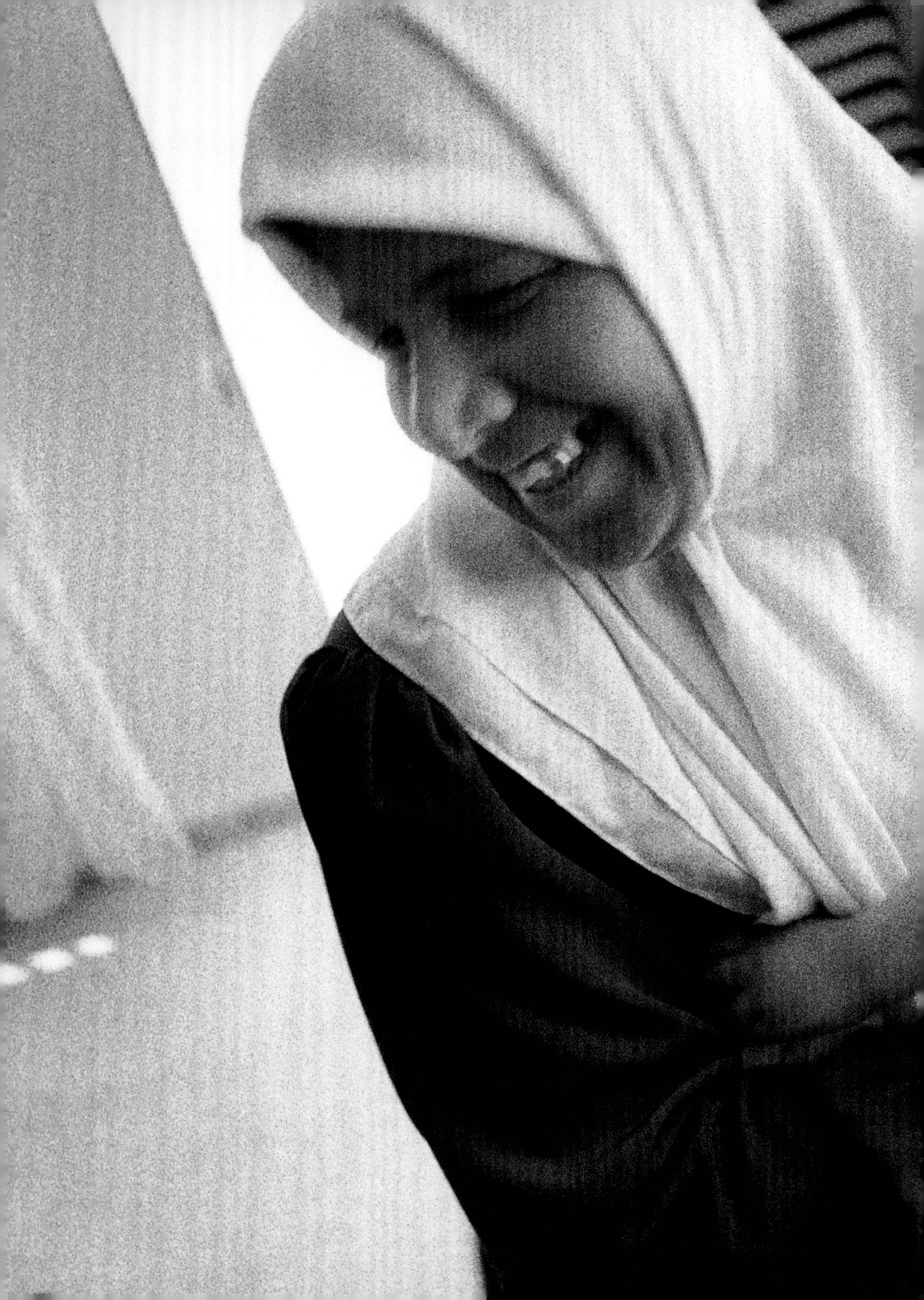

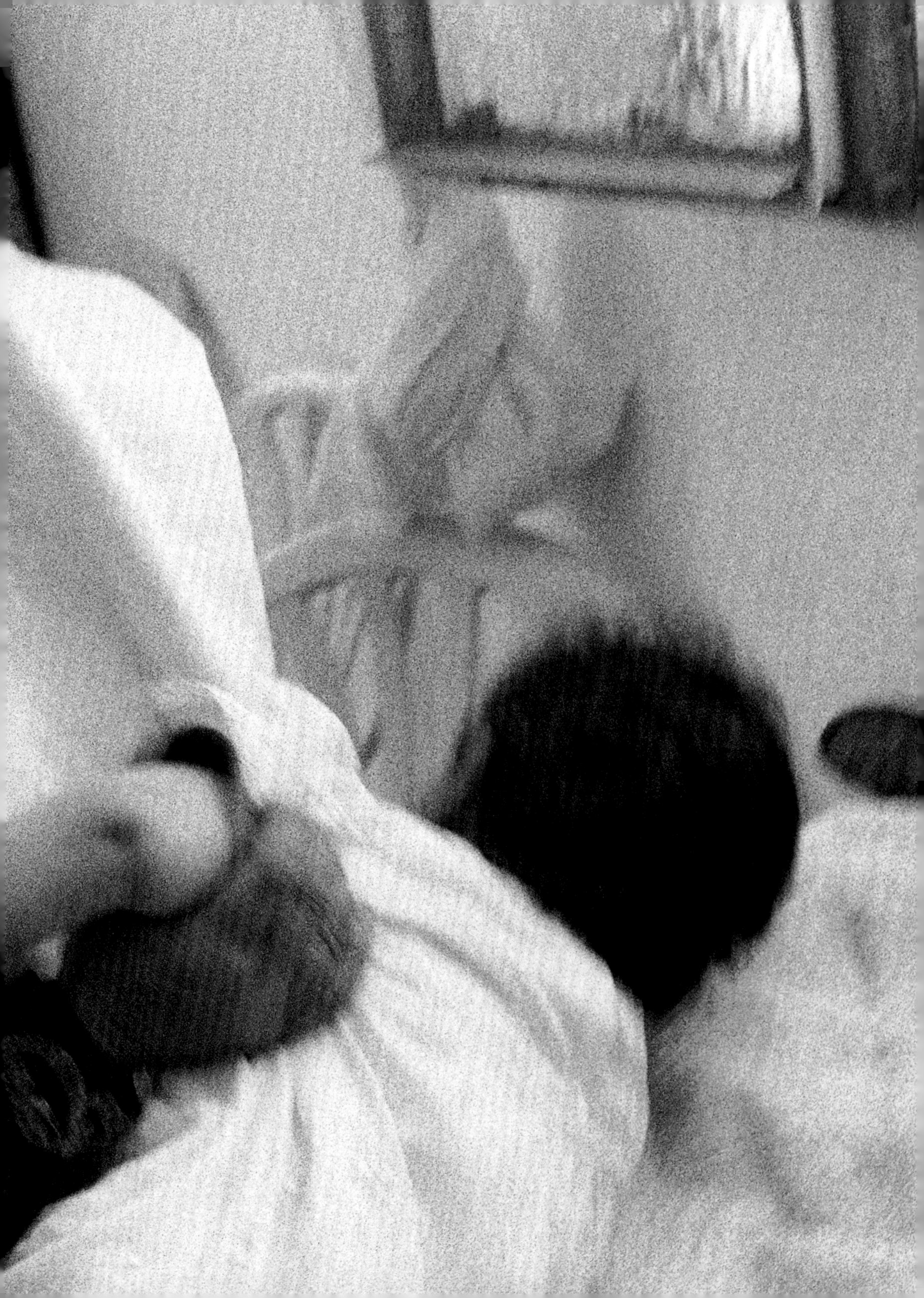

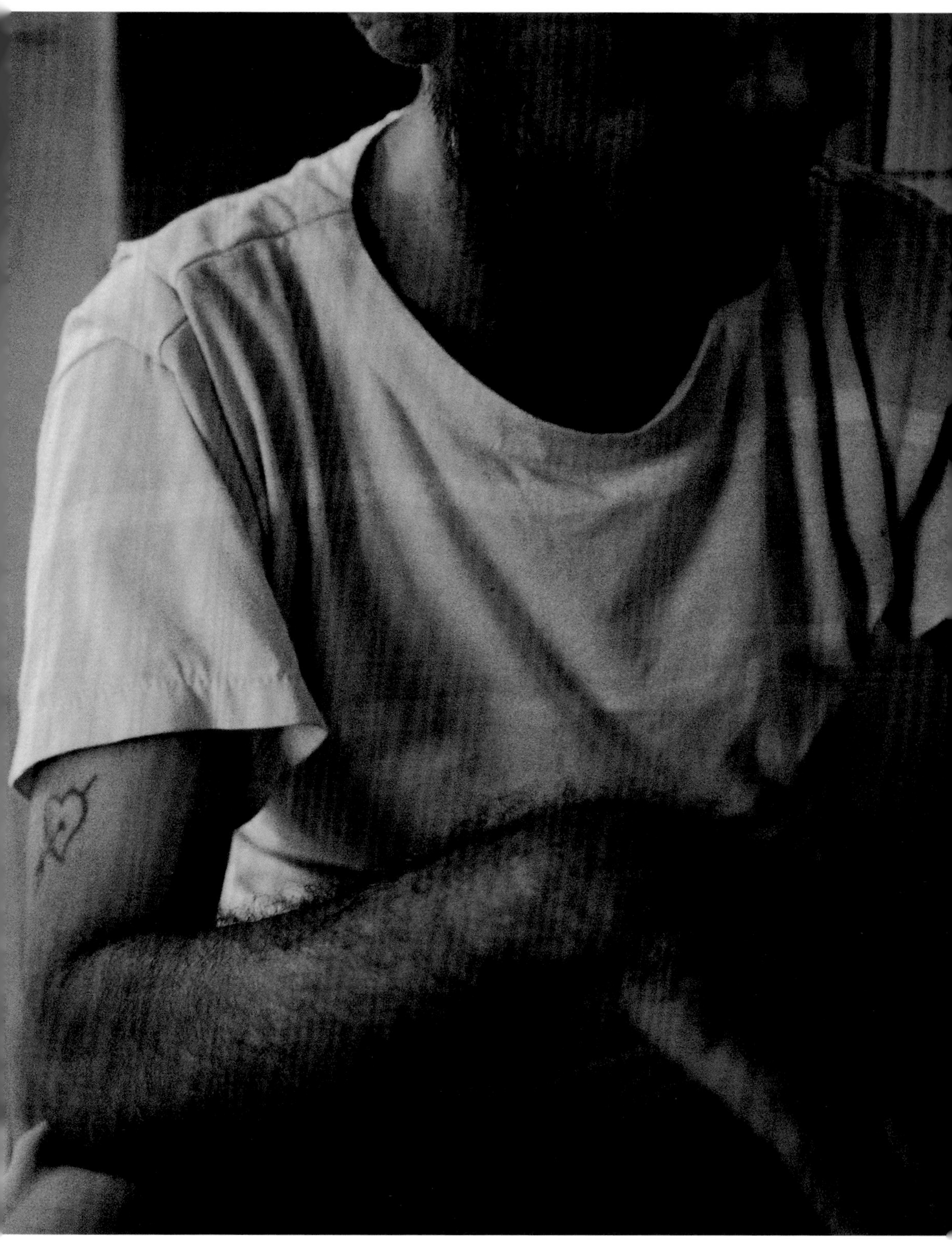

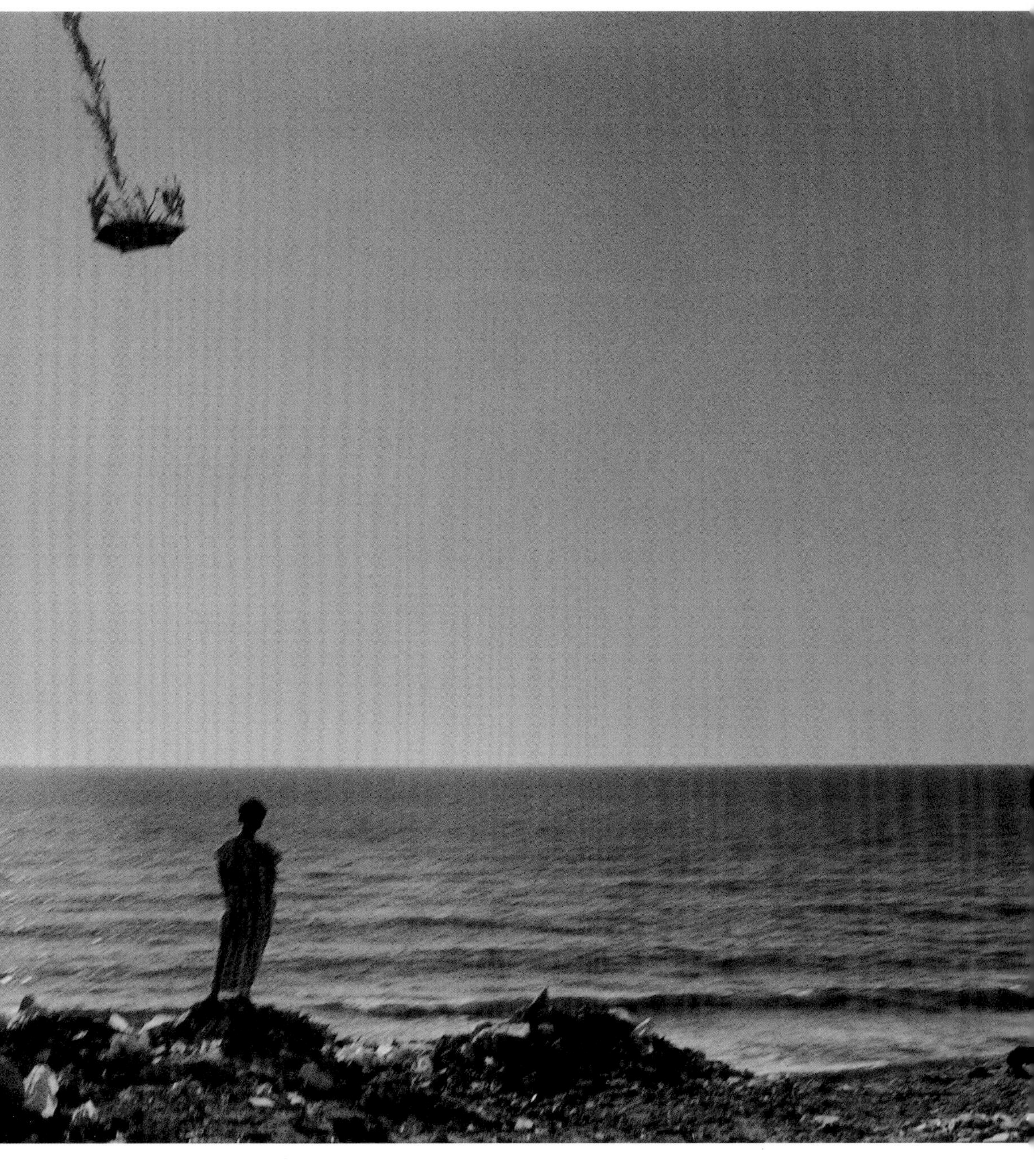

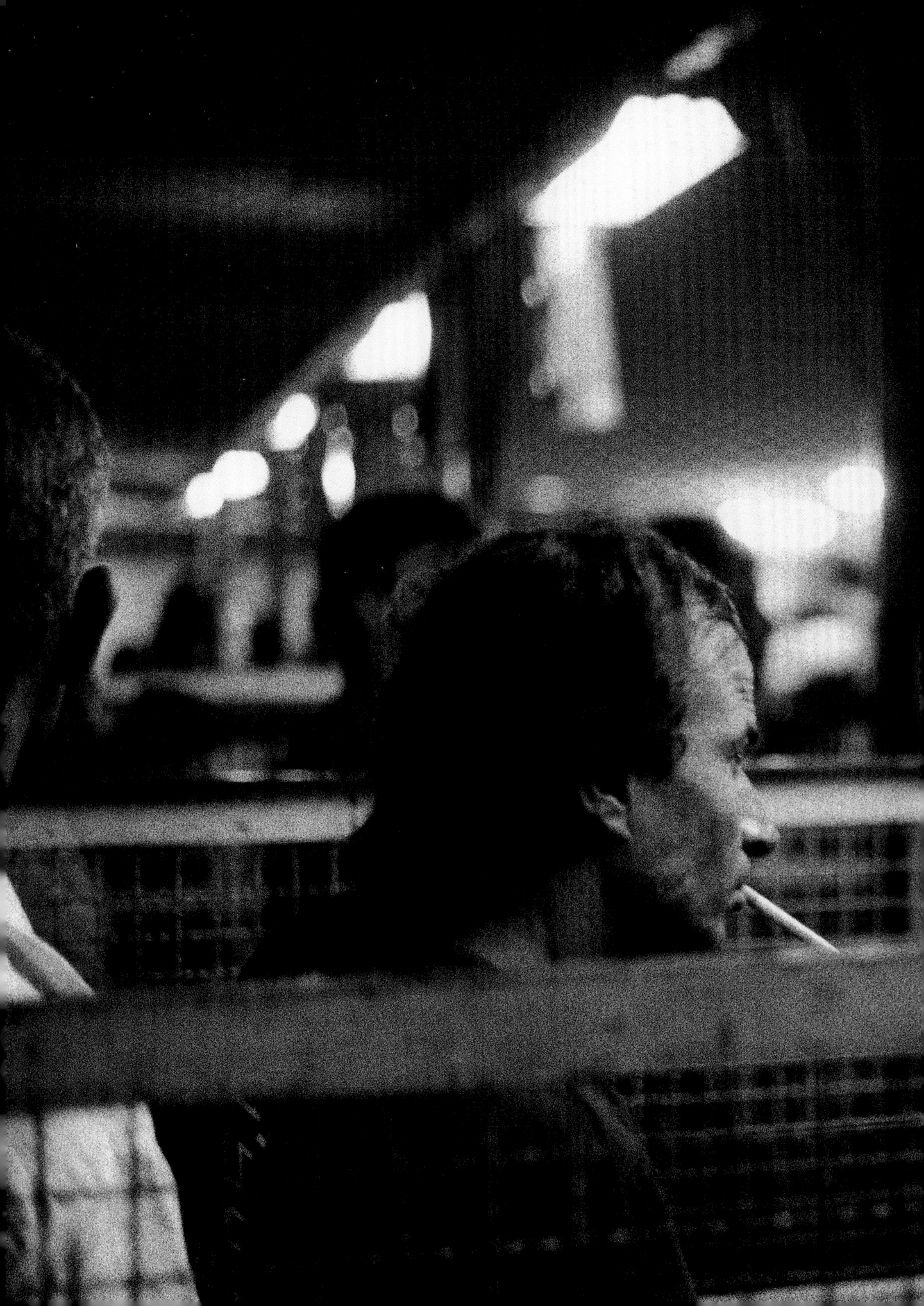

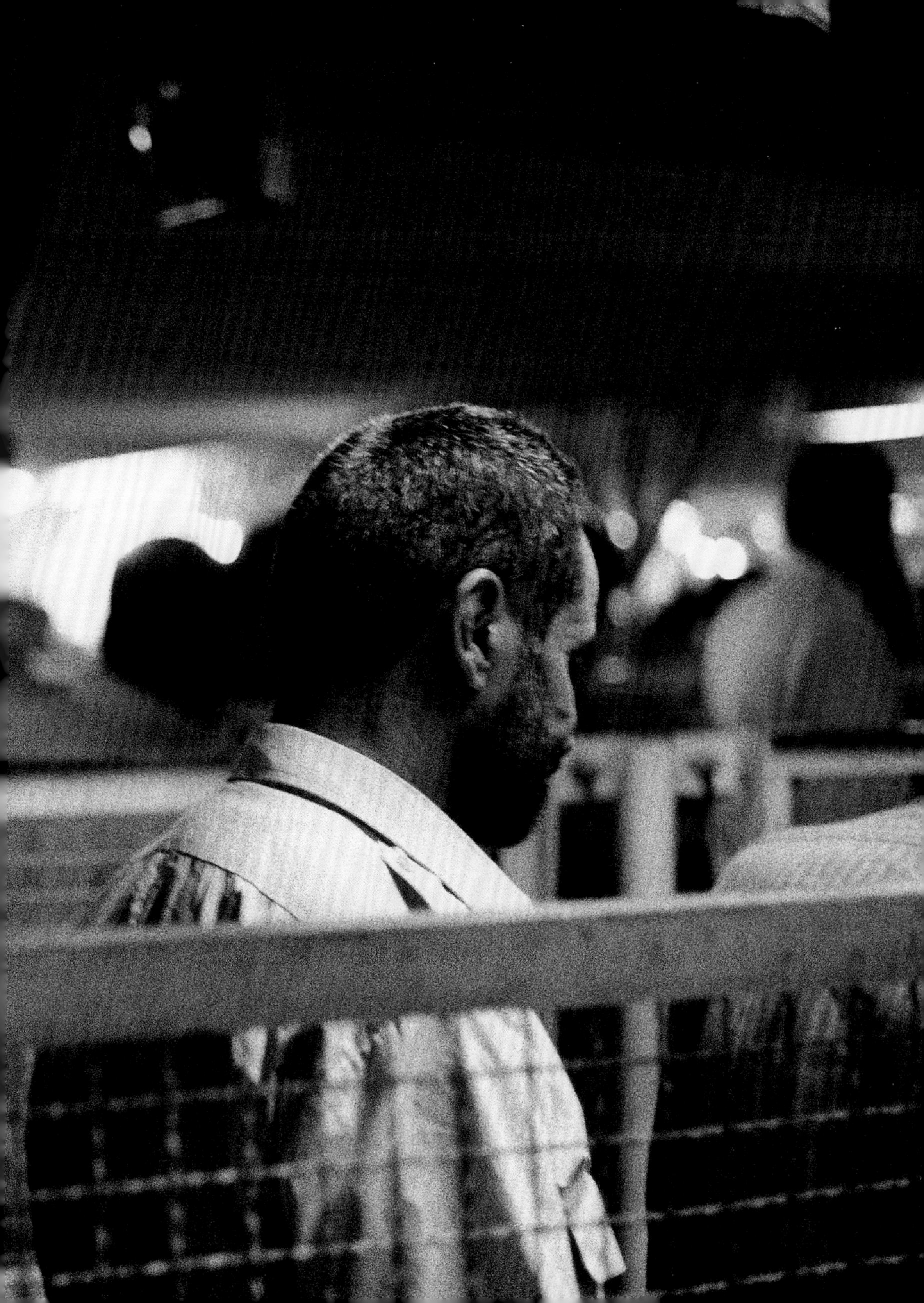

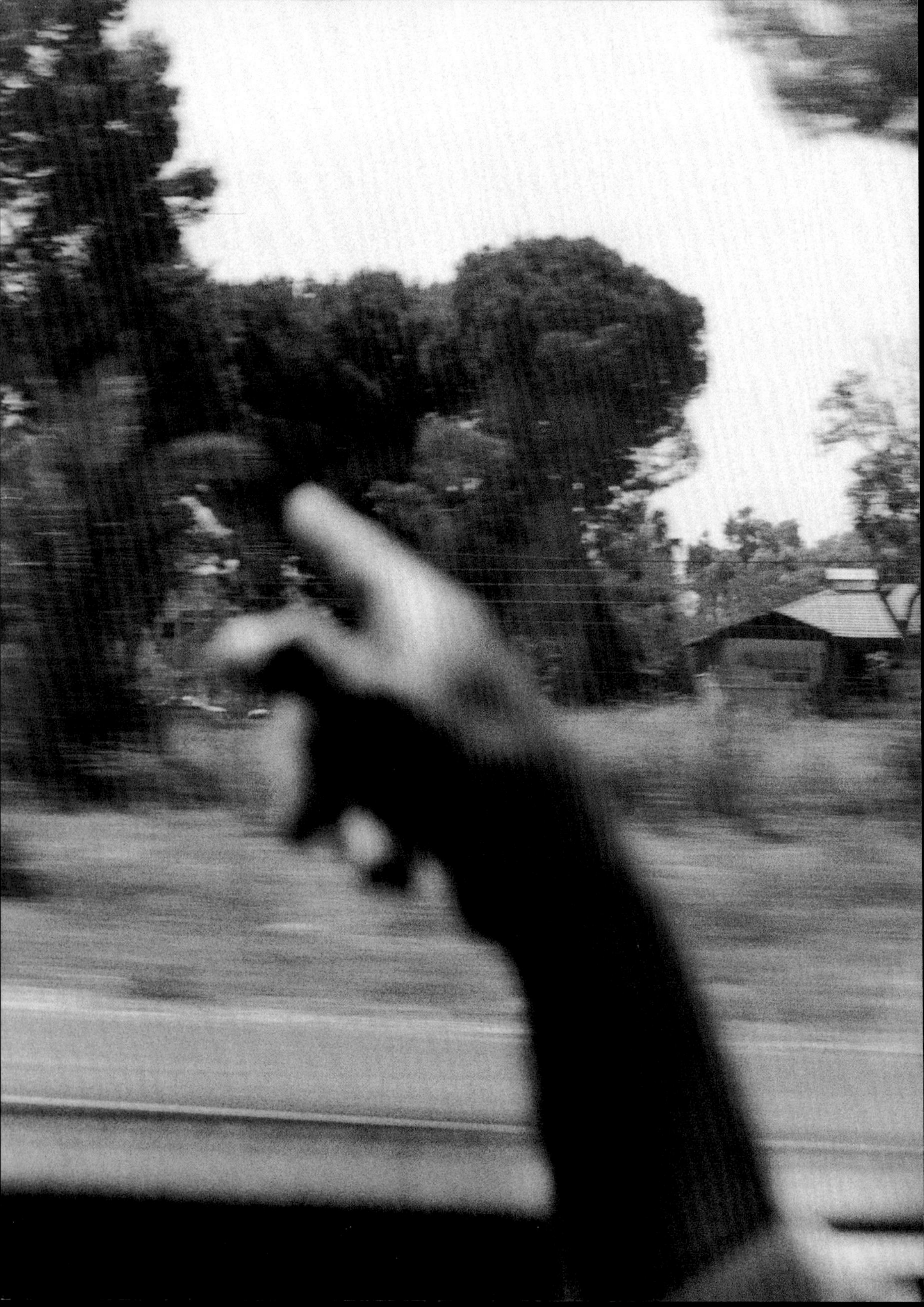

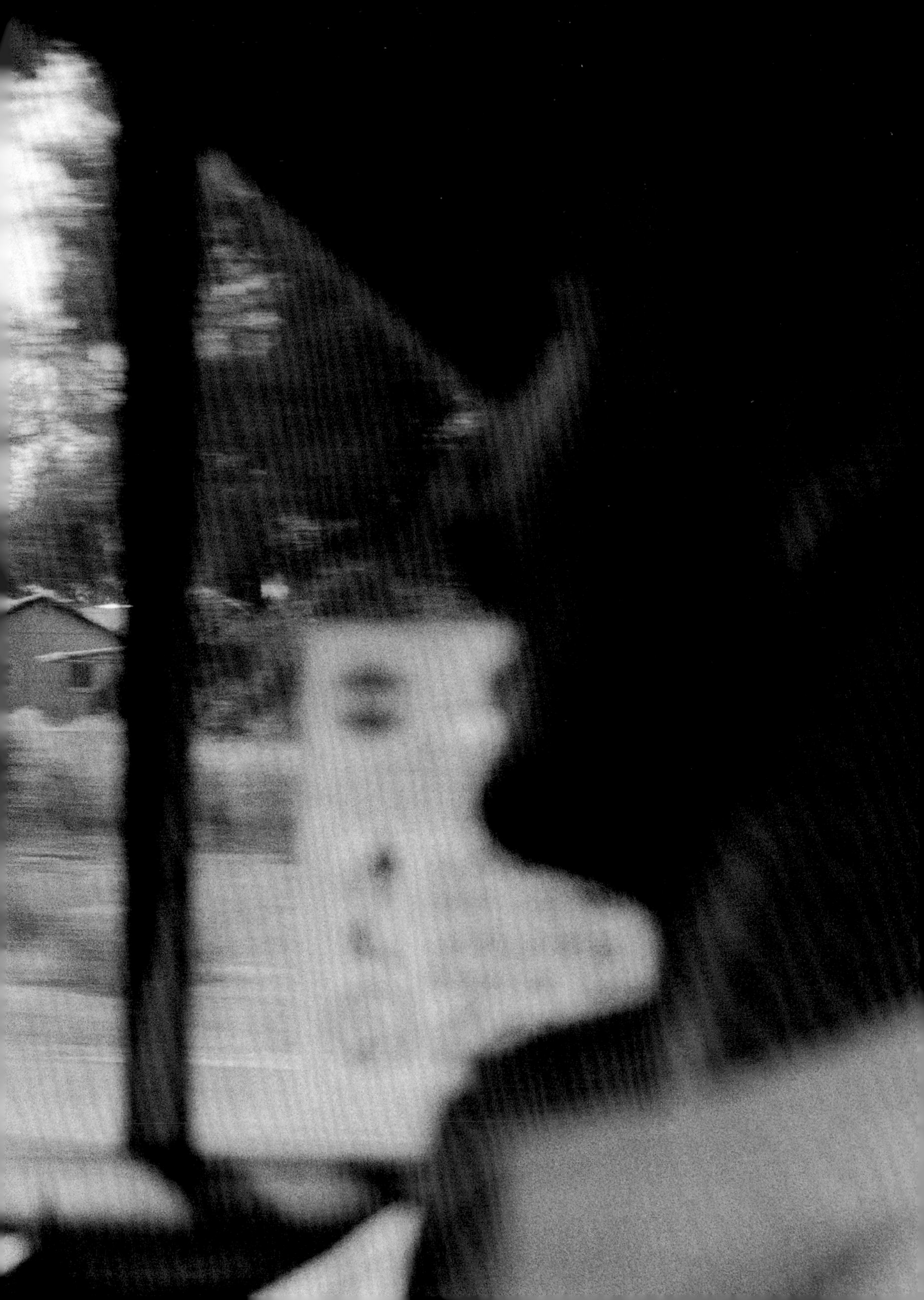

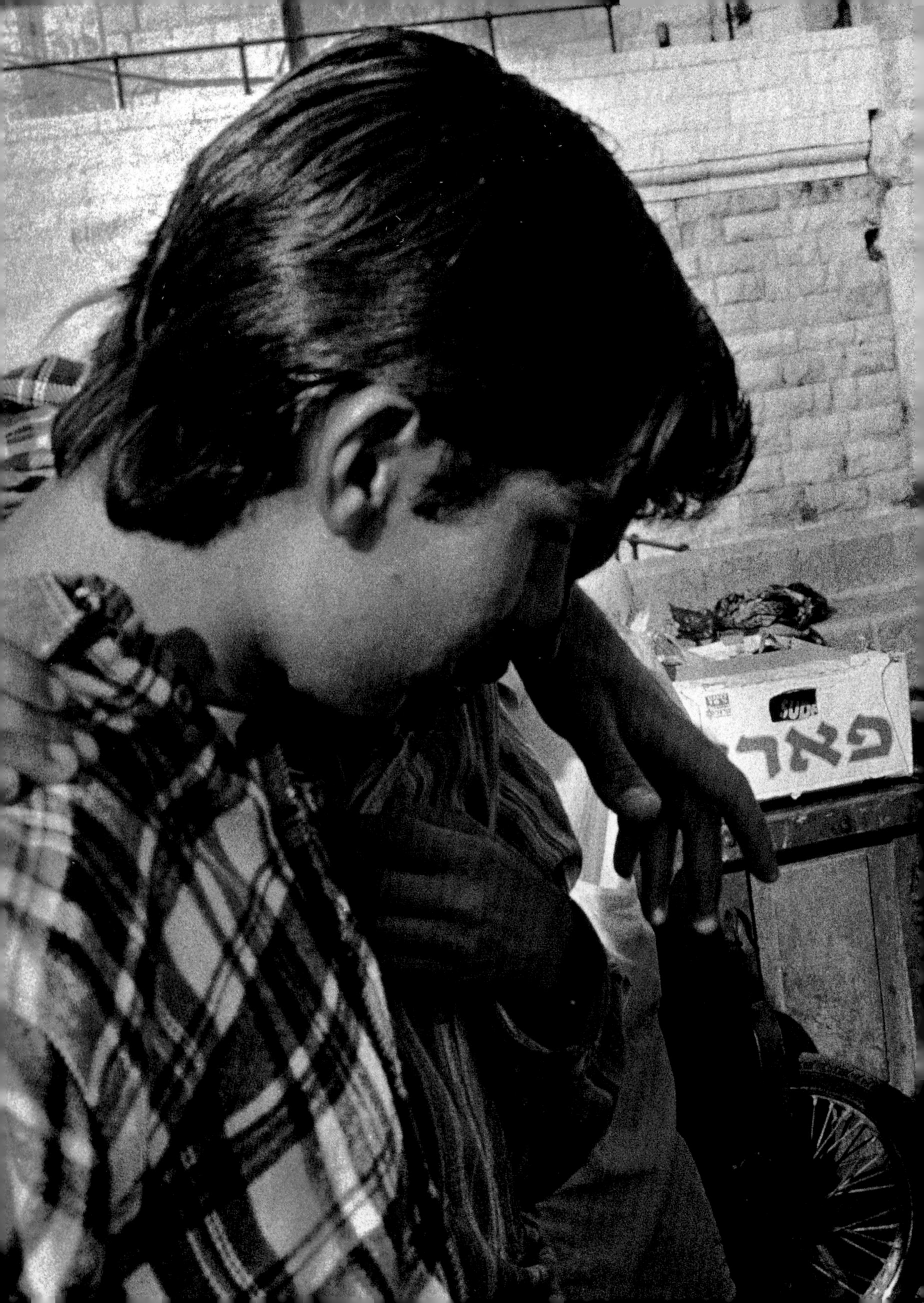
פאר

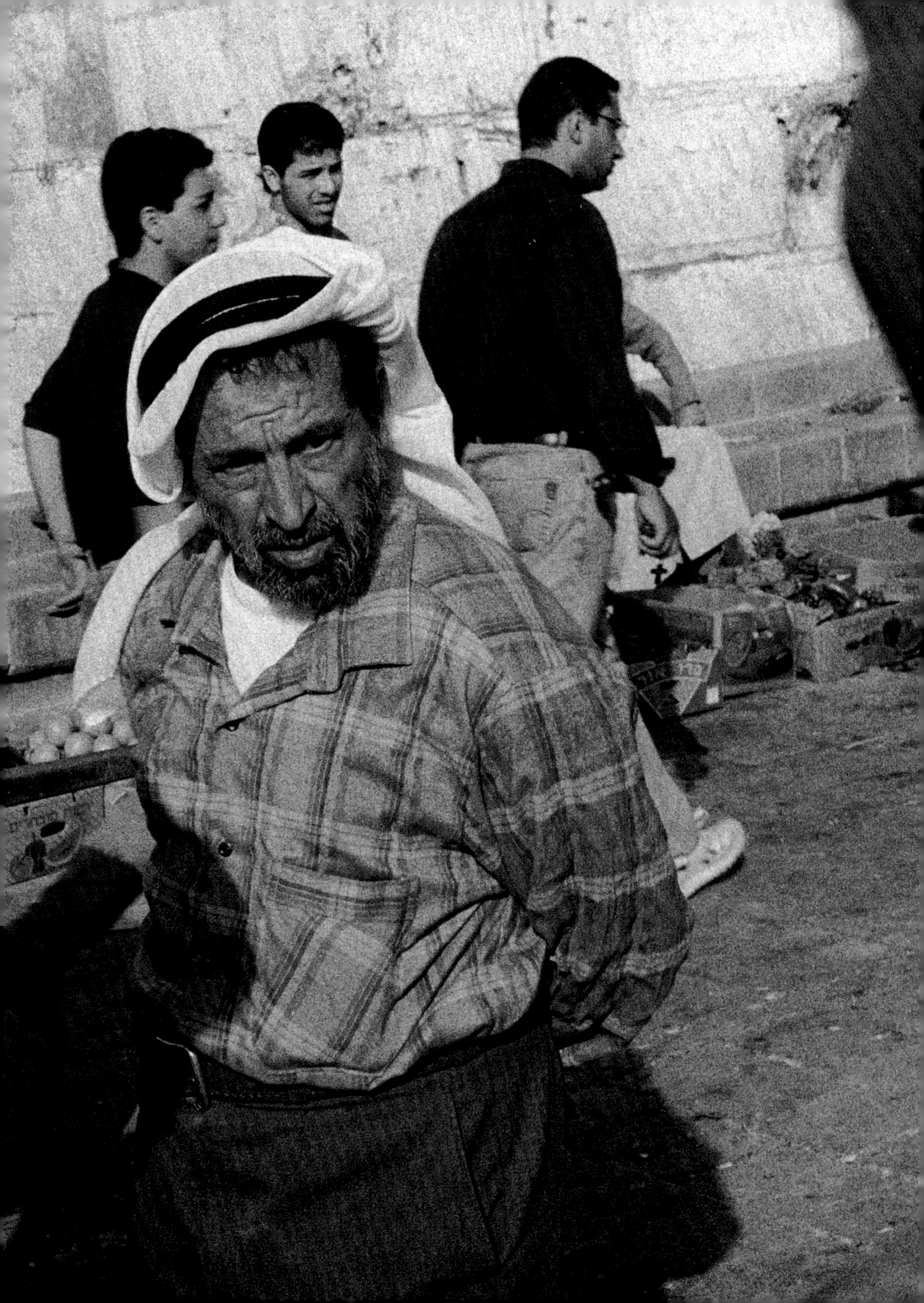

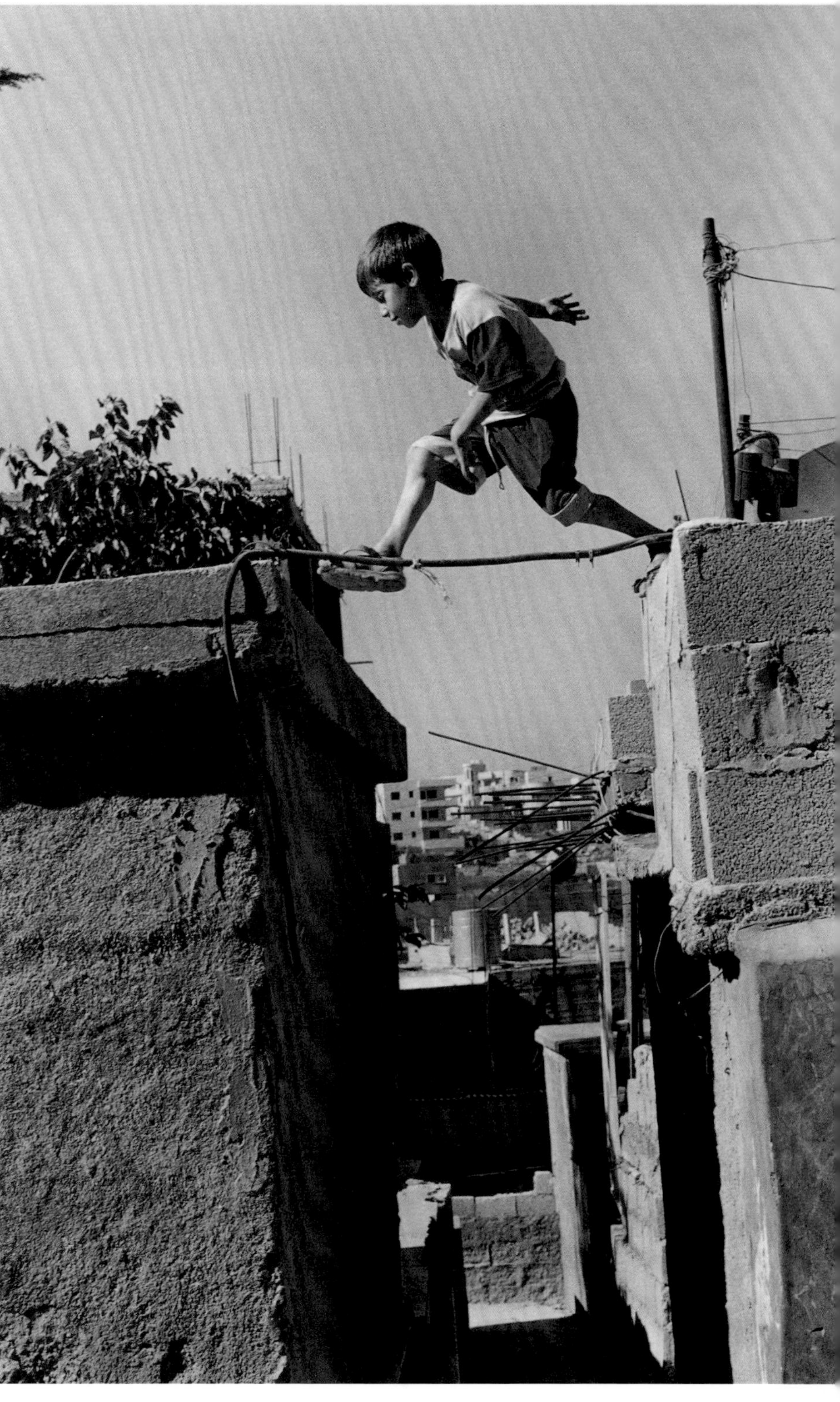

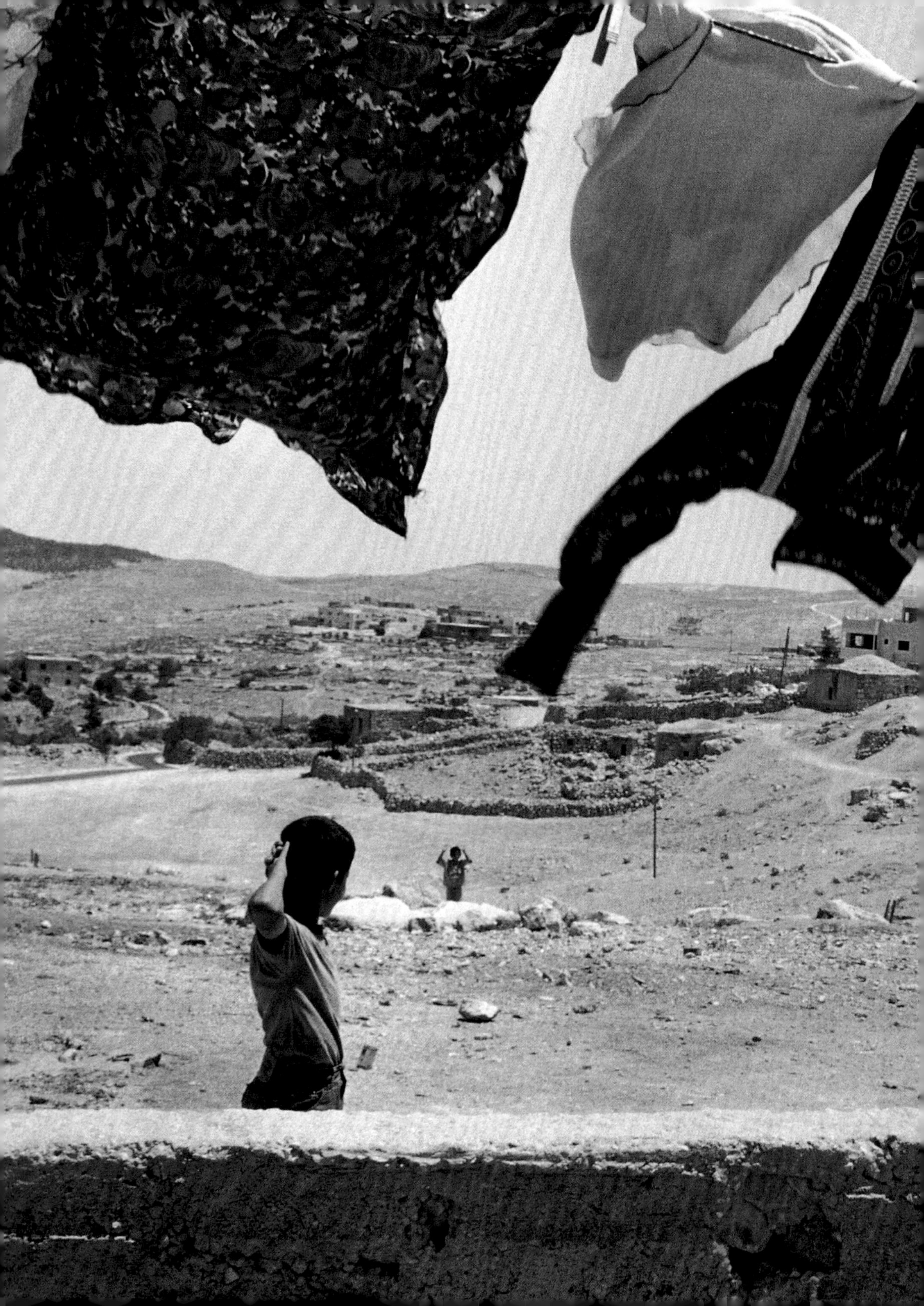

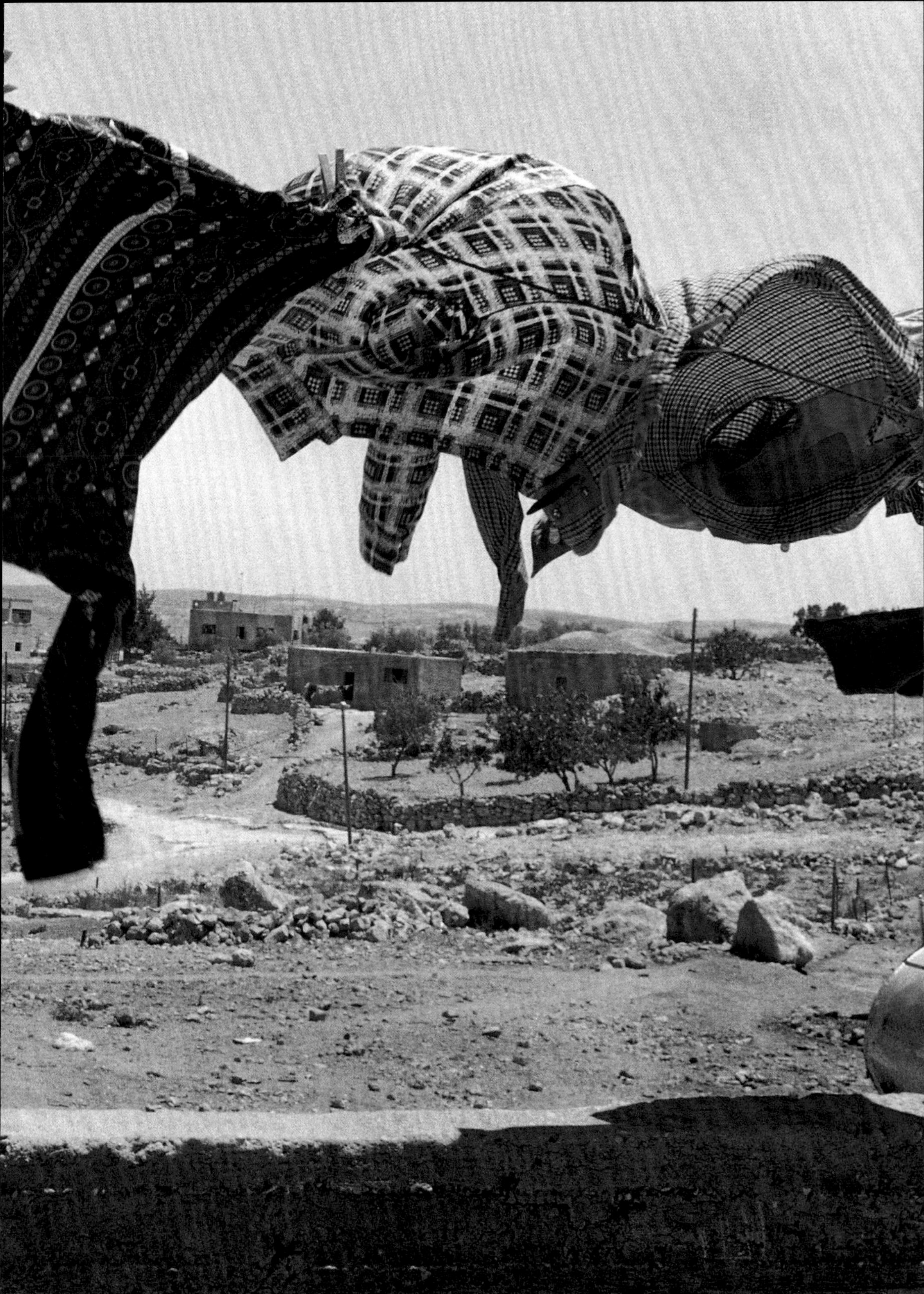

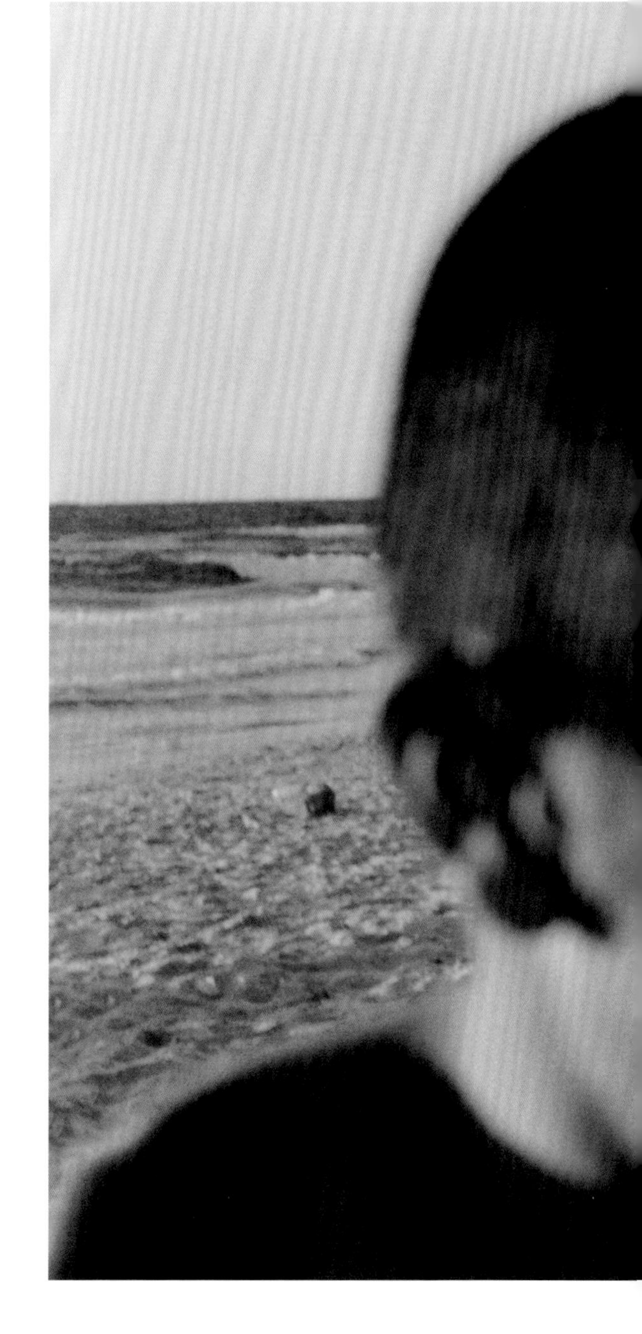

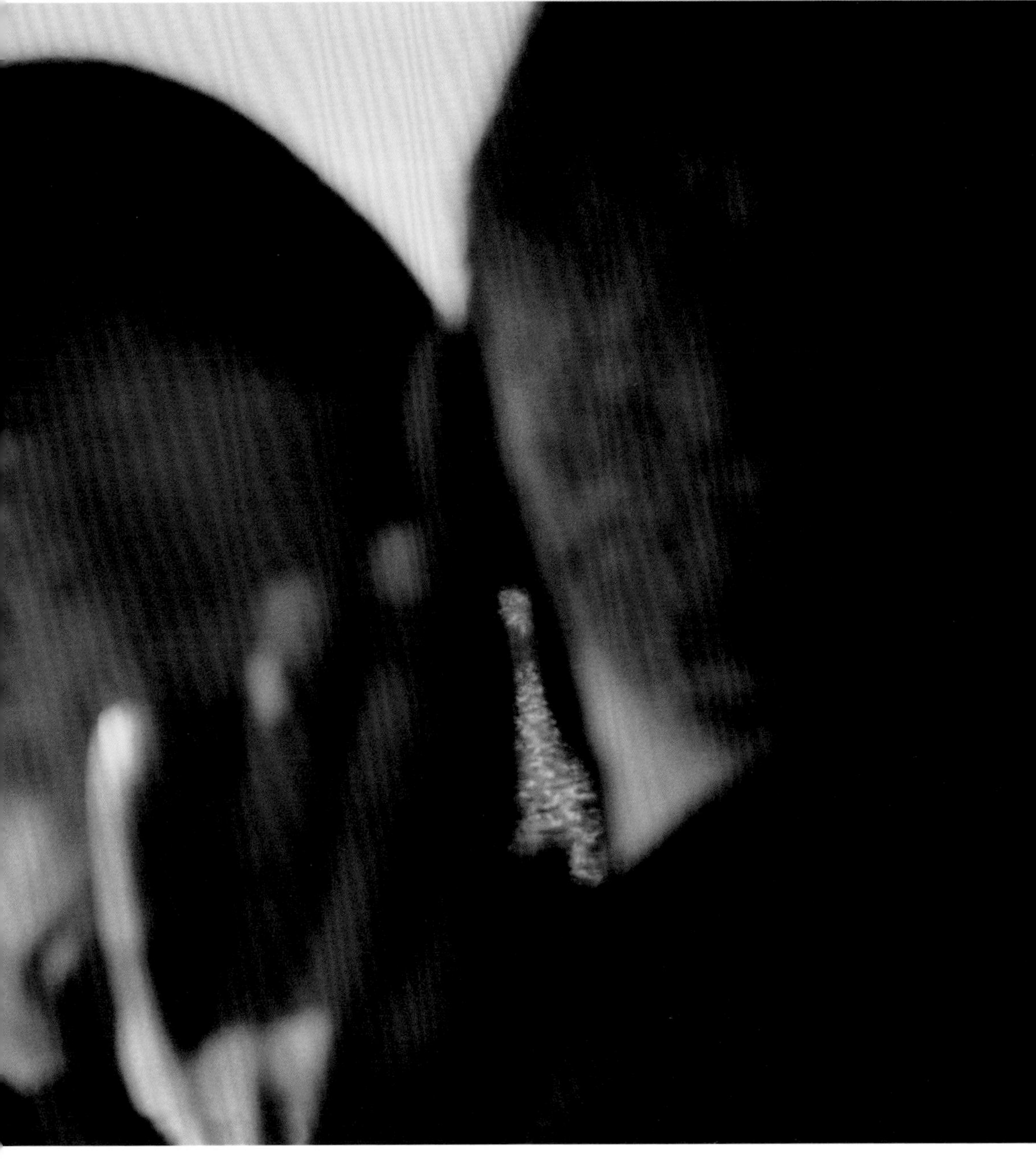

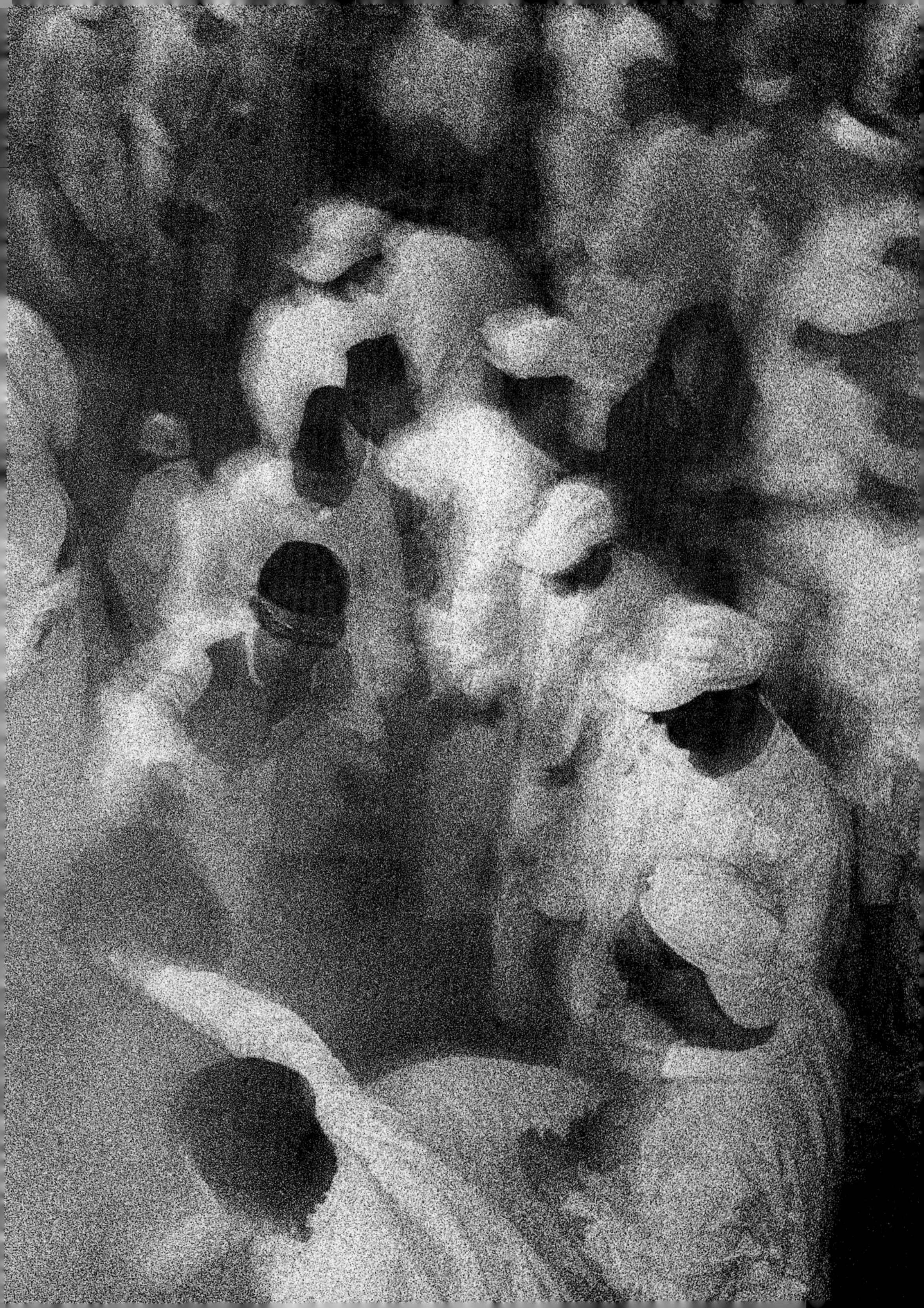

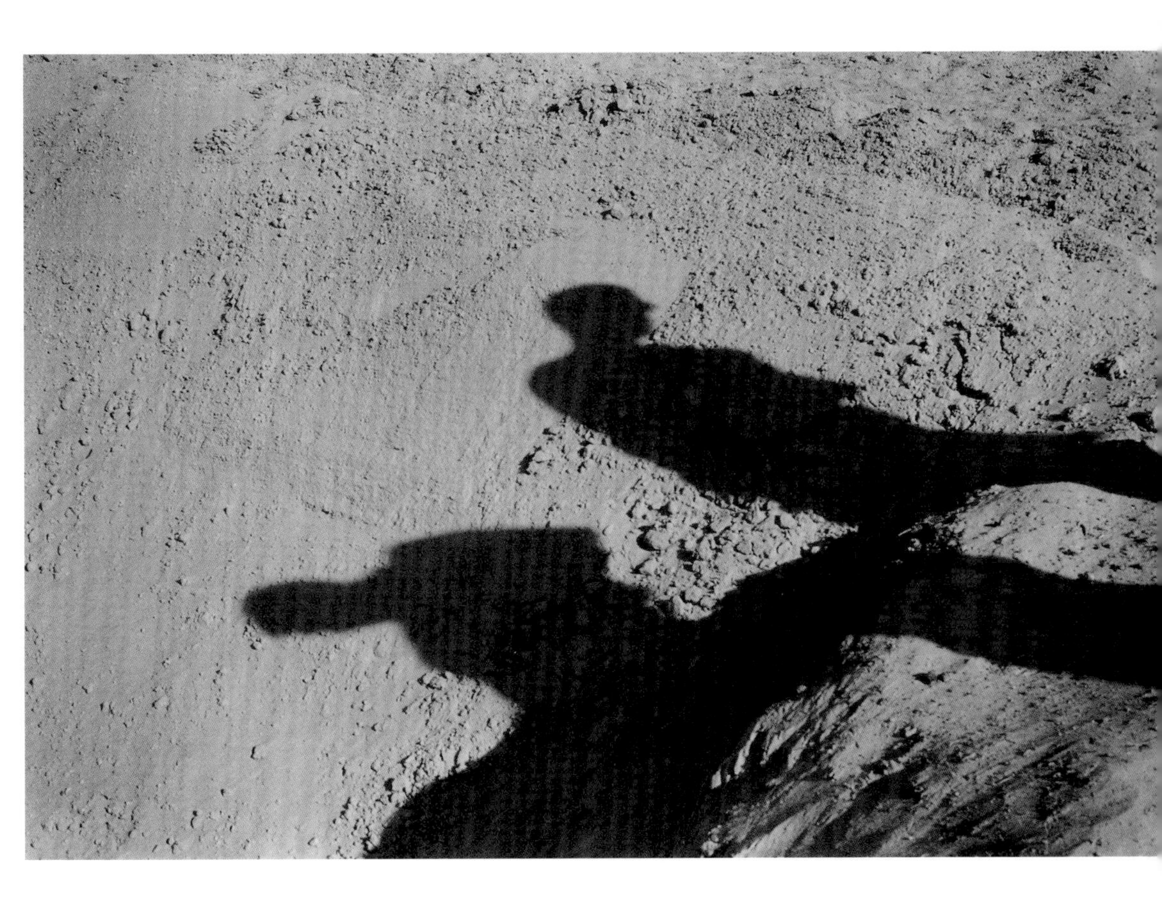

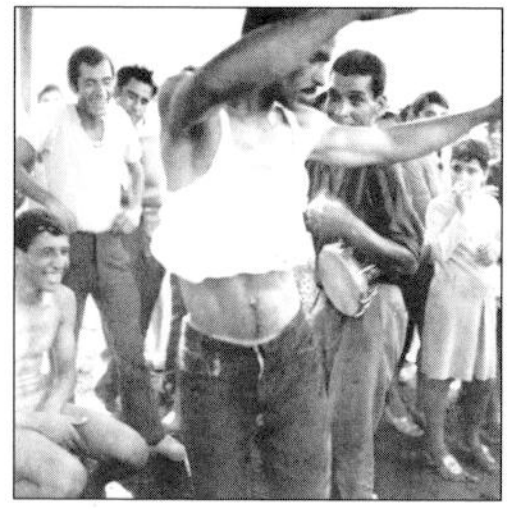

Jericho, West Bank, 1970

The images that follow were made between 1997 and 2001 in the Palestinian Autonomy (the West Bank and the Gaza Strip) and Jerusalem.

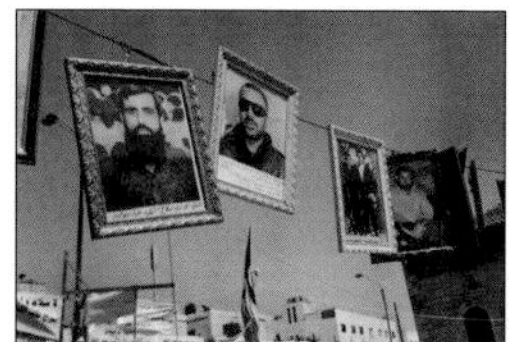

Ramallah, West Bank

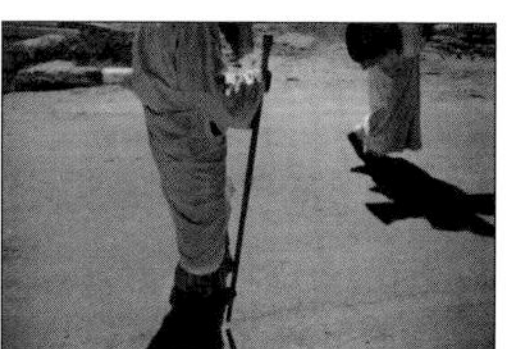

Samaritans, Mt. Gerizim, West Bank

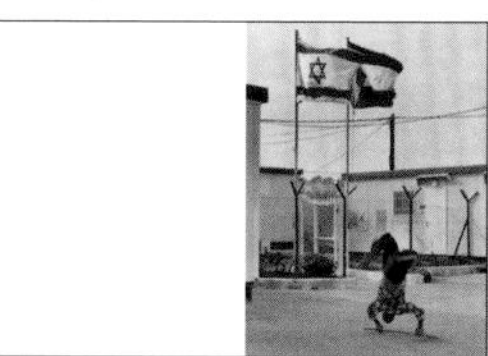

Joint Patrol Base, Ramallah, West Bank

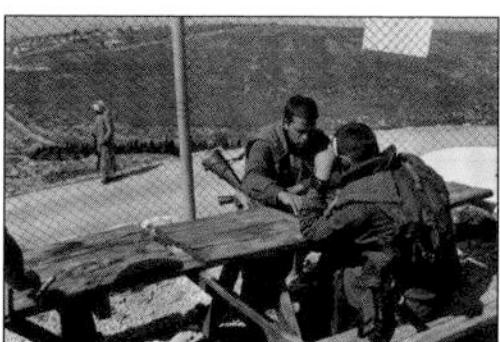

Jewish Settlement, near Nablus, West Bank

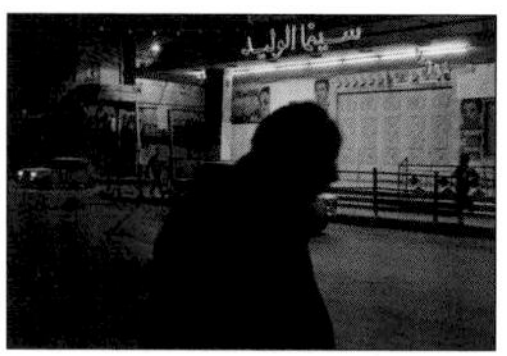

Ramallah, West Bank

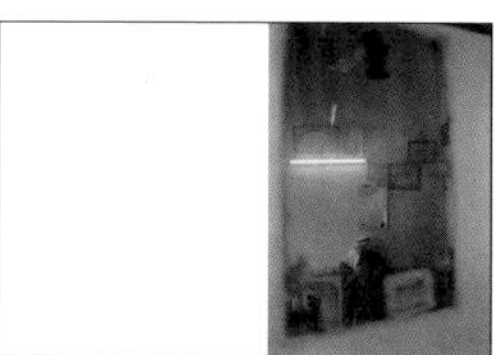

Nablus, West Bank

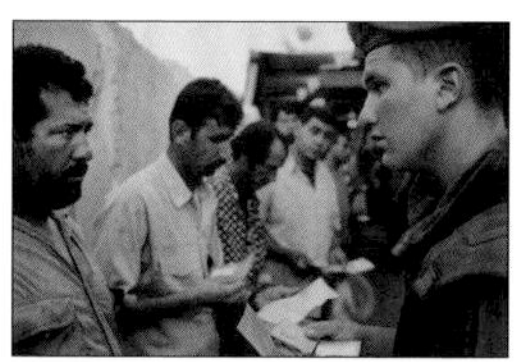

Erez Border Crossing, Gaza Strip

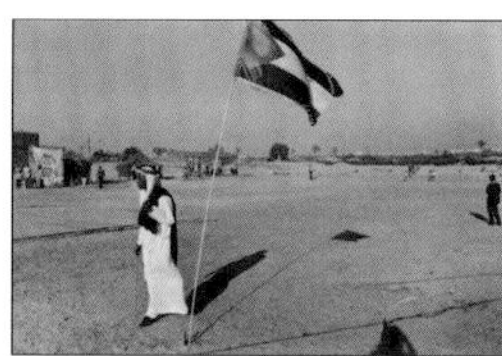

El Mughraqa, Gaza Strip

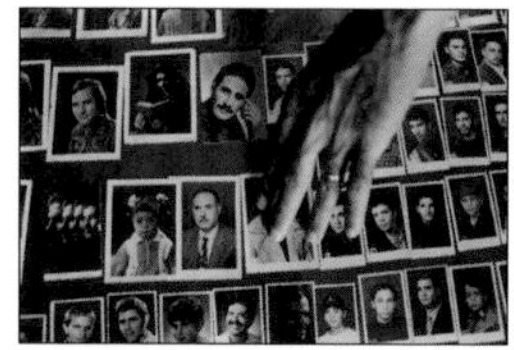

Gaza City

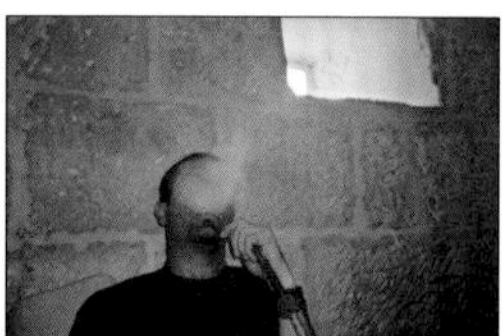

Ramallah, West Bank

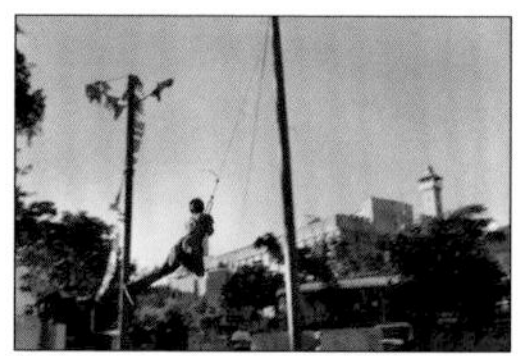

Tomb of the Patriarch, Hebron, West Bank

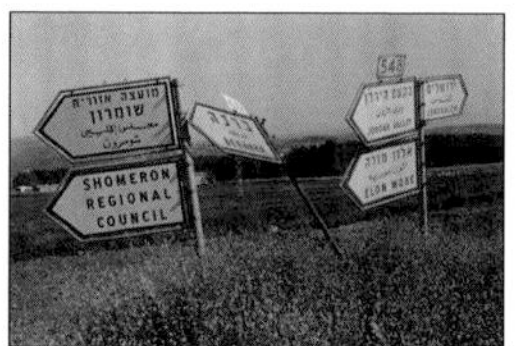

Nablus Checkpoint, West Bank

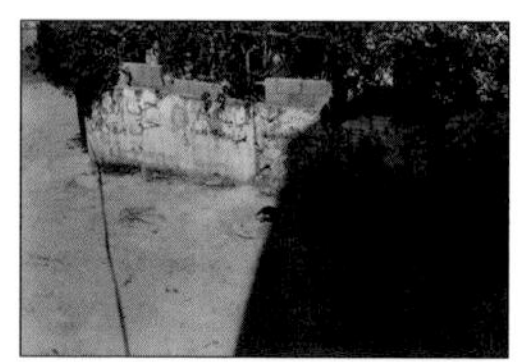

Daheisa Refugee Camp, Bethlehem, West Bank

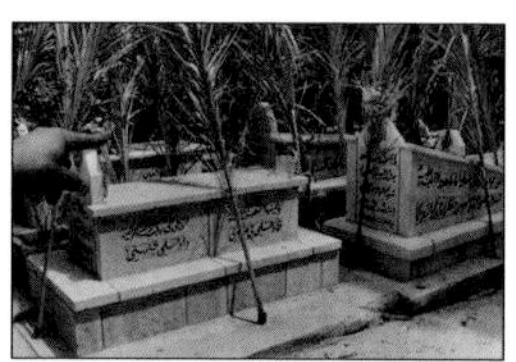

Cemetary for Child Martyrs of the Intifada, Nablus. W.B.

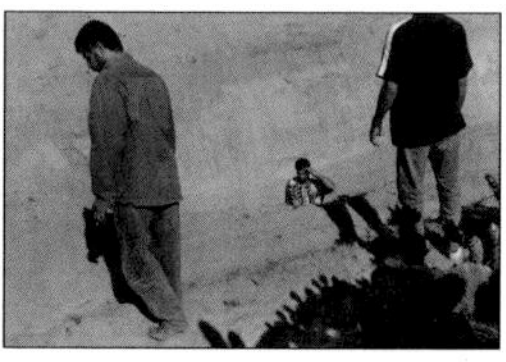

Rafah, Gaza Strip

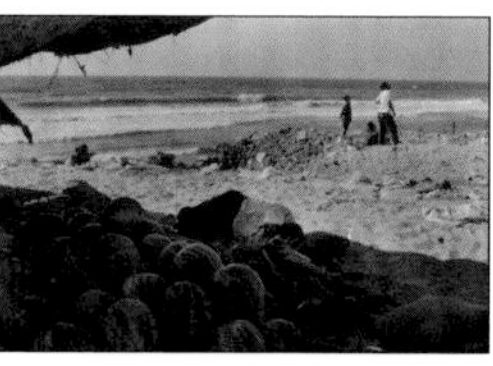

El Shati Refugee Camp, Gaza Strip

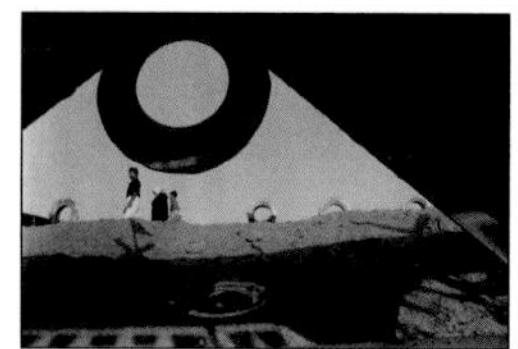

El Mughraqa, Gaza Strip

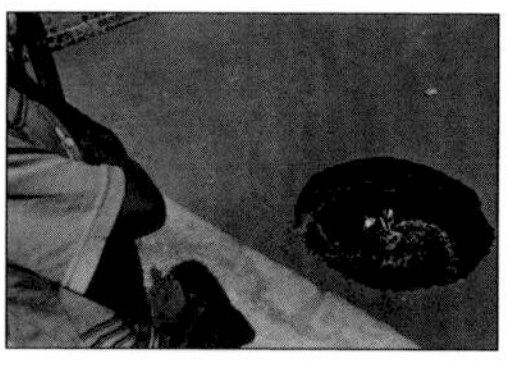

Polluted Reservoir, Carmeil, West Bank

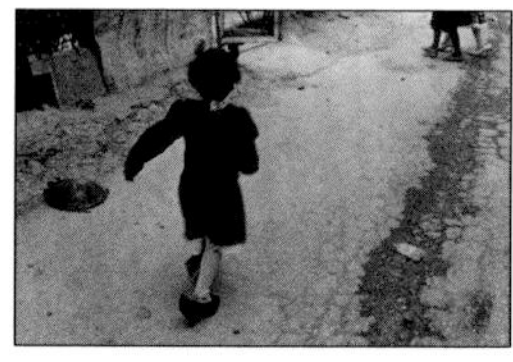

Balata Refugee Camp, Nablus, West Bank

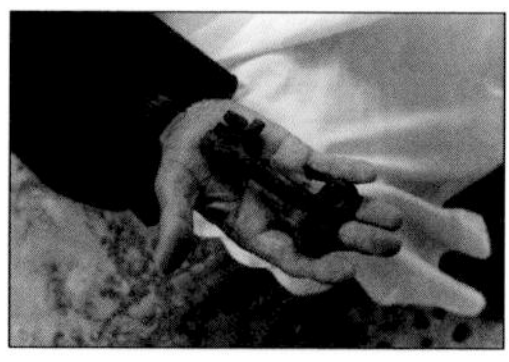

Daheisa Refugee Camp, Bethlehem, West Bank

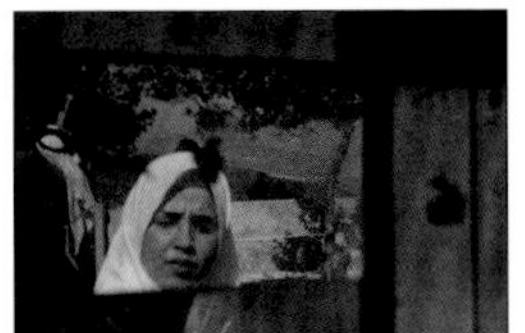

Dir Istia, West Bank

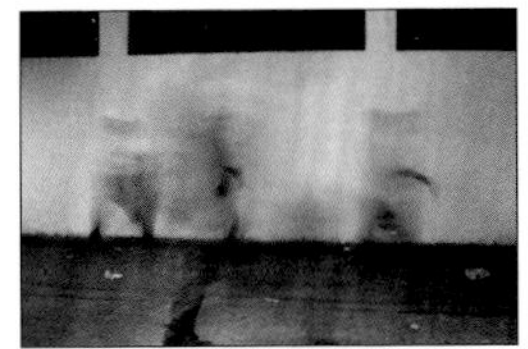

Erez Border Crossing,
Gaza Strip

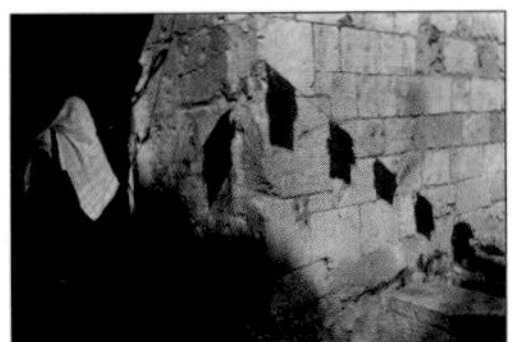

Damascus Gate, Jerusalem

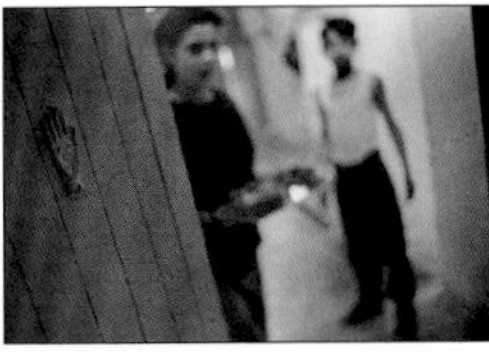

Balata Refugee Camp,
Nablus, West Bank

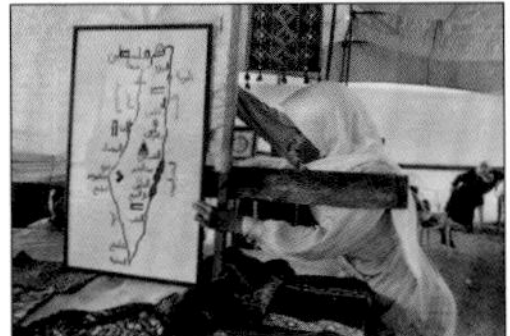

El Mughraqa, Gaza Strip

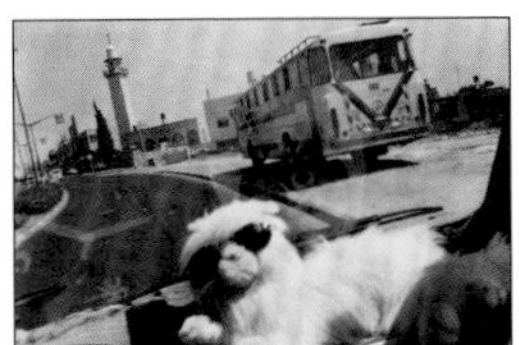

Shofat, Jerusalem

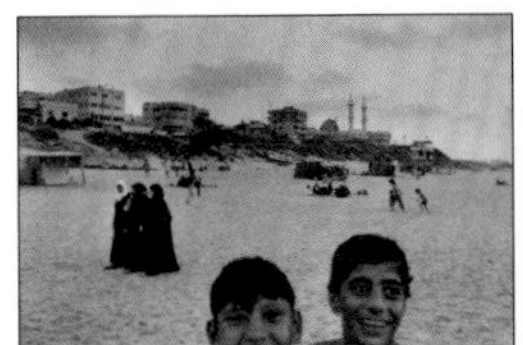

Gaza City

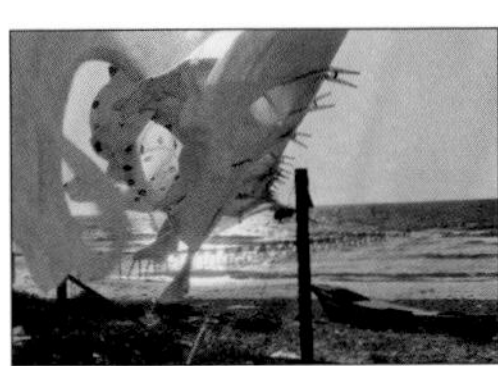

Brazil Refugee Camp,
Gaza Strip

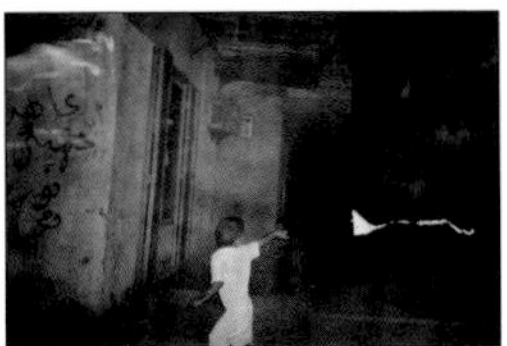

El Zeit, Gaza Strip

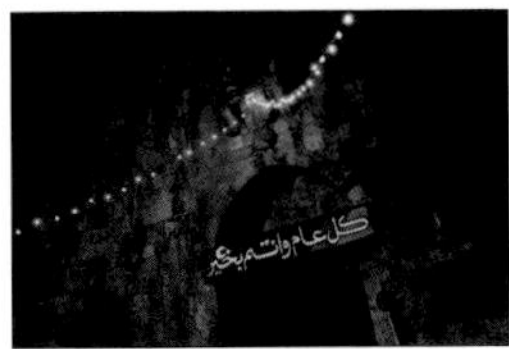

Lion's Gate, Jerusalem

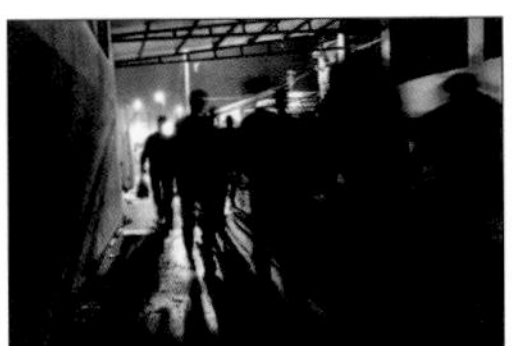

Erez Border Crossing,
Gaza Strip

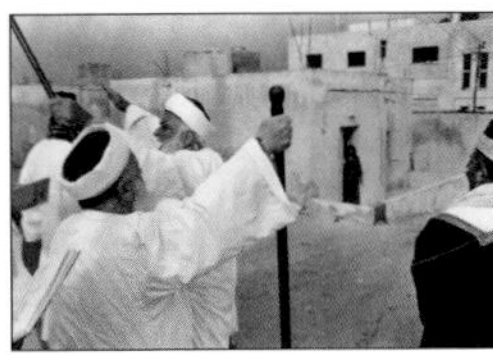

Jebel Atour, Mt. Gerizim,
West Bank

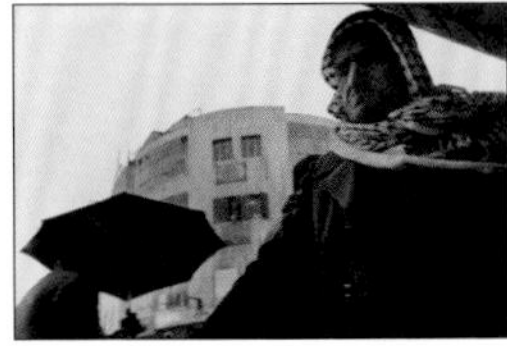

Ramallah, West Bank

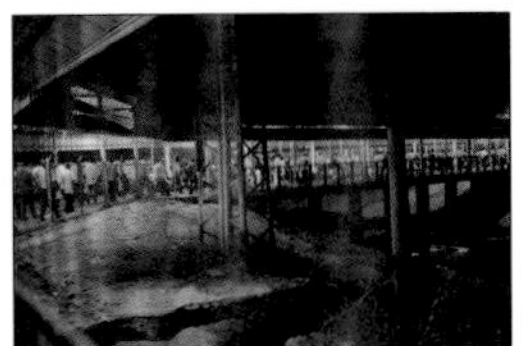

Erez Border Crossing,
Gaza Strip

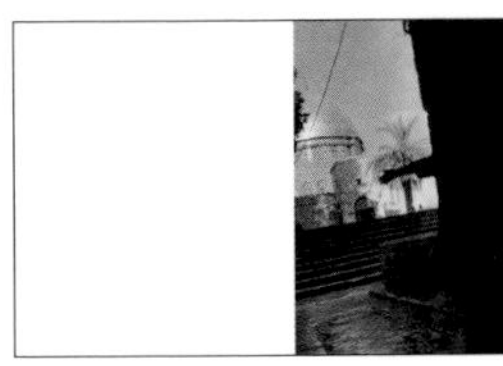

Haram Al Sharif,
Jerusalem

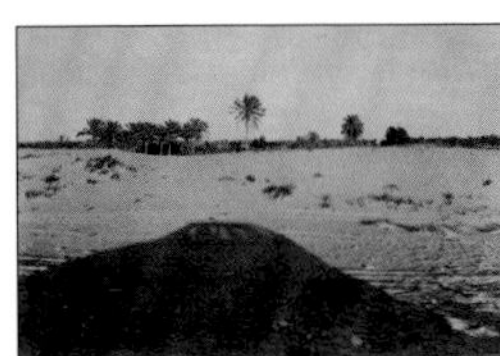

Dir El Balah, Gaza Strip

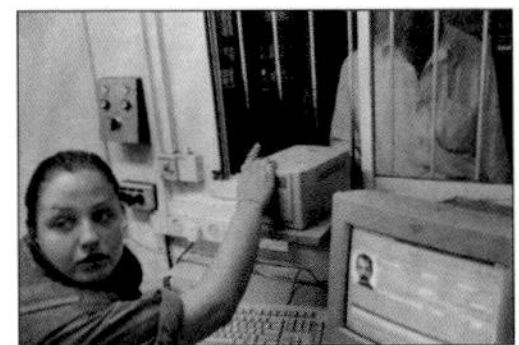

Erez Border Crossing,
Gaza Strip

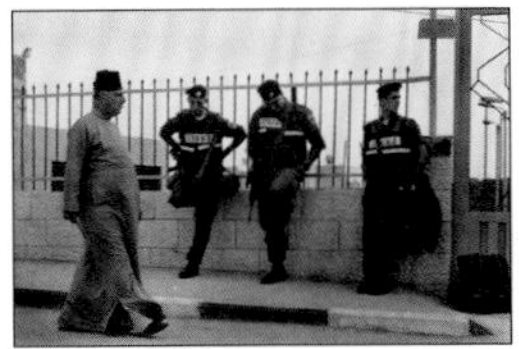

Jebel Atour, Mt. Gerizim,
West Bank

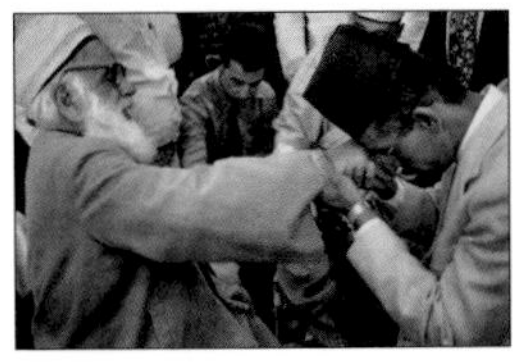

Samaritans, Mt. Gerizim,
West Bank

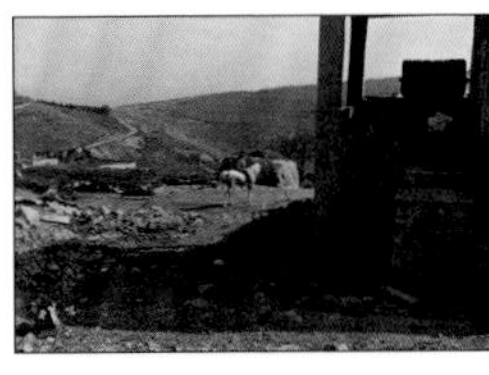

Jebel Atour, West Bank

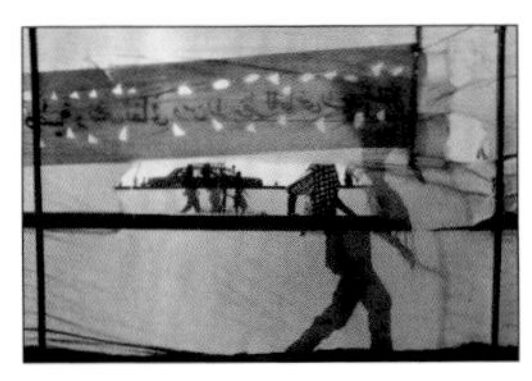

El Mughraqa, Gaza Strip

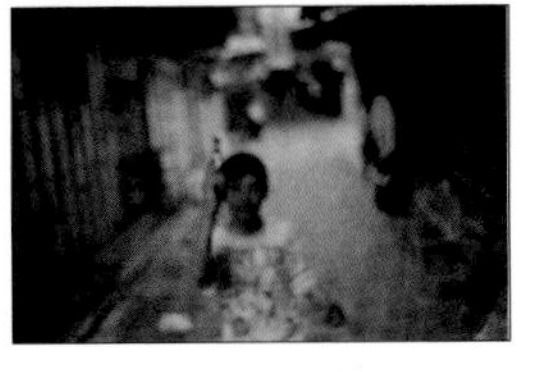

Nablus, West Bank

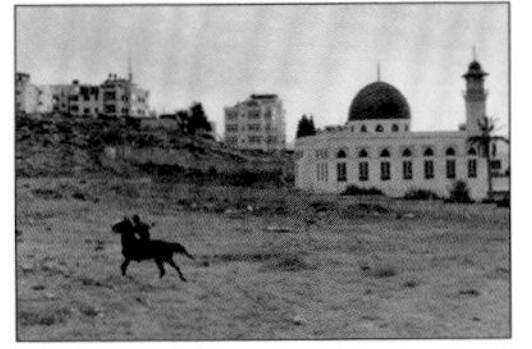

Beit Hanina, Jerusalem

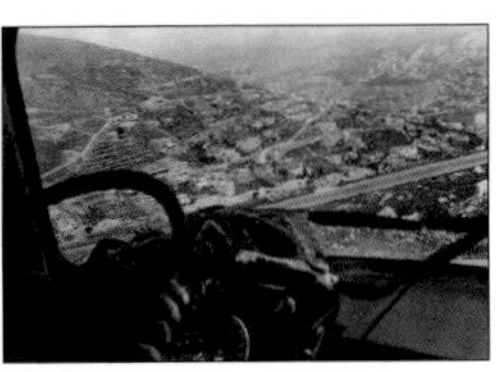

Nablus, West Bank

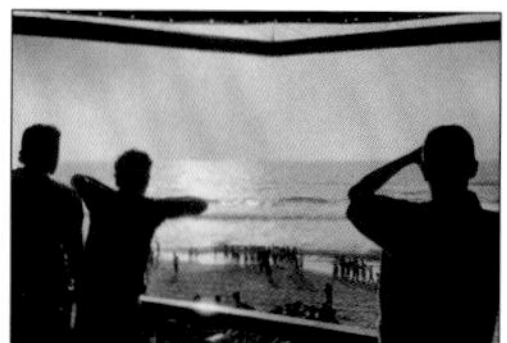

Haifa Beach, Gaza Strip

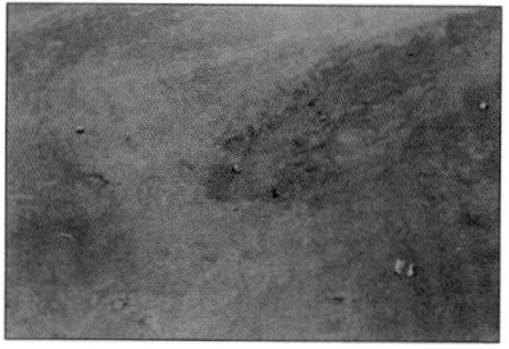

Polluted Reservoir, Carmeil, West Bank

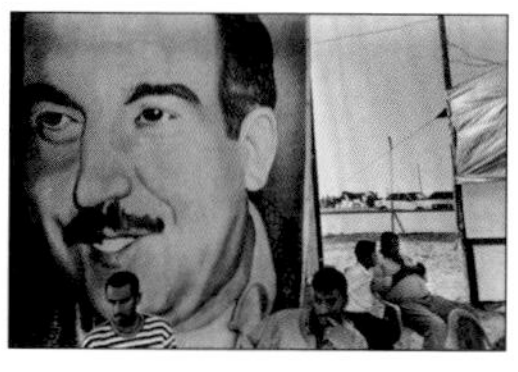

El Mughraqa, Gaza Strip

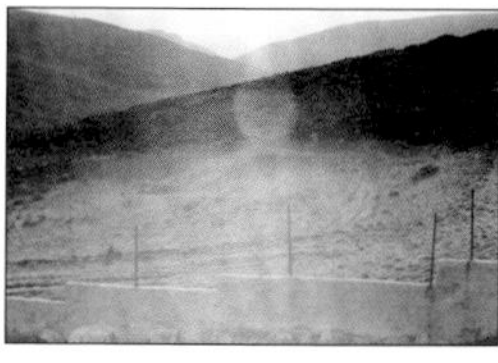

Tulkarem, West Bank

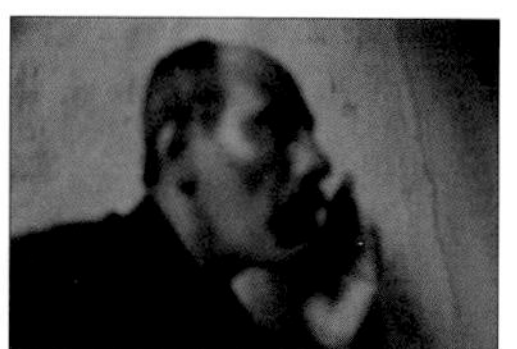

Balata Refugee Camp, Nablus, West Bank

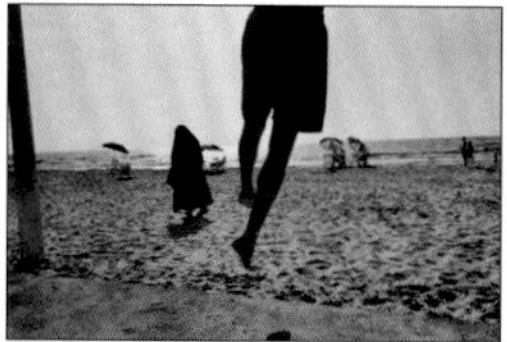

Chalet Club Beach, Gaza City

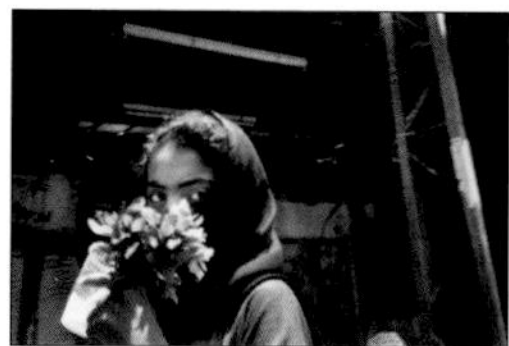

Gaza City

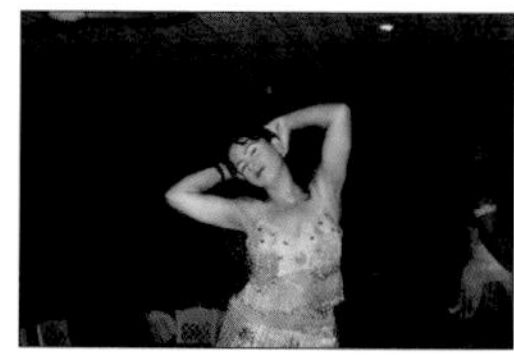

Sherazade Night Club, Gaza City

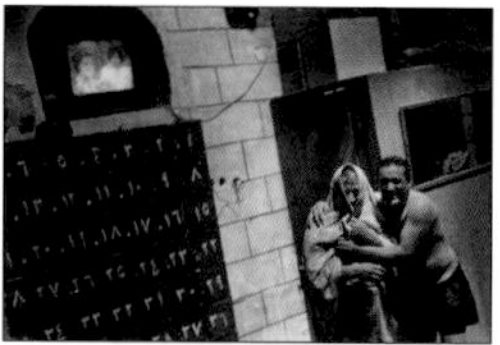

Bathhouse, Nablus, West Bank

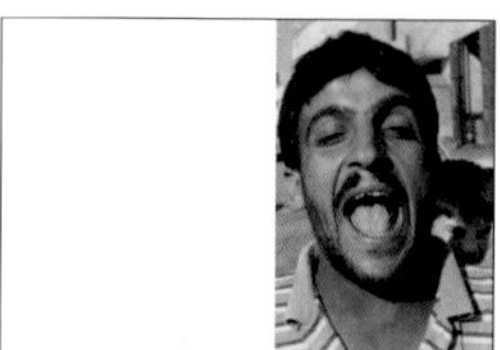

Yata, West Bank

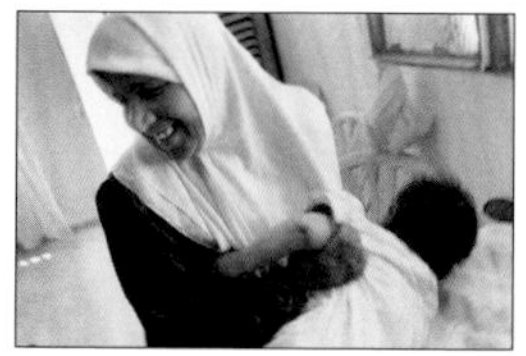

Hebron, West Bank

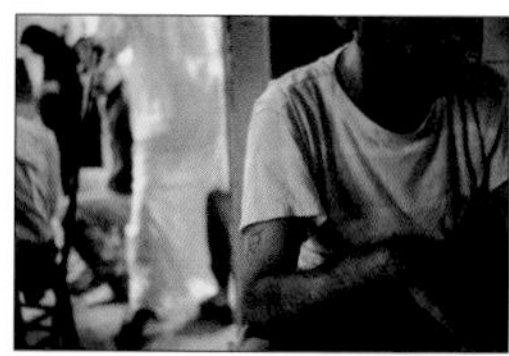

Gaza City

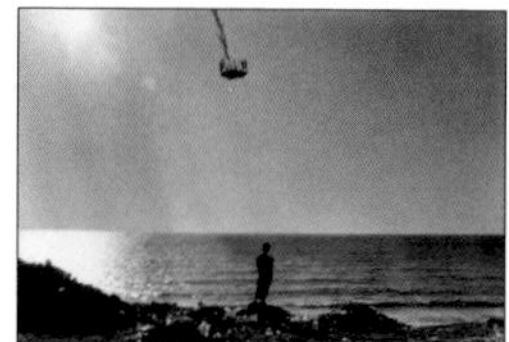

Haifa Beach, Gaza Strip

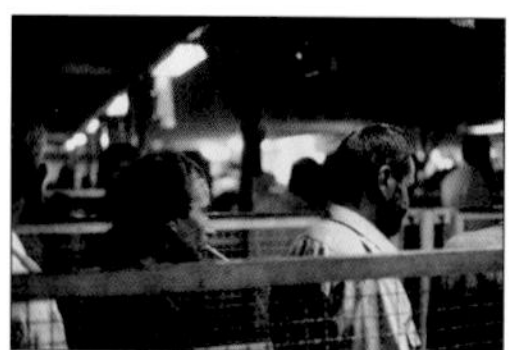

Erez Border Crossing, Gaza Strip

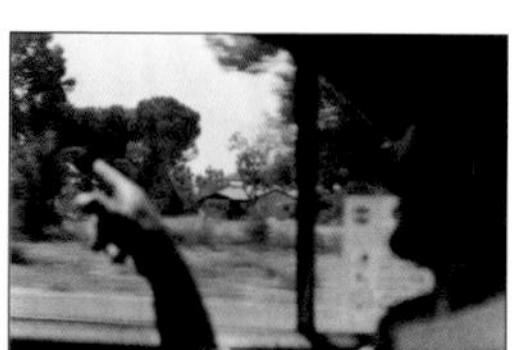

Gaza - West Bank collective taxi

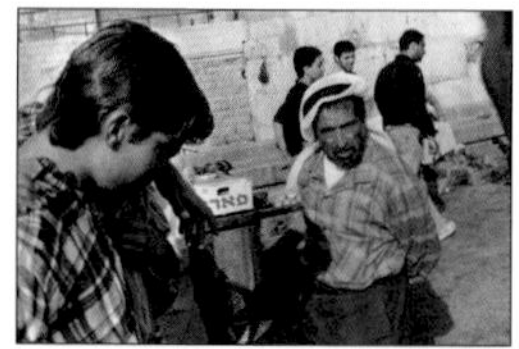

Damascus Gate, Jerusalem

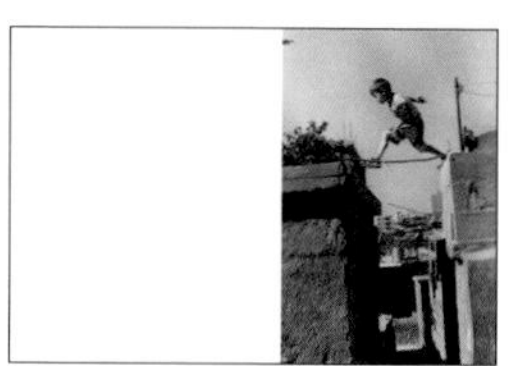

Daheisa Refugee Camp, Bethlehem, West Bank

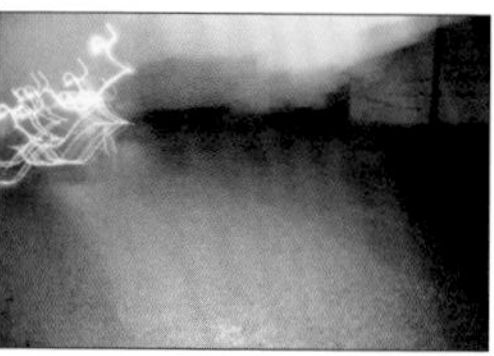

Gaza City

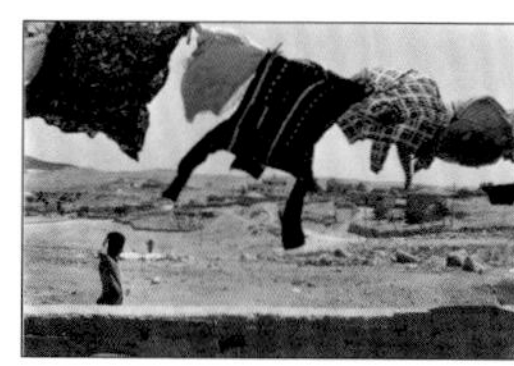

Carmeil, West Bank

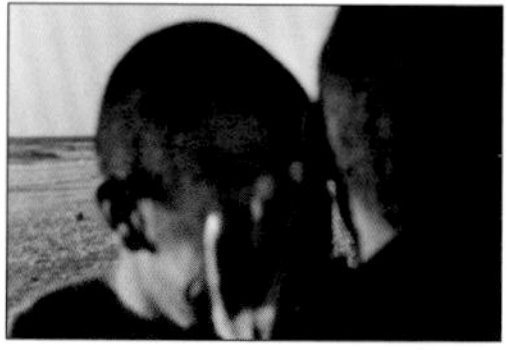

Brazil Refugee Camp, Gaza Strip

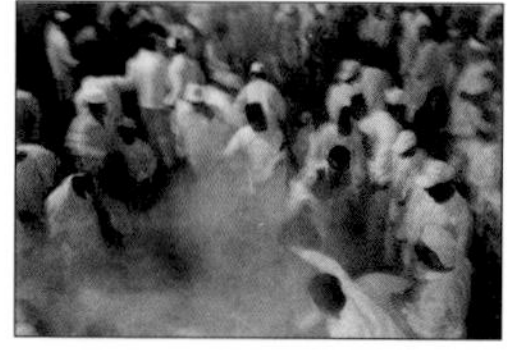

Samaritans, Mt. Gerizim, West Bank

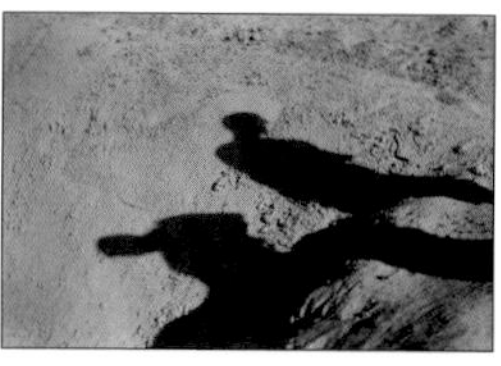

Rafah, Gaza Strip

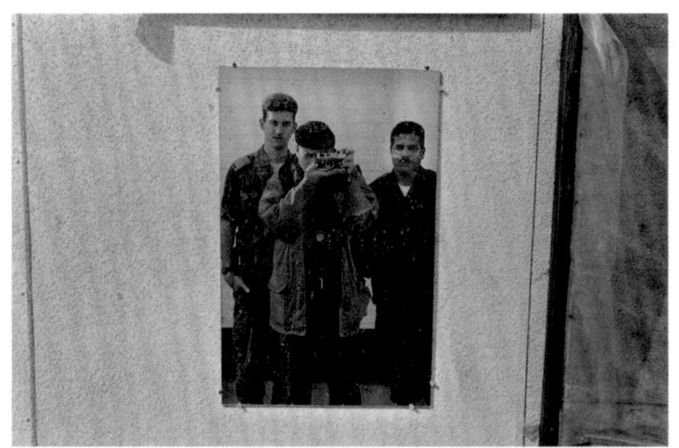

Matei Glass (Joseph Winterfeld) was born in Montreal,
Canada in 1956, the son of Jewish refugees from Romania.
His images, installations and video work have been
widely exhibited and figure in both public and private
collections. Since 1995, he has lived in Barcelona.

acknowledgments

First and foremost, thanks to my partner Angeles Alonso Oliva, without whose advice, collaboration and support this project would never have been possible.

I also wish to thank:

Miriam Smolka,
Abu Akram and the Gaza Office of the Union of Palestinian Medical Relief Committees,
B´tselem, The Israeli Center for Human Rights in the Occupied Territories,
Edouard Libeau of Medcins Sans Frontiers,
Chandra Prakash,
Manel Guerrero,
Miri Scharf,
Maximo Stein-Hofer,
Annie Bats,
Andonis Rigas,
Marie Svindt,
Daniel and Rose-marie Winterfeld,
Maria Isabel Oliva Alonso,
José Antonio Alonso Santos,
Eulalia Bosch,
Ester Hérnandez,
Jacob Langvad,
Joel Kantor,
Meeka Walsh,
Gloria Montero and David Fulton,
Erez Yanuv,
Lluís Arribas,
Abdel Menem Adwan,
Rafael Doctor,
Dante Bertini,
Marcelo Clivati,
Arnau Pons,
Richard Schweid,
Josep Manel, Xavi and the team at Laboratorio Copia,
Paco Salinas,
Asociación Cultural Mercury,
Susana Arias,
Jean Lonay,
Antonio Corral,
Oriol Rigat,
Montse Sagarra,
Ramon Prat,
and last but not least, John Berger.

This book is dedicated to the memory of Dierdre Herrick.

Photography
Matei Glass

Graphic Design
Ramon Prat
Montse Sagarra

Technical Production
Font i Prat Associats

Printing
Ingoprint S.A.

Distribution
ACTAR
Roca i Batlle 2, E-08023 Barcelona
Tel. 0034 934 187 759, fax 0034 934 186 707
info@actar-mail.com, www.actar.es

© 2003 edition Actar
© text Matei Glass
© images Matei Glass

ISBN 84-95951-19-3
DL B-12999-2003
printed and bound in the European Union